D1572539

Hitler's Death Squads

Number Twenty-five:
Eastern European Studies
Stjepan Meštrović, *General Editor*

Series Board:
Norman Cigar
Bronislaw Misztal
Sabrina Ramet
Vladimir Shlapentokh
Keith Tester

HITLER'S Death SQUADS

THE LOGIC OF MASS MURDER

Helmut Langerbein

TEXAS A&M UNIVERSITY PRESS

College Station

The paper used in this book meets the minimum requirements
of the American National Standard for Permanence
of Paper for Printed Library Materials, z39.48-1984.
Binding materials have been chosen for durability.

Library of Congress Cataloging-in-Publication Data

Langerbein, Helmut.
Hitler's death squads : the logic of mass murder / Helmut Langerbein.— 1st ed.
p.   cm. — (Eastern European studies ; no. 25)
Includes bibliographical references and index.
ISBN 1-58544-285-2 (alk. paper)
1. Holocaust, Jewish (1939–1945)—Europe, Eastern. 2. Nationalsozialistische Deutsche
Arbeiter-Partei. Schutzstaffel. Sicherheitsdienst—History. 3. Nationalsozialistische Deutsche
Arbeiter-Partei. Schutzstaffel. Sicherheitspolizei—History. 4. Jews—Persecutions—
Europe, Eastern. 5. World War, 1939–1945—Atrocities—Europe, Eastern.
I. Title. II. Eastern European studies (College Station, Tex.) ; no. 25.
D804.3 .L365 2003
940.53'18'0947—dc21
2003009578

For my mother, Monika Langerbein,
and my son, Ryan Ian Whelan

The essential and inalienable rights of man cannot vary in time and space. They cannot be interpreted and limited by the social conscience of a people or a particular epoch for they are essentially immutable and eternal. Any injury . . . done with the intention of extermination, mutilation, or enslavement, against the life, freedom of opinion . . . the moral or physical integrity of the family . . . or the dignity of the human being, by reason of his opinion, his race, caste, family, or profession, is a crime against humanity.

Report of the VIII Conference for the Unification of Penal Law, July 11, 1947

CONTENTS

ILLUSTRATIONS

ACKNOWLEDGMENTS

Invaluable insight has been received from individuals and institutions, as well as support and cooperation during the research and writing of this book. Peter Kenez, my dissertation adviser at the University of California Santa Cruz, encouraged me to pursue this project. Mark Cioc and Murray Baumgarten, also from the University of California at Santa Cruz, read and efficiently criticized different versions of the manuscript. David Go helped with the charts and tables. The Department of History, the Center for Justice, Tolerance, and Community, and the Institute for Humanities Research at the University of California, Santa Cruz, supplied grants to enable me to visit Germany.

I would also like to express my gratitude to Staatsanwalt (District Attorney) Tönnies and others in Germany who greatly facilitated my research at the Zentrale Stelle (Central Office of the State Justice Administrations for the Investigation of National Socialist Homicide Crimes) in Ludwigsburg; the Bundesarchiv (Federal Archive) in Berlin; the Militärarchiv (Military Archive) in Freiburg; and the Institut für Zeitgeschichte (Institute for Contemporary History) in Munich.

Hitler's Death Squads

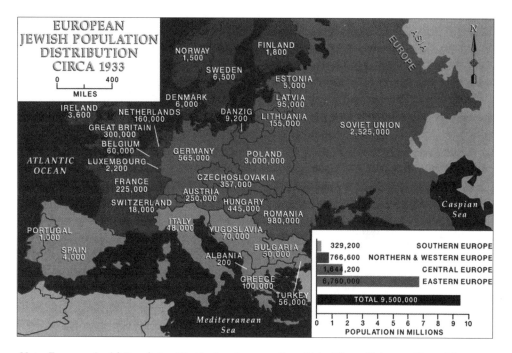

Map 1. European Jewish Population Distribution circa 1933. From United States Holocaust Memorial Museum, *The Historical Atlas of the Holocaust* (New York: Macmillan Publishing, 1995). Used with permission of the United States Holocaust Memorial Museum, Washington, D.C.

INTRODUCTION
The German Einsatzgruppen Trials

*It is with sorrow and with hope that we
here disclose the deliberate slaughter of more
than a million innocent and defenseless
men, women, and children.*

From the Prosecution, Military Tribunal II,
Nuremberg, Germany

 N 1962 the District Court of Berlin
sentenced Dr. Alfred Karl Filbert, a lieutenant colonel in the terrorizing Nazi
SS—the Schutzstaffeln, Elite Protection Squads—for the murder of 6,800 persons. The court judgment read:

> He did not act to aid Hitler, Himmler and Heydrich, but he wanted to participate in the elimination of the Eastern European Jews as a perpetrator. The
> extraordinary enthusiasm with which he participated in the crime proves that
> he felt it to be his own deed.[1]

Filbert was not simply satisfied with following orders, the court determined; he
wholeheartedly wanted to contribute to the eradication of the Jews. With a fanaticism that was noticed by both his commanding officer and his subordinates,
he made certain that every Jew he could find was killed, in the larger cities, and
in the smallest hamlets. "The zeal with which Dr. Filbert obeyed the general
elimination order knew no limits."[2]

Filbert's trial was but one of many German legal proceedings against former
officers in the notorious Einsatzgruppen, the mobile killing units of the SS operating in the Soviet Union beginning in 1941. The Einsatzgruppen had been
tasked with the annihilation of Jews on the eastern front.

The postwar German police and district attorneys' offices investigated more
than 1,770 former Einsatzgruppen members. They indicted and successfully

brought to trial 136, a ratio of little more than 7.5 percent. Most investigations did not lead to a trial because the perpetrators had died or were too sick, or simply for lack of evidence. Others could no longer be prosecuted because the statute of limitations had been shortened in 1968; at that time, the maximum sentence for accessory to murder was commuted from life to fifteen years. Accordingly, the statute of limitation for a crime punishable by a life sentence, which previously had been twenty years, no longer applied. Perpetrators who were charged for the first time in the 1960s fell under the new regulation, and their pending trials had to be suspended.[3] Eight defendants were sentenced to life, and fifty-three received sentences of more than four years. Most of the others were punished with prison terms between two and four years. Twenty-five were acquitted. (See table 1.) For his high-profile zeal, Dr. Filbert was among those who received the maximum sentence, life imprisonment.

The fifty-three judgments recorded during the Einsatzgruppen Trials, between 1950 and 1991, offer a wealth of information on the social background, education, and political opinions of the defendants, and, most important, the reasons why they had participated in mass murder. On the basis of that material this study establishes the various types of killers (table 2), the various explanations why they acted as they did, and their postwar careers.

THIS RESEARCH on the motivations of middle- and low-level Nazi Einsatzgruppen criminals builds on the scholarship of Christopher Browning and Daniel Jonah Goldhagen.[4] Whereas both scholars used records from the District Court in Hamburg concerning only one particular Reserve Police Battalion, this study draws on a different and more comprehensive data base, that of an entire group of perpetrators, from the 1950–91 trial records of the indicted Einsatzgruppen officers. From this body of knowledge it is possible to present more fully developed case histories, more subtle character studies, and ultimately a larger perspective on the motives of the perpetrators.

Before turning to the Einsatzgruppen cases, however, it is necessary to examine more closely the arguments of Browning and of Goldhagen, to reflect on the nature of the sources and the administration of justice against former Nazi criminals in West Germany, and to relate the latter issue to the major historiographical approaches to Nazi Germany and the Holocaust.

The Browning-Goldhagen Debate

In his pioneering 1991 work, *Ordinary Men. Reserve Police Battalion 101 and the Final Solution in Poland,* Christopher Browning studied the detailed interrogations of 210 of 500 original members of Reserve Police Battalion 101 and their

TABLE 1
Einsatzgruppen Officers before the German Courts

1. EDUCATION (HIGHEST DEGREE RECEIVED)	
Law	44 (4 Ph.D., 16 incomplete)
Other Areas	24 (1 Ph.D., 13 incomplete)
Gymnasium	20 (4 incomplete)
10 years of school (Mittlere Reife or Equivalent)	8
Apprenticeship	38
8 Years of school (Volksschule or Equivalent)	12
Total	146*
2. LAST POSITION BEFORE ARREST IN GERMANY	
Police	25
Other Civil Servants	19
Independent/Business Owner	15
Employee (White Collar)	52
Worker	12
Attorney	3
Writer/Editor/Journalist	3
Retired/Unemployed/Unknown	7
Total	136
3. SENTENCE	
Acquitted/No Penalty/Trial Discontinued	31
1 Year, 6 Months–2 Years	8
2 Years, 6 Months–4 Years	35
4 Years, 3 Months–6 Years	29
7–8 Years	11
9–10 Years	5
11–15 Years	8
Life	8
Total	136

* Ten officers held multiple degrees.

TABLE 2
The Einsatzgruppen Perpetrators

Category	Number
Confirmed killers	8
Officers from eastern German borderlands	13
Specialists	12
Acquitted officers	25
Obedient officers	78

initiation to mass murder. He found that the policemen did not have a Nazi back-ground; in fact, they had joined the Police Reserve to avoid service in the German army, the Wehrmacht. They had no previous war experience and had spent only three weeks in occupied Poland before they assisted in the elimination of the Polish Jews. Most of the Battalion 101 policemen came from the lower classes; they had families, and were old enough to have formed their political opinions independently, before the Nazis came to power. They were the quintessential "ordinary men," and certainly the least promising material out of which to create mass murderers. Yet, when they had to choose whether to shoot and then to continue shooting thousands of Jews—a task which they obviously abhorred—or whether to be utilized for other work without retribution for their decision, a vast majority chose to murder.

In his last and most important chapter of *Ordinary Men,* Browning discusses the relevant psychological concepts that account for such perplexing behavior, and he relates these concepts to the evidence. He concludes that although factors such as general wartime brutalization, careerism, compartmentalization of tasks, alcohol, deference to authority, anti-Semitism, and propagandistic indoctrination were relevant, conformity to the group and peer pressure were the single most potent motivations for the men of the battalion. Their willing participation in mass murder was not wholly atypical of the behavior of humanity at large, a point Browning especially re-emphasizes in his Afterword to the second edition of his book, which is a rebuttal to Daniel Goldhagen's work of 1996, *Hitler's Willing Executioners. Ordinary Germans and the Holocaust.*

Browning's meticulously researched and well-argued presentation offers important insights into the motivations of average Germans who contributed to the torture and murder of the Jews. Nevertheless, some of his points were not as carefully considered. It is certainly correct that most members of Reserve Police Battalion 101 were not fanatical Nazis, and they opted for service in the Police Reserve to avoid being drafted into the military, but they cannot have been as naive as Browning claims. If indeed they were mature enough to form their personalities independent of Nazi influence, as Browning argues, they also must have been experienced enough to realize that the branches of the German police had come under increasing SS control after 1933. In their choice of the Police Reserve over a military-front assignment, they also must have known that they had entered an organization under the command of the ruthless and unscrupulous Reichsführer SS (Reich Leader of the SS) and Chief of German Police Heinrich Himmler, and that they could be used for his nefarious purposes.

Moreover, it seems that Browning's conclusion—at least in the original edition of the book—does not sufficiently recognize the significance of pervasive anti-Semitism and the impact of Nazi propaganda, which had systematically denigrated the Jews and other groups of "undesirables" to less-than-human status for many years preceding the events in Poland. (He does, however, focus on the importance of anti-Semitism and cultural influences in the newly added Afterword to his second edition.) And even if the policemen were more resistant than other groups of perpetrators to the philosophies put forth in Nazi stereotypes, even with only rudimentary ideological training, nevertheless, their generally low level of education certainly might have made them more vulnerable to constant Nazi propaganda. Thus, even the battalion commander's simplistic and devised justifications before these large massacres—excuses such as, the Jews were being punished for starting the war or for the bombing of the policemen's hometown and other German cities—might have allowed these very ordinary men to validate their own behavior once they had been sent to occupied Poland.

In stark contrast to Browning's multi-level explanation, Daniel Goldhagen sees eliminationist anti-Semitism as the sole key to understanding the motives of the Reserve policemen. Goldhagen studied the material on Reserve Police Battalion 101 four years after Browning and came to very different conclusions. *Hitler's Willing Executioners* is a broad reinterpretation of the Holocaust in general, and a reply and refutation of Browning's thesis in particular. Goldhagen contends that the men of Reserve Police Battalion 101 did not come from the lower social strata; rather, they roughly represented an average occupational profile of the entire German population. Goldhagen's subtitle, *Ordinary Germans and the Holocaust,* suggests that the Reserve policemen were not "ordinary" in Browning's sense, but only insofar as they came from within the extraordinary culture of Nazi Germany. And this culture was ingrained, according to Goldhagen, with deeply rooted and radically eliminationalist anti-Semitism. Therefore, the behavior of the policemen, once they had been exposed to mass murder and did not turn away from it, only underscores that the vast majority of the German population were actual, or at least potential, Jew killers.

In a rather lengthy and repetitive book, Goldhagen uses two methods involved in the annihilation of European Jewry, labor camps and death marches, to substantiate his point. Nevertheless, Goldhagen's often overly simplistic and monocausal thesis must be rejected. As most serious Goldhagen critics have pointed out, even virulent and lethal anti-Semitism is insufficient to explain all aspects of an event of the magnitude of the Holocaust, as Goldhagen claims to do.[5] Moreover, the instances of Germans taking pleasure in torturing and killing Jews, compiled by Goldhagen, as real and horrible as they are, simply do not prove that the entire population consisted of Jew haters, torturers, and murderers only waiting for the opportunity. Most important, however, if many Germans were "Hitler's willing executioners," as Goldhagen's title implies, the sweeping claim must be valid for every group of perpetrators. Certainly the Einsatzgruppen officers, who mercilessly killed tens of thousands of innocent men, women, and children, and thereby implemented the Nazi ideology in its most uncompromising and personal form, should confirm his theory.

Yet the German court records reveal that both Christopher Browning's "ordinary men" and Daniel Goldhagen's "willing executioners" theses are overly simplistic. Many different types of perpetrators existed within the Einsatzgruppen, ranging from enthusiastic sadists to those who refused to shoot civilians on grounds of conscience. Age, background, education, profession, and many other factors played a part, but no clearly identifiable particular set of circumstances is seen to have turned so many of these men into routine killers. The psychological concepts—brutalization during the war, careerism, compartmentalization of tasks, alcohol, obedience, propagandistic indoctrination, anti-Semitism, and conformity to the group—put forth by Browning indeed go a long way toward explaining the often perplexing behavior of these men. The callous attitude of the Einsatzgruppen officers, however, suggests an even more disturbing truth: situations exist that bring out the worst in human behavior. For the Einsatzgruppen, service in the Soviet Union gave the officers an opportunity to exercise unrestrained power over an entire group of human beings.

The latter conclusion seems to correspond with the results of Yale University psychologist Stanley Milgram's famous obedience experiments.[6] From the very beginning of his research in the 1950s and 1960s, Milgram associated his experiments with the mass killings of the Jews. He writes:

> Obedience . . . is of particular relevance to our time. It has been reliably established that from 1933-45 millions of innocent persons were systematically slaughtered on command. . . . These inhumane policies could only be carried out . . . if a very large number of persons obeyed orders.[7]

Milgram then created a laboratory situation designed to study how ordinary people react when confronted with the decision to control the fate of other human beings. He had an apparently legitimate authority figure instruct "subjects" to administer increasingly stronger electric shocks whenever a "learner" failed to give the correct answer to a subject's questions. The learner was a trained actor who responded with escalating degrees of protest to the growing level of punishment. Of course, he did not actually receive the electric shocks, but his cries of pain and requests to stop the procedure did not prevent half of the subjects from following through with the experiment and inflicting even the highest and potentially deadly voltage levels.

From the evidence collected in the experiment and a number of control tests,

Milgram concluded that obedience is deeply ingrained in the functioning of human society and that ordinary people can rather easily become part of a terrible destructive process. As one of his control experiments showed, the test subjects' propensity to inflict pain and suffering was even stronger if the victim was considered "unworthy" or lowly regarded. Following the history of the Jews in Nazi Germany until the outbreak of World War II, it is obvious that they had been denigrated to such a status.

Critics of Milgram's conclusions, however, object that it is impossible to relate the outcome of his laboratory experiments to the realities of the Holocaust.[8] But it is worthwhile to examine how Milgram's experiments relate to the behavior of the Einsatzgruppen officers in particular (see chapter 6).

Court Records, Historiography, and Legal Distinctions

Relying on court records presents a particular challenge to the historian. On the one hand, it is problematic to determine whose testimony should be credited or disregarded. Everyone connected to Nazi crimes certainly had strong reason to minimize or at least distance himself from all such deeds. Moreover, ten, twenty, and sometimes thirty or more years after the events, both witnesses and defendants could not always rely on their memory. Most important, in many instances the legal principle *in dubio pro reas,* "When in doubt, then in favor of the accused," forced juries to accept assertions that could not be factually refuted. Although the German legal system does not have jury trials in the American sense, and there is no jury of the defendant's peers, District Court trials have a jury consisting of three judges and at least three lay persons.

Court records, on the other hand, have some clear advantages over other types of sources. A trial's very purpose is to determine "what really happened, and how." Therefore, the judge does the same groundwork as the historian, critically evaluating sources, analyzing facts that the sources convey, and assessing contradictory information. Unlike the historian, however, the judge has the authority to gain access to material and secure the cooperation of persons who would otherwise not volunteer their information.

The presence of both the prosecution and defense at a trial offers two perspectives on the same event, which is rarely available in historical research. In addition, juries in the German courts made sure that witnesses did not incriminate others only in order to save themselves, and that in cases of possible mistaken identities more than one witness independently linked the defendant to the pertinent events. According to a legal commentator, most indicted officers were willing to cooperate with the courts because they expected to receive mild sentences, at least by international standards. Thus, the prospect of leniency not only made these officers come forward with precise information, it also helped to accurately document the activities of the Einsatzgruppen.[9] For these reasons the judgments are the most reliable source on the activities and the character of the Einsatz-gruppen perpetrators.[10]

It is obviously important that historical investigations attempt to recreate a situation including the names of the main characters as accurately and authenti-cally as possible. Nevertheless, this has not always been achievable in this study because of German privacy laws. Unfortunately, therefore, the names of perpe-trators and witnesses will appear in three different forms:

1) The original name is used if it has been published. That has been the case for the officers indicted in Nuremberg, other well-known SS per-sonalities, the Einsatzgruppen officers sentenced in trials before 1966, and some witnesses.
2) A last name initial will be given if a defendant was acquitted in a trial before 1966. A last name initial or abbreviated version of the name is also given to witnesses from these trials.
3) Finally, a pseudonym will be used if a defendant was charged, or if a wit-ness appeared, in a trial after 1966, in order to maintain anonymity. In such cases, an asterisk (*) after the name of the person indicates that the original name was changed.

The 616 judgments from the trials of all Nazi homicide crimes, including the Einsatzgruppen cases that were concluded between 1945 and 1965, have been published.[11] The remaining 219 judgments from the trials conducted between 1966 and 1991 are available through the district attorneys' offices that held the pertinent proceedings, or the relevant state archives. Copies of the complete trial records are also available at the Central Office of the State Justice Administra-tions for the Investigation of National Socialist Homicide Crimes (Zentrale Stelle der Landesjustizverwaltungen zur Verfolgung nationalsozialistischer Gewaltver-brechen) in Ludwigsburg, where it is possible to obtain the records of the Ein-satzgruppen trials held after 1965. The Central Office was founded by the Secre-taries of Justice in the German states in 1958 in order to facilitate the uniform prosecution of Nazi crimes. Since then, the Central Office has initiated more than 7,000 pre-investigation motions and has referred them to the appropriate District Courts.[12]

The opinions of the judges (Urteilsbegründung) in the German courts dem-onstrate how historical interpretation of the destruction of the European Jews influenced the administration of justice. All courts accepted the testimony of their main expert witnesses, Helmut Krausnick and Hans Buchheim, both from

the influential Munich Institute for Contemporary History (Institut für Zeitgeschichte). These historians argued that the decision and the plan to murder
the Jews originated from Hitler, Heinrich Himmler, and Reinhardt Heydrich
(some judgments also mention Hermann Göring and Josef Goebbels), and that
before the 1941 invasion of the Soviet Union, Heydrich had transmitted a general
order to the Einsatzgruppen leaders to kill the Soviet Jews.

During the 1960s when most of the trials were held, the expert witnesses' versions of the events corresponded with the prevailing historical attitude about the
nature of government, exercise of power, and origins of the Final Solution in the
Third Reich. Krausnick, Buchheim, and other "intentionalists," as this school
of thought was called, believed that Hitler's ideology and his position as the
Führer at the top of the Nazi hierarchy determined all German politics, and especially the decisions that led to the annihilation of the European Jews. The intentionalists contend that Hitler harbored radical anti-Semitic thoughts from the
very beginning of his political career in the early 1920s and only waited for the opportunity to transform them into actions. The intentionalists use evidence from
Hitler's books, the Nazi Party program, and speeches such as Hitler's declara-
tion of January 30, 1939, in which he told the German Legislature (the Reichstag)
and the world:

> At the time of my struggle for power, it was mostly the Jewish people who
> laughed at the prophecy that one day I would attain in Germany the leadership
> . . . and that among other problems I would also solve the Jewish one. . . .To-
> day I want to be a prophet again: If international finance Jewry inside and out-
> side Europe succeeds in precipitating the nations into a world war, the result will
> not be the Bolshevization of the earth, and with it the victory of Jewry, but the
> annihilation of the Jewish race in Europe.[14]

Thus, a straight and inevitable connection existed between Hitler's earliest anti-Semitic proclamations, the massacres of the Einsatzgruppen, and the
factory-style killings of millions of Jews. Ernst Nolte, one of the early intentionalists, succinctly stated, "The hard monomaniacal core of his [Hitler's] being,
did not change one iota from Vienna to Berlin."[14]

The American criminal code does not distinguish between the mastermind
and the executors of a murder plan, and the prosecution may indict either party
with the charge of murder. This possibility, however, does not exist in the German justice system. In fact, an important legal distinction is found in Germany.
The German penal code stipulates that the authorities must differentiate between perpetrators (Täter), who have the will and intention (Täterwille) to commit a crime, and accomplices (Gehilfen), who help with the perpetration of a

crime yet lack the independent will to commit it. Following this logic, the panel of judges in the German trials in general condemned only Hitler, Himmler, and Heydrich as the main perpetrators (Haupttäter). With the exception of Dr. Filbert and a few others, the Einsatzgruppen officers were charged as accomplices, which warrants lesser penalties.

Clearly the judges acknowledged Krausnick's and Buchheim's intentionalist interpretation because they accepted that the vast majority of the Einsatzgruppen officers did not make an independent decision to kill the Russian Jews. They determined that the SS officers merely obeyed the orders of Hitler and other superiors, and therefore they were less culpable for their deeds, even if they actually had been more personally involved.[15] Unfortunately, the courts continued to adhere to the intentionalist model and indicted the Einsatzgruppen officers only as accomplices until the conclusion of the last Einsatzgruppen trial in 1991, even though other scholars soon began to discredit the intentionalists and the central role of Hitler and his ideology.

Obviously the intentionalist position offered a rather convenient defense for many former Nazi and government officials involved in the Holocaust. As a result, beginning in the late 1960s, the search for a larger circle of culprits became an important incentive for a new generation of historians in order to find alternative explanations. These historians were called "functionalists" or "structuralists" because they focused on the structures of the Nazi movement and explained the cumulative radicalization of anti-Jewish policy as a function of the anarchistic power struggles between different groups, factions, and institutions within the Nazi system. Ideological motivation and Hitler's position were of lesser importance, and some went as far as to describe Hitler as "a rather weak dictator."[16] To functionalists, the initiatives of countless decision-makers in an intricate bureaucracy let to piecemeal anti-Jewish measures and improvised temporary solutions, until finally physical elimination of the Jews seemed to be the only way out of a series of self-imposed crises. Therefore, historian Karl Schleunes writes about a rather "twisted road to Auschwitz" in his 1970 work.[17]

According to funtionalists, the Nazis implemented an anarchic system of government immediately after the seizure of power in 1933. They tried to place their officials in decisive state positions, and at the same time they created entirely new, parallel institutions such as the Office Ribbentrop (a Nazi Party organization with similar tasks as the Foreign Office, led by the future Foreign Minister Joachim von Ribbentrop) or the Commissioner of the Economy (with the same duties as the Secretary of the Economy). One scholar described this process as "National socialist shadow growths [Schattengewächse] springing up next to the traditional state bureaucracy and almost every state office received a brown watchdog."[18] Yet more than simply guarding each others' interests, state and Nazi bureaucracies, often encouraged by the lack of clear directives from the Führer, soon engaged in a struggle for power and influence. As a result, by 1938 the most ruthless Nazi officials and offices had secured the important decision-making positions. The built-in dynamic of such a process, the principle of permanent revolution, the tearing down of fixed structures, and the creation of ever-new organizations ultimately led to the proliferation of arbitrary decisions and acts of violence. Beneath Hitler, who unified the leadership of party, state, and people, no overall responsibility existed. Such a polyocracy, based on Hitler's absolute power, as Martin Broszat argues, could not be reconciled with normal conduct of government and inevitably led to complete destruction.[19] To functionalists, the Final Solution thus evolved from the functioning of the system and not, as the intentionalists thought, from Hitler's ideological aspirations.

Although at least until the early 1990s most German historians rather strictly seemed to adhere to these polarized models, both schools are certainly not mutually exclusive. International scholars such as Christopher Browning and Ian Kershaw, for example, were among the first to reconcile the opposing arguments. In two short yet important essays, Browning lays out what he calls his "moderate functionalist" synthesis.[20] He contends that elements from both schools, "the conjuncture of Hitler's anti-Semitic obsession, the anarchical and competitive nature of the Nazi state, the vulnerable status of the European Jews, and the war ultimately resulted in the Final Solution."[21]

Browning argues that Hitler made the decision to murder the Russian Jews during the planning phase for the invasion of the Soviet Union in 1941. The SS and other agencies, however, replaced previously existing resettlement schemes with extermination of all European Jews only after Hitler gave them a "green light" during the euphoria of the German Blitzkrieg victories in the late summer of 1941. Coincidentally, at this decisive juncture, when German victory seemed imminent, Himmler also quickly moved to strengthen the Einsatzgruppen and other killing units behind the lines in the Soviet Union.

Ian Kershaw's famous principle of "working towards the Führer" offers a similar and logical reconciliation of intentionalist and functionalist positions.[22] Drawing from the intentionalist arguments, Kershaw clearly places Hitler at the center of the Nazi system: "His essential, unchanging, distant goals became the driving-force of the entire Nazi regime."[23] At the same time, and corroborating functionalist thought, Kershaw also emphasizes that Hitler usually did not issue direct orders and often did not intervene in the development of events at all. Rather, different functionaries and influence groups knew that they could count on Hitler's support if their interests coincided with his often vaguely stated and distant goals. The functioning of the Nazi system thus left room for local and regional initiatives and offered opportunities for those officials who interpreted the Führer correctly and implemented his "wishes" in their most radical form.

In terms of the "Jewish Problem," the war with Poland and later the Soviet Union opened entirely new and increasingly radical avenues, while it simultaneously closed others until the Nazis had maneuvered themselves into a cul-de-sac because the war in Russia could not be concluded within a few months and the Einsatzgruppen could not "handle" the masses of Soviet Jews. At this point, Hitler signaled to the SS leadership and other organizations involved with the Jews in the eastern territories that it was time to fulfill his prophecy of January 1939. Thus, no further and precise orders were necessary to set in motion the Final Solution and the establishment of the death camps. Arthur Greiser, the regional Nazi Party official (Gauleiter) of the newly annexed Polish territory, the Poznan-Lodz area called the Wartheland (named for the Warthe River), understood this logic well. He explained, with regard to consulting with Hitler before including 30,000 Poles in his extermination program: "I myself do not believe that the Führer needs to be asked again in this matter, especially since at our last discussion with regard to the Jews he told me that I could proceed with these according to my own judgment."[24]

The Einsatzgruppen Study

This examination of the Einsatzgruppen officers is divided into three parts:

- background information on the Einsatzgruppen— their conception and origins, training, indoctrination, orders, activities, and place within the overall framework of the Holocaust;
- analysis of the attitude and behavior of the different categories of perpetrators as they emerge from the court records—the confirmed killers, the officers from the eastern borderlands, the specialists, the officers who were acquitted, and the officers to whom obedience to authority was the principal motivation to participate in the extermination campaign;
- and summation relating these observations to the pertinent literature. Because the German judgments provided the basis for this work, the Afterword offers a brief evaluation of the legal proceedings against the former Einsatzgruppen officers and how they reflect that country's continuing efforts in dealing with its Nazi past.

I. THE HISTORY OF THE EINSATZGRUPPEN

If it had a historical effect,
then everything—even and perhaps
especially the most despicable—must be
examined and revealed objectively.
That is still the first task of
the historical discipline.

Eberhard Jäckel

HE CRIMES of the newly formed Ein-
satzgruppen against the Soviet Jews and other "enemies" of the Third Reich
began with the German attack on the Soviet Union on June 21, 1941. Four Einsatzgruppen of the Security Police (Sicherheitspolizei) and the Security Service
(Sicherheitsdienst, or SD), part of the SS, immediately followed the invading
armies. Their main task was to eliminate the Soviet Jews, Communist Party (KP)
officials, prisoners of war, and everyone deemed dangerous to the interests of
the National Socialist (Nazi) state.

During the time the Einsatzgruppen operated in the territory of the Soviet
Union, they combined with other SS, military, and police units to kill approximately 1.5 million people—it is impossible to give the exact number of victims.
From the German point of view, the Operational Situation Reports (Ereignismeldungen) of the Einsatzgruppen, which detail and itemize these killings, are
thought to be exaggerated, and thus it is often no longer possible to determine
whether the victims were executed by the Einsatzgruppen proper or by the associated SS, police, and military formations. From the Soviet perspective, the
numbers listed in the reports also are not reliable; the number of Jews in the
occupied territories is difficult to estimate because of the Soviet annexations after September 1939 and the subsequent population shifts. In addition, it is difficult to distinguish between the general destruction of a brutal war and the even
more horrible reality of the planned massacres. And finally, although the Situation Reports do distinguish between Jews and other victims, the differences are

not always clearly indicated. Therefore, the estimates given in the literature range between 1 million and 2.35 million for the victims in all parts of the Soviet Union after 1945.[1]

Although the Holocaust is usually associated with the factory-style gassing in the extermination camps, the Einsatzgruppen and other mobile execution squads accounted for almost one fourth of all Holocaust victims.[2]

Preparations and Precedents

The primary sources and the literature are rather limited regarding the origins, personnel, and training of the Einsatzgruppen. Judging from the available material, however, it seems that a career in the various branches of the German police or previous experience with terror in Austria, Czechoslovakia, or Poland were the only required qualifications for an Einsatzgruppen officer. It would seem that such a background must have prepared the perpetrators well, given that the Einsatzgruppen in the Soviet Union achieved a deadly effectiveness, although they had been assembled only one month before they were unleashed.

Map 2. The Occupied Eastern Territories, Spring 1942. Map by Brian Fulfrost.

Holocaust and SS scholars Heinz Höhne, Helmut Krausnick, and Hans-Heinrich Wilhelm suggest that the general training of the police, the SS, and the Security Service had a significant influence on the attitude and performance of the Einsatzgruppen.[3] With the Nazi seizure of power, all branches of the German police had come under increasing SS influence and had turned away from the principles of a state of law (Rechtsstaat). The first step toward this change was the April 26, 1934, appointment of Reich Leader SS Heinrich Himmler to Inspector and Deputy Chief of the Prussian Secret State Police Office. Himmler, thus, simultaneously occupied a National Socialist Party and a state position. Subsequently, by Hitler's decree of June 17, 1936, Himmler became the Chief of the German Police. From then on he carried the official title of Reichsführer SS and Chief of the German Police, which outwardly signified the merger of party political activity with a state office. In the following years, Himmler further coordinated the police services. He abolished the State Police budgets and consolidated them under a central Reich Police budget, which gave him decisive control over personnel, organization, and equipment of the entire German police. On June 26, 1936, shortly after his new appointment, Himmler reorganized the existing police branches under the Main Office Order Police (Hauptamt Ordnungspolizei) and the Main Office Security Police (Hauptamt Sicherheitspolizei). The latter agency combined the Gestapo (Secret State Police) and Criminal Police (Kripo) detectives under the command of Reinhardt Heydrich, who was also in charge of the Security Service.

Himmler defined the tasks of the three Security Police branches:

- the Gestapo would monitor and investigate all hostile political activities directed against the German people and the state;
- Criminal Police detectives would deal with hostile activities against the German people that were not motivated by political goals (a loose and rather arbitrary definition of "political activity" that left enough leeway to use the Criminal Police later in the persecution of the Jews);
- the Security Service primarily would serve to collect foreign intelligence.[4]

On September 27, 1939, Himmler merged these three organizations into one umbrella organization, the Reich Security Main Office (Reichssicherheitshauptamt, or RSHA) under Heydrich, who became Chief of the Security Police and the Security Service.

Since 1937, Himmler further had augmented the consolidation of the police and the SS under his position as Reich Leader SS and Chief of the German Police, and Heydrich as Chief of the Security Police and the Security Service,

FIGURE I
Reorganization of the German Police under Heinrich Himmler

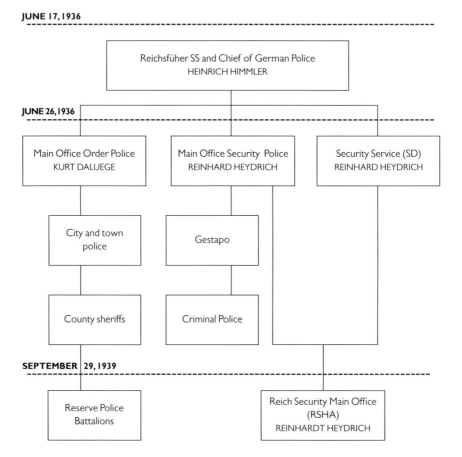

JUNE 17, 1936

Reichsfüher SS and Chief of German Police
HEINRICH HIMMLER

JUNE 26, 1936

Main Office Order Police
KURT DALUEGE

Main Office Security Police
REINHARD HEYDRICH

Security Service (SD)
REINHARD HEYDRICH

City and town police

Gestapo

County sheriffs

Criminal Police

SEPTEMBER 29, 1939

Reserve Police
Battalions

Reich Security Main Office
(RSHA)
REINHARDT HEYDRICH

[1] For an organizational chart of the RSHA, see Raul Hilberg, *The Destruction of the European Jews*, vol. 1, table 7-4 (New York: Holmes & Meier, 1985), 282–83.

with the creation of yet another institution, the Higher SS and Police Leaders (Höhere SS und Polizeiführer, or HSSPF). The Higher SS and Police Leaders guarded Himmler's interests, serving as his "watchdogs" within the army districts, and coordinated the work of the SS, the Security Police, and the Order Police (Ordnungspolizei).

With the subsequent establishment of the Reich Security Main Office in 1939, Himmler forged a large security organization that practically perverted normal police work.[5] Although its name indicated that it was to protect the German people from crime and enemies, in practice this new security super agency soon became Heydrich's instrument for preventive and repressive terror against German and foreign peoples.

To complete the organizational and ideological restructuring of the German police, Himmler, Heydrich, and the higher police leaders preferred that the members of their Security Police join the SS. As an incentive, SS members received the preferential treatment of better salaries and larger houses.[6] In a letter to Himmler, the Chief of the SS Race and Resettlement Main Office (Rasse und Siedlungshauptamt) states: "Apartments measuring 62 to 86 square meters are certainly sufficient for the broad masses. But for our SS families we must apply different standards. I recently inspected an apartment measuring 110 square meters, and I had to conclude that even this size is definitely not too large."[7] Of course, this evaluation also reflects the hoped-for expectation that SS families would produce more children than the average German family.

Himmler handled recruitment, selection, and promotions in the SS according to strict racial and ideological principles. All marriages had to be approved by the SS Race and Resettlement Main Office and members were expelled from the SS if they had married an unsuitable woman.[8] Ideological education dominated the training at the Security Police Leadership School, and promotion often depended on this training. Moreover, all policemen were expected to approach situations with a "practical Nazi orientation," which meant that they disregarded the still-existing—at least on paper—legal framework and the notion of due process. All future officers were furthermore required to completely acknowledge and accept the principles of Nazi ideology.

Training and indoctrination in various SS organizations prepared the majority of the Einsatzgruppen officers for their future tasks. The basic guidelines of the SS were quasi-religious devotion to the Führer, unconditional obedience, and continuing struggle and vigilance. These guidelines were expressed in numerous publications, including the illustrated book *The Path to Obedience,* the honor code of the SS, bestowed by Hitler on November 9, 1931, the eighth anniversary of his failed coup, and in a pamphlet entitled *The Struggle Is Ours.*[9] The guidelines were also strictly emphasized in the SS summer solstice celebrations, part of a series of pagan festivals staged by Himmler to replace Christian traditions. The "twelve promises," the statements of faith for the SS, were recited during these rituals. These promises shed light on the self-perception of the members of the SS, or, as Heinz Höhne called this organization, "the order under the death's head." The name is fitting, as Himmler ironically used the Jesuit order, with its tight discipline and rigid command structure, as a model for his SS.

The Path to Obedience also contains maps and pictures from German history, and its epigraph states: "Our people had to suffer the difficulties of the last two thousand years because of its own faults until it learned in its entirety the path to obedience,"[10] implying that obedience is the key to a better future.

Excerpts from the other sources further underscore the importance of blind obedience:

> Faith, honor, obedience and courage determine the behavior of the SS man. His weapon bears the inscription bestowed by the Führer: "My Honor Is Called Faith. [Meine Ehre heisst Treue]." Both virtues are intertwined. Whoever disregards these virtues is unworthy of membership in the Protection Squad.
>
> Obedience is unconditional. It is based on the conviction that the national socialist ideology will rule supreme. Whoever has that conviction and acts accordingly voluntarily follows this obligation. Thus the SS man is willing to blindly obey every order from the Führer or from his superiors, even if it demands the greatest sacrifice.[11]

Promises number 11 and 12 of the SS guidelines state:

> 11. The Protection Squad is the fighting and kinship order of the new Germany. The enemies of the Reich will be annihilated by its fighting spirit. Its honor is called faith! Its light shall shine!
> 12. Our love and our oath tie us to Adolf Hitler, the leader of the German Reich. We believe in him because he personifies Germany. His light shall shine![12]

> We were armed from the first day. In the beginning the word was our sword. We fought for everyone of our blood in order to win him for the Führer. We jealously guarded over our party comrades so that no one would enter into our ranks who did not believe in the holy struggle of the Führer. . . . The individual is nothing, our people are everything. Our personal goals disappear before the objectives of the Führer. Our free will becomes obedience. . . . We give up our private lives. Our lives belong to the community. . . . We do not know privilege, only duties that we have to fulfill.. . . Our task began with the protection of the Führer. We protected the believers to whom he spoke during the rallies. . . . For a people stops living if it stops fighting. The protection squad will be the fist at the sword during the struggle for the future of the German people![13]

While SS members were being conditioned to live according to such doctrines; anti-Semitic propaganda and the image of the elite SS in the forefront of the battle against World Jewry played another important role in their education. A slide show entitled "Jewry. Its Blood-Related Character in Past and Present" ends with a frame called "SS in the Struggle Against the World Enemy, Juda." It depicts a typical blond, Nordic SS man in front of a swastika flag. Clenching his weapon, he looks vigilant and ready; his eyes seem to be fixed on a glorious future. The summary of the slide show then reads:

> Every SS man has to know the following: Jewry and the Jewish spirit have always been deadly enemies of the Nordic race. As the Jew was thousands of years ago, he is today and will be in the future; it is the law of his blood. If we purge the Jew from the body of our people, it is an act of self-defense. . . . We will try everything to prepare ourselves as quickly as possible to defend our borders and our sovereignty, our people and our nation against all Jewish attacks. Make sure that all German people's comrades recognize the Jew as the deadly enemy of every nation and every ideology that is born from our blood.[14]

To complement the ideological indoctrination, SS training furthermore emphasized physical fitness and the endurance of hardship. Himmler expected that SS members would set high standards for themselves. They learned to apply the most brutal of many possible tactics and believed that terror itself was a cure-all measure for political and military problems.[15]

The SD, the Nazi Party Security Service, was considered an elite branch within the SS. Heydrich intended for it to become the General Staff, and the Gestapo the fighting troops, of the Reich Security Main Office.[16] Security Service officers were generally better educated and even more ambitious than common SS officers, and they usually had joined the Nazi movement very early. It was, therefore, no coincidence that eight Einsatzgruppen and Einsatzkommando leaders held Ph.D. degrees. According to the SS Main Office, Security Service officers who wanted to achieve leadership ranks also were required, among other conditions, to have proof of Aryan ancestry back to the year 1750, and were to have demonstrated political reliability in leadership positions of the Hitler Youth (Hitlerjugend, or HJ).[17]

As did most other Einsatzgruppen officers, Security Service members received job-specific practical instructions in subjects such as criminology, intelligence and counter-intelligence, bureaucratic procedure, and court strategy of the Gestapo, Criminal Police, or Security Service. In addition, they underwent extensive theoretical training at the Security Service Leadership School that included classes in proper SS attitude, demeanor, and behavior; history; biological and racial science; ideology; philosophy; foreign studies and languages; law and state science; and physical education.[18]

Battle-tested at the Night of the Long Knives on June 30, 1934, and the attack on the Gleiwitz radio station (located on the German-Polish border) on September 1, 1939, Security Service officers had gained a reputation for ruthlessness and devotion to Nazi ideology that surpassed even the SS. It was on June 30, 1934, that Hitler had Storm Trooper (SA) leader Ernst Röhm and many other former allies shot, among them the former Reichchancellor Gen. Kurt von Schleicher, claiming that Röhm was plotting a putsch to betray his German fatherland. Although Röhm indeed wanted to transform his Storm Troopers into a "people's army," Röhm had always remained loyal to Hitler. This so-called Night of the Long Knives was the first time that Hitler had openly revealed his murderous capacity, and the result was that the Storm Trooper organization was essentially emasculated, whereas the role and the power of the SS and Himmler increased significantly.[19] On the night of the attack on the Gleiwitz radio station, a Security Service command had been responsible, dressed in Polish uniforms. But Hitler blamed the attack on Poland, and on September 1, 1939, ordered his Wehrmacht "to shoot back," thus beginning the Second World War.[20]

All members of the Security Police, regardless of their membership in the SS, wore a uniform similar to the SS with the characteristic Security Service diamond on the left sleeve. Because of this distinguishing marker, the other German occupation forces in the Soviet Union commonly referred to all mobile and later stationary units of the Security Police and the Security Service, including the Einsatzgruppen, simply as the Security Service. The non-SS and Security Service members of the Einsatzgruppen were allowed to hold a so-called Angleichungsdienstgrad, the SS equivalent to their rank in the police. Thus, for example, a commissar in the Criminal Police became an SS Obersturmführer or Hauptsturmführer (the equivalent U.S. ranks of first lieutenant and captain), depending on the years served on the force (see table 3).[21]

Whereas the decision to murder the Soviet Jews was a decisive step for German Jewish policy, for the designated perpetrators it was not. The SS, Gestapo, and Security Service officers already had acquired experience in the control of "enemies of the state" within Germany since 1933. And forces from the three Security Police organizations had entered the territory of a previously independent country for the first time after the annexation of Austria in the spring of 1938. For the five days it took to establish permanent Security Police control, mobile detachments from the Main Office Security Police and the Security Service ruthlessly eliminated all resistance in political, military, and economic matters. The two branches of the Security Police served as instruments to implement the will of the Führer; they had no legal boundaries.

The term "Einsatzgruppen" had appeared for the first time in the preparations for the dismemberment of Czechoslovakia in May 1938.[22] The activities of an "independent"—a Nazi euphemism for not bound to normal legal stan-

TABLE 3
SS, German Police, and American Army Ranks

SS	Criminal Police	Order Police	US Army
SS Mann		Unterwachtmeister	
SS Sturmmann		Rottwachtmeister	Private
Rottenführer			Private First Class
Unterscharführer		Wachtmeister	Corporal
Scharführer		Wachtmeister	Sergeant
Oberscharführer	Kriminalassistent	Oberwachtmeister	Staff Sergeant
Hauptscharführer	Kriminaloberassistent	Hauptwachtmeister	Technical Sergeant
Sturmscharführer			Master Sergeant
Untersturmführer	Kriminalsekretär/	Polizeimeister/	Second Lieutenant
	Kriminalobersekretär	Polizeiobermeister/	
		Leutnant	
Obersturmführer	Kommissar/	Polizeiinspektor/	First Lieutenant
	Kriminalinspektor	Oberleutnant	
Hauptsturmführer	Kriminalrat	Hauptmann	Captain
Sturmbannführer	Kriminaldirektor/	Major	Major
	Regierungsrat		
Obersturmbannführer	Oberregierungsrat	Oberstleutnant	Lieutenant Colonel
Standartenführer	Regierungsdirektor	Oberst	Colonel
Oberführer		Generalmajor	
Brigadeführer		Generalmajor	Brigadier General
Gruppenführer		Generalleutnant	Major General
Obergruppenführer		General der Polizei	Lieutenant General
Oberstgruppenführer			General

Source: Werner Best, Die deutsche Polizei (Darmstadt: L. C. Wittlich Verlag, 1941), pp. 78–87; Fritz Bauer et al., Justiz und NS-Verbrechen. Sammlung Deutscher Strafurteile wegen nationalsozialistischer Tötungsverbrechen 1945–1966, 23 vols. (Amsterdam: Amsterdam University Press, 1976); National Archives and Records Administration, Finding Aids for National Archives Microfilm Publication T 175 (Washington, D.C.: NARA, 1989), T733, roll 8, frame 0008/0357.

dards—political police during the conquests of Czechoslovakia and Poland set important precedents for the invasion of the Soviet Union.

While the Wehrmacht planned the destruction of the Czechoslovakian state, Reinhard Heydrich worked on the future political repression and domination of its Czech parts, Bohemia and Moravia. He proposed close cooperation between the Operational Task Headquarters (Einsatzstäbe) of the Security Service and the Gestapo. Both organizations were to be protected by Action Groups (Aktionsgruppen) from the Common SS (SS Verfügungstruppe) or the Waffen (armed) SS and supervised by Heydrich himself. This organizational structure for the first time reflected the main sources of manpower tapped for the future Einsatzgruppen: Security Service, Gestapo, and Waffen SS. The Einsatzgruppen in the Soviet Union, however, in order to round out their strength, had also drafted Lithuanian, Latvian, Estonian, Ukrainian, and ethnic German auxiliaries. These Hilfswillige—Hiwis—often committed the most cruel and bloody massacres. In one case, Lithuanian Hiwis had locked up Jewish women in a stable and had ordered them to undress and come out one by one for "medical examination." The Lithuanians then immediately pounced on the unsuspecting victims, clubbing them with iron rods and finally bayoneting them to death.[23]

During the occupation of Bohemia and Moravia in the spring of 1939, the three independent branches of the Einsatzgruppen operated under a uniform command for the first time. The idea of the Einsatzgruppen was, thus, as Einsatzgruppen Commander Otto Ohlendorf expressed in his Nuremberg interrogation, "invented by Heydrich."[24]

The reports the Einsatzgruppen sent to their superiors from Czechoslovakia no longer exist. The accounts of a military counter-espionage officer of the Abwehr, the German military intelligence service, are the only remaining source of knowledge on Einsatzgruppen activities within these lands. The Abwehr, the military intelligence service under Admiral Wilhelm Canaris, had been a rival to the Security Service in terms of counterespionage and the gathering of foreign intelligence.[25] According to Maj. Helmut Groskurth, who traveled in the former Czech territory on behalf of his superior, Admiral Canaris, the Einsatzgruppen followed in the wake of the invading armies in order to control political life and secure the important Czech armaments industries. As an overture to what was to come, Einsatzgruppen operations in Czechoslovakia began with a massive wave of arrests, primarily directed against German emigrants and Czech Communists, and subsequently intensified acts of violence and terror. After the beginning of the Second World War, hundreds of Czech citizens fell victim to summary executions.

In Czechoslovakia, the Einsatzgruppen operated independently from the jurisdiction of the German civilian authority of Governor (Reichsprotektor) Franz von Neurath. The Security Police had no problems asserting its authority over the weak governor, who was succeeded by Heydrich in 1941, but it had considerable discord with the Wehrmacht. An agreement existed concerning executive jurisdiction and responsibilities in the rear combat zone, yet the army was unwilling to relinquish part of its executive authority. Army commanders gave operational orders to the Einsatzgruppen, and the German troops in general despised the Security Service and Gestapo units. The SS, however, would not forget the restrictions the army had imposed on its activities.[26]

The relatively subsidiary position of the Einsatzgruppen, as well as their organization and tasks, changed during the subsequent conquest of Poland. There the cover of the war for the first time would offer the opportunity for the brutal elimination of racially undesirable elements. As Ian Kershaw noted, Poland became a "training-ground" where the Einsatzgruppen could operate loosened from all remnants of law and constraint that had still existed within Germany or even Czechoslovakia.[27] On September 1, 1939, five (later six) Einsatzgruppen pushed into Polish territory directly behind the victorious armies, this time again under a uniform command structure and led by Security Service officers, among them the later leader of the Reich Security Main Office Personnel Department, Bruno Streckenbach.[28]

As in Czechoslovakia in 1938 and later in the Soviet Union, the Einsatzgruppen in Poland reported back to the Reich Security Main Office. Their reports were shorter and not as precise as the later Operational Situation Reports from the USSR, the Ereignismeldungen aus der UdSSR, but they included the most pertinent information. In the early days after the attack, the Einsatzgruppen primarily registered and arrested the Polish elite and all persons potentially hostile to Nazi Germany, in particular the Communists, nationalists, and Catholic priests. By September 7, 1939, Heydrich had talked about "eliminating the leading strata of the population." He explained what he had in mind only a day later: "We want to spare the little people, but the nobility, the priests and the Jews must be killed."[29]

The Einsatzgruppen were also involved in the vast Nazi resettlement schemes that expelled Jews and Poles from the German incorporated territories and dumped them into the newly established Nazi General Government territory (Generalgouvernement). This territory was composed of the former Poland minus the areas incorporated into Germany (Wartheland, western Prussia, southeastern Prussia). It was governed by Hans Frank, renowned for his brutality, corruption, and inefficiency and executed at Nuremburg for presiding over a relentless extermination of Poles and Jews. Frank had converted to Catholicism after his postwar arrest, and at his trial had declared that a thousand years could pass and still Germany's guilt would not be erased.

Heydrich had instructed his Einsatzgruppen in a special letter dated September 21, 1939, stipulating that they should register the Jews and their property and establish ghettos with a liaison Jewish self-government—the notorious and sometimes morally questionable Judenräte, the Jewish Councils—until the Jews could be resettled in the east. Heydrich left the extent and timing of such measures to the discretion of the Einsatzgruppen leaders, but in general he still demanded that the Einsatzgruppen not interfere with military operations.[30]

In Poland, the behavior of the Wehrmacht again determined the limits of the activity of the Einsatzgruppen. And as in Czechoslovakia, the relationship between the military and the Einsatzgruppen remained strained, but it already had developed into the general direction it would take during the invasion of the Soviet Union. During the preparations for the Polish war, Heydrich and the Wehrmacht's then Col. Eduard Wagner agreed that the Einsatzgruppen would receive orders from the army command. The subordination, however, existed only on paper. In practice, the army was all too busily engaged in the conduct of military operations and willingly left the unpopular policing tasks to the Einsatzgruppen. It even handed over suspects. And because the Wehrmacht did not know of Heydrich's exact orders to the Einsatzgruppen, most officers still regarded the SS atrocities as a necessary, though despicable, by-product of the war. They did, however, consider the executions a threat to military discipline, as they were conducted without the proper military procedure of a trial and firing squad. The Wehrmacht did not realize that the Einsatzgruppen were carrying out a full-fledged genocidal program.

Initially the Einsatzgruppen were interested in good relations with the Wehrmacht, and they exercised remarkable constraint in the very early phase of the war. But by September 3, Himmler had ordered the Einsatzgruppen to shoot all armed Polish rebels. In addition, they began to execute "insurgents" without reporting it to the responsible army commands, as the agreement had stipulated. The Wehrmacht protested the open encroachments on its jurisdiction, but grudgingly accepted increasingly radical Einsatzgruppen activities. The army tolerated the formation of on-location courts (Standgerichte) set up by the Einsatzgruppen to condemn insurgents and partisans. But when Himmler unleashed an additional Einsatzgruppe zbV (zur besonderen Verwendung, [for special purpose]) on the industrial areas in Upper Silesia and western Galicia in order to "radically subdue the exploding Polish insurgency," vehement army protests forced its withdrawal.[31] Nevertheless, to characterize the overall conduct of the Wehrmacht, it appeared that the army was content with the conduct of combat operations and left the required policing and ideological duties to the Einsatzgruppen.

Yet that general attitude changed in the time between the end of the military administration on October 25, 1939, and the consolidation of the civilian administration of Governor Hans Frank in early 1940. The Einsatzgruppen were only too eager to fill the legal vacuum and extend their areas of jurisdiction. Their activities against the Polish population became increasingly radical, and they presented the responsible authorities with faits accomplis. After the military operations had ceased, however, the by then idle Wehrmacht soldiers finally had more time to notice the violence and terror spread by the Einsatzgruppen. Protests and interventions increased from officers of the occupation army, in particular from the commanding officer, Col. Gen. Johannes Blaskowitz, on behalf of the Jews. Army officials even arrested and court-martialed some SS perpetrators, but Hitler granted them amnesty on October 4, 1939. Moreover, the Army (Land) High Command (Oberkommando des Heeres, or OKH) and Field Marshal General von Brauchitsch, the army supreme commander, did not back the arrests by their courageous subordinates and looked for appeasement with the SS. Blaskowitz was quickly transferred to France and later quietly relieved of his command.

On November 20, 1939, the Einsatzgruppen in Polish territories were officially disbanded and the personnel used to fill the newly created positions in the Security Service offices in the integrated territories and the General Government. These stationary Security Service organizations then again tightened the screws and intensified radical activities against the Polish intelligentsia and the Jews.[32] In the end, the Polish case had proven that because of the still relatively negative attitude of the Wehrmacht as the executive power, the implementation of racial policies could not yet be fully executed as planned by Himmler and Heydrich. Hitler's personal intervention on behalf of the SS and the failure of the Army High Command to make a decisive stand when it was still possible, as the withdrawal of the Einsatzgruppe zbV demonstrated, however, did not bode well for the upcoming war with the Soviet Union.[33]

A scholarly consensus indicates that either during the planning phase for this war or shortly thereafter, Hitler and his closest paladins in the Nazi leadership decided to eliminate all parts of the civilian population they thought either dangerous to their interests or that did not fit into their radical racial, political, and demographic schemes. For this purpose Heydrich and the Reich Security Main Office began to lay the groundwork for four new Einsatzgruppen. Because the expanding SS and police organizations perennially had suffered from a shortage of personnel, the Einsatzgruppen that had been in operation before were dissolved after every successful German military campaign.[34] For these new Einsatzgruppen, however, they could provide valuable experience in the domination of "lesser" peoples.

During the preparation for the invasion of the Soviet Union, former Hamburg Gestapo Chief Bruno Streckenbach, by this time an SS colonel and head of the Reich Security Main Office personnel department, again had to man new Einsatzgruppen with members from the existing Security Service, Gestapo, Criminal Police, Order Police, and Waffen SS formations. Streckenbach conscripted specialists such as drivers, mechanics, interpreters, radio operators, and others based on the "Third Emergency Decree to Secure Manpower for Tasks of Special State-Political Significance" (Dritte Notverordnung zur Sicher-

stellung des Kräftebedarfs für Aufgaben von besonderer staatspolitischer Be-
deutung).[35] The ethnic Germans Eberhard von Toll and Peter Gehfluss* were
drafted as interpreters in the Einsatzgruppen under this law.[36]

Due to the personnel shortages, but also because of their unique qualifications, many high-ranking Einsatzgruppen officers were pulled directly from the
Reich Security Main Office organization, such as the leaders of Einsatzgruppe B
and D, SS Brig. Gen. Arthur Nebe and SS Col. Otto Ohlendorf, respectively,
and the leader of Sonderkommando 4a, SS Lt. Col. Paul Blobel. Because the
Reich Security Main Office members already knew about the plan for the eradication of the Jews, the circle of the "initiated" was kept small. Other officers, such
as the leader of Einsatzgruppe A, Franz Walter Stahlecker, actively sought assignment to the Einsatzgruppen on their own, to revitalize a dwindling SS career.
Stahlecker had been reassigned to the Foreign Office, but would force his way
back into the Reich Security Main Office. And the commanding officer of Sonderkommando 7a, SS Lt. Col. Albert Rapp, had volunteered for the Einsatzgruppen because he had no military training or experience.[37]

According to the testimony of Streckenbach, Heydrich had hand-picked
the commanding officers and the personnel for the Einsatzgruppen headquarters, who would in turn request their most loyal subordinates to follow them
into their new assignments. They thus formed a leadership nucleus that was
usually able to coerce the less-experienced and fanatical members of the new
units. SS Lt. Col. Dr. Erich Ehrlinger, leader of Sonderkommando 1b, for instance, had asked for the services of SS 2d Lt. Max Brünnert, who already had
worked under him in the Warsaw Security Service office; and SS Brig. Gen.
Otto Rasch convinced SS 1st Lt. Hagen Weber* to join the headquarters of his
Sonderkommando 4a.[38] Weber* was the mastermind of the notorious Babi Yar
Massacre, a wooded ravine near Kiev, where over 33,000 Jews were gunned
down in a brutal execution.

Another source of manpower for the Einsatzgruppen came from the Security
Police Leadership School, from which entire classes were directly transferred to
the assembly points in Pretzsch and Bad Düben. Thus, for example, most junior
officers of Sonderkommando 4a came from the same leadership class.[39] Many
faculty members from the Border Police School in Pretzsch also had to go to the
Soviet Union.[40] Finally, other Einsatzguppen officers were pulled from a variety
of civilian occupations. SS Capt. Werner Schönemann and the SS 1st Lt. Hans
Graalfs were studying law, and SS T. Sgt. Martin Weiss had just returned to his
plumbing business, when their draft notices arrived.[41]

Hilberg, Höhne, and Wilhelm also suggest that Heydrich drafted men to the
Einsatzgruppen as a form of punishment and a way of securing the undivided
loyalty and commitment of officers with other professional interests.[42] Heydrich

furthermore gave instructions to rotate the Einsatzgruppen personnel so that every Security Service leader had an opportunity to show his devotion and prove himself in the "rough wind of the east." However, despite some pressure to serve in the Einsatzgruppen, SS men were sent home without further consequences, including high-ranking officers who, before or during their time in the killing fields, were declared to be unsuitable—too weak—for their tasks. Yet, no one was ever severely punished for refusing to participate in the executions. On the contrary, as the German courts often found, the outwardly tough and disciplined SS leadership generally displayed much leeway in its interior functioning and could almost be considered caring toward its members.[43]

In May 1941 Einsatzgruppen members assembled in the Border Police School in Pretzsch and in the neighboring towns of Bad Düben and Bad Schmiedeberg. They formed four Einsatzgruppen, each further divided into independently operating Sonderkommandos and Einsatzkommandos—special commando units—and designated to the sectors of the Wehrmacht. Einsatzgruppe A was to follow Army Group North into the Baltic States and to Leningrad; Einsatzgruppe B was assigned to Army Group Center with Moscow as the objective; Einsatzgruppe C was to follow Army Group South into the Ukraine; and Einsatzgruppe D operated in the extreme south with the independent German Eleventh Army and Hungarian and Romanian forces.[44]

In the meantime, General Wagner (by then the quartermaster general of the Wehrmacht who earlier had negotiated with the Security Service before the Polish campaign), and Heydrich reached an agreement regarding the military operating area and the tasks to be performed by the Security Police and the Security Service. Field Marshal Walther von Brauchitsch set forth the terms in a secret order dated April 28, 1941. According to the order, the Sonderkommandos were to operate in a zone directly behind the lines of battle, where they would secure the matériel, archives, and files of organizations, groups, and other "enemies of the state," and, most importantly, of leading individuals such as emigrants, saboteurs, and terrorists. The Einsatzkommandos were to operate in the rear army area, where they would conduct espionage measures such as reconnaissance and gathering of information, and fight against "hostile activities" as long as such activities were not committed by members of the opposing armed forces.[45] Yet the Brauchitsch order additionally gave both Sonderkommandos and Einsatzkommandos the right to conduct executions of the civilian population if it fell into the framework of their previously outlined tasks. Thus, in practice, there existed no difference in the primary task of these formations; despite the different names, both conducted the elimination of the Jews.

The organization of these zones delineates the varying degrees of executive, legislative, and judicial powers of the military over civilian populations. On one end of the scale, the commanders of the individual German armies exercised nearly unlimited control in the combat zone and in the directly adjacent rear area; and the powers of commanders in the rear army area were almost as unfettered. Yet, on the other end of the scale, the army had hardly any control over the civilian population in the Reich.

The regulations concerning the activities of the Einsatzgruppen were part of a cluster of criminal directives issued in preparation for the invasion of the Soviet Union.[46] In conjunction with the Hitler decree on military jurisdiction (Kriegsgerichtsbarkeitserlass), dated May 13, 1941, that withdrew the Soviet civilian population from the military justice system, the Einsatzgruppen regulations essentially gave them unlimited jurisdiction over the civilian population.[47] In addition, the army was to grant logistical support to the Einsatzgruppen. In time, the army renounced much of its power in the rear areas and in return received only the assistance of the Einsatzgruppen in the fight against partisans and subversive elements.

Why then did the army consent to such a lopsided agreement? From the very beginning, when Hitler decided to turn on the Soviet Union, he made it clear that the military administration should be as limited in time and space as possible in order to give the SS a free hand and avoid the complications of the Polish experience. The desire to work "towards the Führer," and the willingness to accept Hitler's often vague statements as binding orders certainly helps to explain the army behavior, even for the traditional conservative and less Nazified generals who, until the triumphant victory in the west, still had looked down upon Hitler with some sort of disdain. However, after the quick defeat of France on June 16, 1940—the ancient enemy and the symbol of the hated Versailles Treaty—these less radical army leaders were ever more willing to cooperate with Hitler and the Nazis. Opposition against Hitler's megalomaniac goals declined, doubts about Hitler disappeared, and even former skeptics increasingly identified with Nazi objectives. Like their fellow conservative Ernst von Weizsäcker, the Undersecretary in the Foreign Office, many thought "there was some consolation in the knowledge that very often in history great transformations have been wrought by criminals."[48] Believing in the myth of German invincibility, the generals expected another quick and easy victory in Russia, and certainly no one would ask questions once the war came to its inevitable successful conclusion.

The army was content to leave the necessary pacifying and security tasks behind the front line to the Einsatzgruppen so that it could fully concentrate on its primary and more glorious task, fighting the enemy army. The German army particularly feared that without the Einsatzgruppen, partisans, Communists, and saboteurs behind the line could significantly hurt its military operations. Thus, the Einsatzgruppen "watched the army's back" so that there could be no renewed spoiling of the army's success, as had allegedly happened at the end of World War I when the German army had been victorious on the battlefield but had to sue for peace because of the undermining activities of Communists and saboteurs at the home front. The notorious stab-in-the-back legend, of course, had been a favorite focus of Nazi propaganda since the early 1920s. To compound the army's paranoia in 1941, Stalin's first-ever radio address to the Soviet people, delivered on July 3, 1941, had asked for the creation of partisan units in the German-occupied areas to "create intolerable conditions for the enemy who must be persecuted and destroyed at every step."[49]

The agreement between General Wagner and Heydrich, in addition, made easier the Wehrmacht's distancing of itself from the atrocities committed by the Security Service, which the army had been forced to witness in Czechoslovakia and Poland.

Yet, there is another explanation for the Wagner-Heydrich agreement. Because the army—and especially its High Command, which regarded itself as the rightful heir to the famous Prussian General Staff—had already lost much of its distinguished position in Germany in the years under the Nazi regime, and certainly had not contributed much to the previous German successes, was now eager to reassert its once powerful status. Not only would it achieve the defeat of the hated Bolshevik arch enemy, but the Army High Command also saw the chance to prove itself in terms of Nazi racial politics and thereby possibly recover the ground lost to the OKW, the overall Armed Forces High Command, and the SS. Thus, the army willingly agreed to close cooperation with the Einsatzgruppen. Moreover, on its own initiative, the Army High Command issued a series of orders that clearly ran against the accepted rules of warfare, including the "Principles for the Behavior of the Troops in Russia," a decree which, against all international agreements, gave the German soldiers unchecked powers regarding the treatment of the civilian population. In the end, it remains unclear whether or not the High Command (OKH) actually realized that its more than accommodating behavior only facilitated its entanglement in the increasingly radical racial policies of the Nazis.[50]

When individual army commanders later learned the terrifying dimensions of the massacres, they often distanced themselves from such activities. As in Poland, however, an order issued by Generalfeldmarschall Gerd von Kluge on September 11, 1941, proves that the generals primarily feared for the reaction and discipline of their troops and never stopped the ongoing genocide.[51] On the contrary, many Einsatzgruppen operations, such as the one at Babi Yar, had been planned and carried out with the help of the Wehrmacht.[52] Wehrmacht units often helped the SS in the registration and rounding up of the Jews, especially in the operating area of Army Group South.[53] In other regions and cities, army soldiers were so eager to participate that Einsatzkommando 5, for example, complained that the "systematic execution of an action suffered greatly and many Jews and functionaries managed to flee" because of the premature and random violence perpetrated by Wehrmacht members and the indigenous population.[54]

In some places, Wehrmacht soldiers killed Jews on their own and without an Einsatzkommando nearby.[55] In Augustowo, Poland, an anonymous Wehrmacht unit shot one hundred Jews and Communists at the recommendation of the local Security Service commander, SS Capt. Wolfgang Ilges.[56] In other cases, Wehrmacht soldiers and engineers helped to search the cities for hidden Jews and then prepared and closed the mass graves.[57] Without specific orders, individual army soldiers from all ranks volunteered to participate in the massacres and contributed in other ways to the killing operations.[58] Moreover, the army allowed the Einsatzgruppen to screen its POW camps for Jews, political commissaries, and other "undesirables."

These are only a few, selected examples from a vast complex of activities and orders testifying to the successful cooperation of the German army and the SS. It is not surprising then that in contrast to the Polish experience, relations between the Einsatzgruppen and the Wehrmacht were cordial and friendly. "The attitude of the Wehrmacht to the Jews is downright heartening,"[59] recorded Sonderkommando 4b on July 6, 1941, from Tarnopol. In August 1941, another report indicated no changes. "The relations are still excellent, the Wehrmacht personnel are showing interest and understanding for the activities of the Einsatzgruppen, especially toward the executions."[60]

In all fairness to the German army, however, relations with the SS were not always cordial. Many officers and men detested the slaughter of helpless civilians. Commander of the Rear Army Area Middle General von Schenckendorff, for example, released the following order: "I hereby repeat that participation in the special measures and executions of the SD is forbidden for all soldiers in my area of responsibility."[61] On another occasion the army commander in the town of Welish refused to hand over the Jews of the city to a detachment of Sonderkommando 7a for execution.

That SS 1st Lt. Kurt Matschke received a uniform with the higher insignia of a captain in order to enable him to "pull rank" with the Wehrmacht, when necessary, indicates that the planners in the Reich Security Main Office had anticipated confrontations.[62] In general, most German army units did not become directly involved. Yet considering the atrocities committed in the Wehrmacht's area of operation, keeping a neutral stance and pointing to a questionable agreement was a crime, at least from an ethical point of view. It is also worthwhile to consider that without the military conquests, the Einsatzgruppen could not have inflicted their destruction.

The invasion of the Soviet Union, however, puts us ahead of the story. Shortly before the planned attack, Heydrich, Streckenbach, and the Gestapo Chief, SS Maj. Gen. Heinrich Müller—"Gestapo Müller"—briefed the leaders of the Einsatzgruppen, their subordinated command leaders, and the other staff members on their duties. All three cited Hitler and Himmler as the original source of their order. Heydrich then disclosed that the invasion was imminent and that the Einsatzgruppen were to secure the army rear areas through "special treatment" of "potential enemies."[63]

Heydrich repeated the directive in an Operational Order (Einsatzbefehl) to the Einsatzgruppen and elaborated it in a July 2, 1941, decree to the four Higher SS and Police Leaders designated for the occupied territories. With regard to "special treatment," the decree indicated execution for "all functionaries of the Comintern (including all communist career politicians), the higher, middle and the radical lower functionaries of the party of the central committees, the regional and local committees, peoples commissaries, the Jews in the Soviet party and state positions, and other radical elements (saboteurs, propagandists, snipers, assassins, agitators, partisans etc.)."[64] The euphemistic term "partisans" provided a useful cover for the extermination of the Jews and other "racially inferior elements," the disabled, as well as "eastern and asian peoples" such as Gypsies, Mongols, Armenians, and Muslims.[65]

As a preparation for the final destruction of the Soviet Jews, the individually operating commands attempted to incite pogroms, established the ghettos and Jewish Councils, and forced the Jewish population to wear a yellow star or patch. Screening commands were also sent to the POW camps to eliminate the Jews and "racially inferior" eastern elements from among the hundreds of thousands of Soviet soldiers the German army had captured during the first months of the invasion. Moreover, the Einsatzgruppen also was tasked with crime prevention and the fight against political organizations, and to extend Security Service influence on the newly formed local civil administration, organize indigenous police units, and in general monitor and supervise public life in the conquered territories. In short, the Einsatzgruppen were indeed smaller, mobile versions of the Reich Security Main Office.

Heydrich, the Reich Security Main Office, and Hitler had placed a special emphasis on detailed information about the activities of the individual Einsatzgruppen commands and the political, cultural, and economic conditions that they met in their respective operating areas. Heydrich instructed each Kommando unit to send reports to its Einsatzgruppen leader. The leaders in turn forwarded each report received and their own individual report via radio, telegraph, or messenger to the Reich Security Main Office where the incoming messages were evaluated systematically and drawn together into a uniform document. The head of Department IV, Gestapo Müller, then read the summarized reports and made some minor changes. The reports were numbered and classified as Geheime Reichssache, the highest level of secrecy, then distributed to the departments of the Reich Security Main Office and other interested Nazi Party and government offices. Only a small circle of individuals knew about the ongoing extermination program, and public discussion or dissemination of information was strictly prohibited.

These Operational Situation Reports from the USSR were succeeded by the Reports from the Occupied Eastern Territories (Meldungen aus den besetzten Ostgebieten).[66] Both have been the standard source of information for the activities of the Einsatzgruppen and German occupation policy in the east. An Ereignismeldung usually contains lists of locations of each Einsatzgruppe, Einsatzkommando, and Sonderkommando reporting as well as accounts of operations, including liquidation of Jews. In the sections on the executions, the reporters often used statements such as "not wearing the correct identity marker," "dissemination of anti-German rumors," "insubordinate behavior," and similar pretexts as legal justifications.

The Ereignismeldungen are a valuable historical source because they were drafted at the time of the events, and all incidents mentioned were later corroborated by other sources. The historical limitations of the Ereignismeldungen, however, include the tendency of individual commanders to exaggerate the number of victims to emphasize their personal achievements, and chronological mistakes due to the time elapsed between the actual and the finalized report, as well as due to problems of transmitting the reports and clerical errors.[67]

Killing Operations

The purpose of this work is to explain why the Einsatzgruppen officers became mass murderers, and thus this section concentrates on the killing operations as they can be discerned from the Situation Reports and the court judgments. The tactics of the Einsatzgruppen are reviewed, along with the destruction inflicted upon the victims.

The horrifying efficiency of the Einsatzgruppen was facilitated by a number of favorable factors, the first of which was the distribution of the Jewish population. Because of the historical developments in Russia and the Soviet Union, in particular the restrictions on movement imposed on the Jews under Catherine the Great in 1791, four out of five Soviet Jews still lived within the country's western parts—the former Pale of Settlement—which were now quickly overrun by the German invaders. The high concentration of Jews had aroused the existing anti-Semitism among the indigenous peoples ever since the creation of the Pale.

These sentiments were exacerbated early in the twentieth century by the per-ceived visibility of Jews among the Bolsheviks during the revolution and the sup-pression of Ukrainian national independence in the Civil War, and then by the later Soviet occupation of the Baltic Republics. In addition, the Jews were highly urbanized and could be reached easily.[68]

It is, therefore, no surprise that the Einsatzgruppen easily incited pogroms and found many willing accomplices among the people of the Baltic and the Ukraine. The rural populations regarded the Jews with suspicion as well. If the Jews managed to escape from the Einsatzgruppen, they usually received no sup-port from local peasants. Thus, many Jews who had fled the cities chose to re-turn to their homes and die with their families rather than die of hunger and exposure in the countryside.

Map 3. Einsatzgruppen Massacres in Eastern Europe: June 1941–November 1942. From United States Holocaust Memorial Museum, *The Historical Atlas of the Holocaust* (New York: Macmillan Publishing, 1995). Used with permission of the United States Holocaust Memorial Museum, Washington, D.C.

The tasks of the Einsatzgruppen were also made relatively easy by the igno-rance and gullibility of the Jews. The speed of the 1941 German advance had ini-tially left the Jewish communities in a state of shock. In addition, at least until the Germans had crossed into the Soviet Union, the Soviet leadership had purpose-fully kept the Jews in the dark about what would happen at the hands of the Ger-mans. Thus, many Jews saw no reason to flee. As during the First World War, many had still oriented themselves to western Europe and Germany, and, un-aware or disbelieving of Hitler's objectives and prophecy, they had expected that the Germans as a "Kulturnation" would finally liberate them from the yoke of Soviet barbarism. Jewish survivors from the former western Russian town of Konin remember: "The old generation thought these were the same Germans who had come in the First World War. My father said, 'Don't worry'." Another woman added, "Mother remembered the Germans from the First World War, a cultured nation. She said it was impossible what the Germans were supposed to be doing to the Jews—she could not imagine it."[69]

Thus it sufficed that the Einsatzgruppen had often relied on speed and de-ception alone. Only when the truth about the massacres had emerged did the strongest and most able-bodied within the Jewish communities manage to flee, at the pain of leaving behind the most vulnerable, the women, children, elderly, and sick. And many of those who fled, often did not find help and had no choice but to return to their certain death.

In order to reach the Jews before they had time to think and react, the Ein-satzgruppen arrived in a city immediately after the heaviest fighting was over—in many instances, even earlier. A report from Einsatzgruppe C stated that "Dur-ing every larger military operation, advance commands of the Einsatzgruppe marched into the newly conquered cities with the fighting troops." In Zhitomir, three vehicles of Sonderkommando 4a rolled into the city directly behind the first tanks; and army units often requested that Einsatzkommandos operate as close to the front as possible so that they did not to have to deal with the civilian population.[70] As a result of this cooperation, the earliest Einsatzkommandos often appeared so quickly on the battlefield that some had to be rescued from dangerous military situations. Records show, for example, that scouting detach-ments of Sonderkommando 4a had reached Lvov and were encircled there to-gether with military units even before the city was finally captured.[71]

Later, during the German retreat in the first winter and after 1942, the Ein-satzkommandos also participated in the defense of cities and the fight against partisans. Individual members like SS 1st Lt. Adam Schild* received medals for bravery.[72] In all cases, however, either during the German advances or later dur-ing the war, as soon as the military operations had ceased, the Einsatzgruppen began their assigned nefarious tasks. They regularly used assurances and lies such as "registration for work and resettlement" before sending the unsuspecting Jews to their graves. On occasion, the Einsatzkommandos arrived at a town and did nothing at first, a deception that convinced the Jews that the rumors about German atrocities were exaggerated and that it was time to return and cooperate.

The Einsatzgruppen method of conducting the actual execution was simple, with little variation. After reconnaissance of the local conditions, the command leader chose a killing site approximately two to three miles outside of the town. The site needed an access road and ideally would be located out of view of the victims. Jewish prisoners assigned as work Kommandos, or other Soviet prisoners of war and indigenous workers, dug mass graves to the required capacity. To save labor, natural inclines, tank ditches, or bomb craters were used. The Einsatzkommando, or parts thereof, then rounded up the Jewish population on a town square or in a synagogue. They searched Jewish houses for weapons and hiding places. Plunder, so-called executions during flight, and other acts of violence were common. While the Jews awaited their executions, they had to witness the Einsatzkommando destroying their holy books and cultural items, and setting fire to their synagogues. The Jews were divided into groups, depending on the size of the execution squad, and were marched or driven to the killing site. Usually the area had been closed off in the meantime, but some executions were open to spectators from the Wehrmacht, civil administrators, and other German agencies.

At the execution site the victims had to undress partially or fully, hand over their valuables, register on a list, and finally line up facing the side of the grave. Many had to wait for hours before it was their turn to die. The victim was killed either by a single shot in the neck, then pushed into the grave, or by machine-gun fire, with the victims falling into the ditch. For those not lethally hit, the officers in charge and other personnel delivered so-called mercy shots—situations that occurred frequently when the executioners' ability had been affected by the influence of alcohol.

In well-prepared executions, each liquidated group was covered with chalk and a thin layer of earth before the killing of the next group commenced. However, there usually was not enough time, because all "actions" had to be over before the end of the day. Cries and whimpers often could be heard for hours after the executions. Time and again some particularly unfortunate victims managed to crawl from the hurriedly closed and poorly covered mass graves, only to be killed by the guards left behind. Most victims died stoically and without resistance. And their executioners often ended the day's work with drinking and celebrating.[73]

Passages from the Einsatzgruppen trial records, translated below, describe the use of specialists skilled at shooting in the neck (Genickschussspezial-isten) and the ingenuity of the Einsatzgruppen in taking advantage of geographic features:

> The execution took place in the court of the asylum. A wall was around the court so that no one could see inside. Members of the Sonderkommando were the assigned shooters. Russian auxiliaries had to assist. In the court, a 3½ to 4-foot wide subterranean creek surfaced. The creek then traveled down a slope of 70 to 80 degrees and disappeared into the ground again. The patients were brought individually from the asylum to the creek. The distance was about 65½ feet. They were shot individually. The police short-barreled pistol, with a 7.65mm caliber, was used as the means of execution. . . .The victims received a single shot in the back of the neck. The barrel of the pistol was placed between the two ligaments at the base of the neck, facing upward. The shot was supposed to come out at the forehead so that the bullet would have traveled through the entire length of the brain. If that succeeded, blood and brains splashed out of the pulsating wound and death occurred instantly. After the shot was fired, the patients were pushed into the creek, and carried away by the strong current; their bodies disappeared.[74]

Other Einsatzkommandos did not practice what they termed these "Bolshevik" methods. They shot their victims from a longer distance:

> The execution ditch, a former Russian defense trench, ran parallel to a partially destroyed stable. During the execution eight to ten victims had to line up in front of the trench, facing the execution squad. . . . The twenty-man squad stood in a double row approximately 65½ feet from the victims. Two policemen always had to shoot at one victim. The single line of victims would be forced to run to the trench. When eight to ten victims had reached the ditch, they stood there or knelt down and the officer in charge gave the firing command.[75]

The brutality and inhumanity of the executions cannot be forgotten:

> Urged to accelerate the execution, the shooters fired more non-lethal shots than usual. Therefore, a relatively high number of victims that were still alive were lying in the grave. They were still moving, and the pile of victims within the grave remained in motion. A woman emerged from the pile of the living and the dead and raised her arms for mercy. . . .Where there were signs of life, the leaders fired additional shots. An examination to determine if the victims were dead never happened.[76]

In certain cases the conditions at the executions site were often so unorganized and chaotic that Einsatzgruppen members were wounded or killed in the crossfire, especially when indigenous Hiwis under the influence of alcohol served in the firing squads.[77]

Subsequently, the killing technique changed. In the latter part of 1941, and especially in 1942, the use of gas vans became increasingly prevalent.

> The prisoners condemned for gassing were loaded into the gas vans and driven to an area with tank ditches to the north of Kiev. When they entered the vans, the prisoners did not know what would happen to them; the doors were closed tightly and the exhaust fumes of the engine were led into the interior. Soon the van started moving slightly; dampened screams and knocks could be heard. The prisoners were fighting with death. When the van stopped moving, it was the sign for the driver that the prisoners were dead. The gas van drove to a destination on the edge of town where the bodies were unloaded by a special command. . . .When the van was opened, the bodies—men, women, children—with distorted faces, covered with vomit and stained with excrement, still carried the visible signs of their painful death.[78]

The use of gas vans demonstrates the connections between the Einsatzgruppen activities and the mass extermination campaign that ultimately led to the development of larger, stationary gas chambers in the extermination camps.

The passages from the Einsatzgruppen reports also shed some light on the repercussions of the massacres on the perpetrators. Apparently for all but the basest members of the Einsatzgruppen, the bloody scenes led to significant psychological reactions. Heydrich and the Reich Security Main Office had trained their men to follow orders blindly and dispose of "subhuman" beings without hesitation. The euphemistic language, the frequent and liberal use of alcohol, the delegation of the most grizzly tasks to the auxiliaries, the pseudo-justifications such as prevention of diseases and historical necessity, as well as the frequent inspections and motivational speeches by the officers in charge were to ease the perpetrators into their assignment.

Himmler and other SS leaders indeed made many commitments to make off-duty life in the Einsatzgruppen as pleasant as possible. A letter from the Reich Security Main Office asked for donations of magazines ("the essential 'lighter' reading material"), and books and games for "Our comrades in the Einsatzkommandos in the east who rarely have an opportunity for relaxation and recreation." Especially sought after were board games such as Chess, Checkers, and Aggravation, card games, dice, table tennis, and record players—all measures designed to create an aura of normality.[79]

Yet, although the killers had experience in employing terror and controlling enemies from prior service in the forerunners of the Einsatzgruppen and the SS, and though many had already committed crimes against humanity and had burned moral bridges long before they came to the Soviet Union, most perpetrators still had problems with the direct and personal method of killing. The neurological examination of SS Capt. Carsten Freund*, after he returned from service in Sonderkommando 7a and Einsatzgruppe B, had concluded: "Nervous exhaustion of the mind, reactive depression. At least four weeks of recuperation necessary, if possible in a sanitarium employing hydrotherapy. To avoid a certain relapse, a completely different assignment required, even after conclusion of treatment."[80] Another officer, SS T. Sgt. Thomas Gevatter*, the driver of a gas van, underwent weeks of psychological treatment before he was able to serve again as a driver for normal duties at the Gestapo State Police office in Brünn.[81]

Amidst this, however, Reich Leader SS Himmler had the welfare of his men in mind. While the Einsatzgruppen were leaving their bloody trails in Soviet territory, the decision to exterminate all European Jews had been made, and the planners in the Reich Security Main Office were already working on psychologically less burdensome and logistically more effective solutions.

With such evidence, we can dismiss Daniel Goldhagen's argument that anti-Semitism was the sole motivating factor for the men of the Einsatzgruppen. Or, at least, it is possible to point to one of the most significant contradictions of his work. Why were Himmler and Heydrich so concerned about the mental state of the members of the Einsatzgruppen if Goldhagen's eliminationist form of anti-Semitism had indeed been the cause to induce tens or hundreds of thousands of average German citizens from a variety of occupations and classes, who were not Nazi zealots, to murder "without pity" utterly defenseless Jewish men, women, and children?[82] They, too, were raised in the anti-Semitic German culture. They had undergone years of training, indoctrination, and experience in the SS that set them apart from ordinary citizens. If we followed Goldhagen's logic, these trained professionals should not have had problems with the killings, and if they did, as the subsequent chapters and Himmler's and Heydrich's concerns will prove, his reasoning must be flawed.

It is, of course, difficult and perhaps morally questionable to assess the "success" and "efficiency" of mass murderers. But in order to evaluate properly the Einsatzgruppen within the machinery of destruction, the historical record must be reviewed. Obviously, the numbers speak for themselves. The small Einsatzgruppen alone accounted for a large percentage of all Holocaust victims. An important factor that facilitated this "success" was the existence of other SS forces and German government authorities in the occupied territories. The four Higher SS and Police Leaders (HSSPF) in the occupied Soviet territories, and their subordinated SS and Police Leaders (SSPF) appointed by a special Führer decree, achieved special notoriety. As with their counterparts within the Reich, these SS officers were the personal representatives of Reich Leader SS and Chief of the German Police Heinrich Himmler. They were supposed to coordinate the activities of the Security Police, the Security Service, the Order Police, and local auxiliary police formations. They were nominally in charge of operational matters, such as the planning of combined operations. Regarding the Einsatzgruppen and its subordinated units of the Order Police, however, the specific directives from the Reich Security Main Office and the Main Office Order Police in all personnel and disciplinary matters had a higher priority.[83] Thus, the relations between the Higher SS and Police Leaders and the Einsatzgruppen remained unresolved from the beginning. The HSSPFs, or "little Himmlers," outranked the Einsatzkommando leaders, or "little Heydrichs," as the court in Koblenz called them, but the orders for mass executions usually circumvented the Higher SS and Police Leaders and came from the Reich Security Main Office directly to the Einsatzgruppen.

The function of the Higher SS and Police Leaders—to secure police control in the occupied territories—also overlapped with the tasks of the Einsatzgruppen. In fact, Heydrich's letter to the HSSPFs is the only source on the directives to the Einsatzgruppen. That the Higher SS and Police Leaders alone could not fulfill their assignments can be surmised from the fact that they had few SS units and primarily only Order Police troops at their disposal.[84] Nevertheless, they initiated massacres of Jews with improvised killing squads of their own, often because many Jewish communities had hardly been touched by the first hurried advance of the Einsatzgruppen.[85] Thus, on November 29, 1941, the Higher SS and Police Leader Russia North, at the time the brutal and ruthless SS Lt. Gen. Friedrich Jeckeln, who had just switched positions with the ineffective SS Lt. Gen. Hans Adolf Prützmann, decided to liquidate the Jews of the Riga, Latvia, ghetto on his own initiative—a massacre that would be called "Riga Blood Sunday." Only after it became evident that Jeckeln's forces were insufficient, did he ask Einsatzkommando 2 for help, a request that was obliged willingly.

To the Einsatzgruppen, the Higher SS and Police Leaders often represented nothing more than liaison officers to army groups and the civil administration, whose purpose remained questionable at best.[86] Individual Einsatzgruppen and even subordinated Einsatzkommando leaders did not hesitate to issue orders to forces under the direct command of a Higher SS and Police Leader, as was the case with the leader of Einsatzgruppe A, Brig. Gen. Franz Walter Stahlecker. Immediately after the German attack on the Soviet Union in June 1941, Stahlecker demanded that the local Gestapo office in Tilsit, part of the Memel area, clear all

Jews from a strip of land extending approximately sixteen miles east of the eastern Prussian border, into Lithuania. The territory ran from the Baltic Sea coast
south to the Memel River. Stahlecker's subordinate, SS Col. Karl Jäger, then
quarreled with the Gestapo office over responsibility to execute the order.[87]

One would expect that the impulsive measures, such as Jeckeln's action
at Riga, would promote contradictions, inefficiencies, and errors, considering
that the controversies between the Einsatzgruppen and the Higher SS and Police Leaders were not the only cases of ambiguous directives or interior power
struggles. Despite the territorial divisions based on the three German army
groups, even the boundaries between the Einsatzgruppen and Einsatzkommandos were not clearly defined. In the end, however, the dualism of competing
SS formations not only gave Himmler and Heydrich an extra channel of control,
it spurred internal competition and contributed to the increased radicalization of
anti-Jewish policies.[88]

With little difficulty, the Einsatzgruppen had indeed butchered approximately 500,000 Jews during their first 600-mile deep sweep into Russian space
in 1941. But because of the speed of the advance and the small size of the Einsatzgruppen, some 2 million of the Soviet Jews were bypassed or forced into
ghettos, and 1.5 million managed to flee. Only when the Germans renewed their
offensive in the following year and advanced even farther east, the situation
changed. The number of Jews who then were still alive in ghettos posed a crush-
ing logistical and psychological problem for the Einsatzgruppen. In addition, it
was much more difficult to hunt down the Jews who had escaped the initial massacres and ghettoization because they then knew their destiny if they would fall
into the clutches of the Einsatzgruppen.[89]

Meanwhile, with the decision to eliminate all European Jews set in motion,
"research" into more "humane" and effective killing methods had led to the
development of the gas vans and the establishment of the first stationary killing facilities in the Government General. The Nazis also began to deport Jews
from the German territories and the Reichsprotektorat—today's Czech Republic minus the Sudeten, the border area to Germany and Austria—as well as from
the Reichskommissariat Ostland (the northern part of the Reich Ministry for
the Occupied Eastern Territories—the RmBO, Reichsministerium für die besetzten Ostgebiete) to the ghettos of Riga and Minsk.[90] These Jews then became
the victims of the Einsatzgruppen's second sweep in late 1941, the clearing of the
ghettos.[91]

Initially conceived to eliminate only Soviet Jews, the Einsatzgruppen thus ultimately became part of the shock troops—the aggressive Stosstruppen units—
in what would become the final German attack on European Jewry.

After German advances had come to a halt in the winter of 1941–42, or soon thereafter, Einsatzgruppe units A and C were dissolved. From their members, and with newly recruited manpower—again from the Gestapo, Criminal Police, Security Service, and Waffen SS—new offices were established: the Commanding Officer of the Security Police and the Security Service on the Einsatzgruppen level (BdS, Befehlshaber der Sicherheitspolizei und des SD), and the Commander of the Security Police and the Security Service on the Einsatzkommando and Sonderkommando level (KdS, Kommandeur der Sicherheitspolizei und des SD). With essentially the same tasks as the Einsatzgruppen, these offices, however, were stationary and no longer operating under the territorial command of the Wehrmacht. They also became increasingly involved in the fight against actual partisan groups behind the German lines.

When the tide of the war turned and a German victory seemed no longer feasible after the battle of Stalingrad, Hitler decided to eliminate all evidence of the mass executions in the occupied eastern territories. The SS planned to open mass graves, burn bodies, crush bones, and thus completely destroy all evidence of German atrocities. Under Decree No. 1005, classified as Top Secret (Geheime Reichssache), a Sonderkommando under Paul Blobel was charged with the planning and execution of these operations. As with the activities of the Einsatzgruppen proper, the Reich Security Main Office insisted on detailed reports. Euphemisms such as "weather report" for the location of the graves and "ceiling" for the number of the burned bodies served to conceal the true activities of these units.[92] Insiders called the exhumations "blobeln," with reference to its leader.[93] Blobel's Sonderkommando 1005 began its duplicitous work in the Ukraine throughout the summer of 1943. Another Einsatzgruppe, "Iltis," (which means "polecat," the flesh-eating animal—indicative of the Einsatzgruppe's nature) later continued similar work in the western parts of the Soviet Union until September 1944, when the military offensive of the Red Army finally pushed all German forces out of the country for good.[94] The exhumation work of these units thus remained incomplete, leaving ample evidence of their murderous activities.

The Einsatzgruppen Operations in Perspective

It is worth interrupting this narrative to recapitulate how Einsatzgruppen activities fit into the overall framework of the destruction of the European Jews. The Einsatzgruppen trial records confirm Holocaust scholar Raul Hilberg's observation that, "With the order to the Einsatzgruppen to liquidate Soviet Jewry, Hitler and the German bureaucracy crossed the threshold from previous anti-Jewish policy to organized killing operations."[95]

Yehuda Bauer, too, saw the planning phase for the invasion of the Soviet

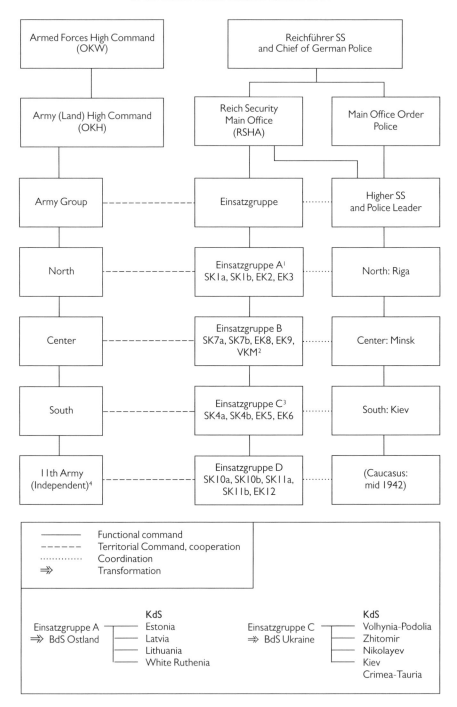

FIGURE 2
German Military and SS Command Structure
in the Soviet Union until November 1944

Union, the spring of 1941, as the critical moment in the decision to murder the Jews. Hans Mommsen interpreted the operations of the Einsatzgruppen as the decisive link between previously existing territorial solutions and the physical extermination of at least a major part of the European Jews. What initially had been one of a number of solutions discussed by Nazi officials, premeditated killing, thus became the new standard. And to Daniel Goldhagen, the Einsatzgruppen evolved from "genocidal scouting parties" to integral parts of the assault on European Jewry. He rightfully establishes that, "With the preparations for the attack on the Soviet Union, Hitler and his subordinates had crossed the psychological and moral Rubicon to genocide—and the die was cast for all of European Jewry."[96]

The available material clearly points to Hitler as the source of this program of annihilation. He must have made the decision before he ordered the attack on the Soviet Union, otherwise the planning concerning the Jews and the delineation of tasks between the SS and the army would not have been necessary. And, therefore, arguments claiming that the Nazis conceived the idea to kill the European Jews only after the reversal of German military fortunes must be dismissed.[97] Himmler and Heydrich subsequently transmitted Hitler's orders to the Einsatzgruppen. As with the Final Solution, except for the reference to Heydrich's Operational Order of July 2, 1941, in the Operational Situation Reports and in the circular letter to the Higher SS and Police Leaders, no written orders to the Einsatzgruppen exist. Disclosure of the information the individual commanders had received in Pretzsch was their responsibility, after their units had been set in motion. That the orders were transferred through the chief of the Reich Security Main Office—down the normal chain of command—and not, as one might expect for such a far-reaching task, directly from Hitler or at least Himmler, also means that the activities of the Einsatzgruppen from the very

---

[1] After November 1941, the mobile Einsatzgruppe A was transformed into the stationary Office of the Commander of the Security Police and the Security Service (BdS) Ostland. Its subordinated units—Sonderkommandos 1a and 1b and Einsatzkommandos 2 and 3—were transformed into the stationary Offices of the Commander of the Security Police and the Security Service (KdS) at Estonia, Latvia, Lithuania, and White Ruthenia.

[2] VKM, Vorkommando: Advance Command Moscow.

[3] Since the beginning of November 1941, the mobile Einsatzgruppe C and parts of Einsatzgruppe D were reorganized into the Office of the Commander of the Security Police and the Security Service (BdS) Ukraine. Simultaneously, its subordinated units—Sonderkommandos 10a and 10b and Einsatzkommandos 5 and 6—as well as parts of Einsatzgruppe D were regrouped into the Offices of the Commander of the Security Police and the Security Service (KdS) at Volhynia-Podolia, Zhitomir, Nikolayev, Kiev, and Crimea-Tauria.

[4] Operating independently from any army group and answering directly to the OKH. All other German armies belonged to one of the three army groups (North, Center, South), but the 11th Army attacked in cooperation with Romanian force at the southernmost part of the front.

beginning were designed to establish an aura of normal and everyday duty. The perpetrators were expected to fulfill this duty with the same devotion as filing a report or conducting a department meeting. Of course, this attitude of normalcy of the operations also helped to lighten the psychological burden and made unconditional compliance of the perpetrators even easier.

It is also clear that Heydrich and his creation, the Reich Security Main Office, masterminded and organized, as well as supplied, large parts of the manpower for the first large-scale killing operations of the Holocaust. This would also explain why the Reich Security Main Office, except from the agreement reached with the army, was not interested in a cooperation with other government agencies. Although Hermann Göring, who alone held the highest German military rank—Reichsmarschall—was the powerful Plenipotentiary for the Four-Year Plan and Hitler's designated successor, it took him more than a month after the attack on the Soviet Union before he commissioned Heydrich to coordinate all measures for the preparation of the Final Solution of the Jewish Question. Yet by this time the liquidation of Soviet Jewry was already well under way. In addition, only in December of 1941 did Heydrich find it necessary to inform Joseph Goebbels's Ministry for People's Enlightenment and Propaganda (Ministerium für Volksaufklärung und Propaganda). Goebbels promptly sent his delegates to the Einsatzgruppen. Almost expectedly, Heydrich established no contacts with Alfred Rosenberg's weak Reich Ministry for the Occupied Eastern Territories, although the institution was supposed to be responsible for "the central questions of the Eastern European space."[98] Testimony in German courts also indicates that the Reich Security Main Office aspired to prove itself "at the front" and win recognition and medals, much like the victorious Wehrmacht had.[99]

As to the Wehrmacht, in Czechoslovakia and Poland it might still have distanced itself from the crimes of the SS and the Security Service with some credibility. Because Hitler depended on the Wehrmacht for his conquests, it could have gained concessions in terms of racial politics. However, this was no longer an option in June 1941. With the acceptance of the Heydrich-Wagner Agreement, the limitation of military jurisdiction, the promulgation of the "Principles for the Behavior of the Troops in Russia," and a cluster of criminal orders, the free rendering of military and logistical support to the Einsatzgruppen, and the participation of soldiers in Aktionen, the army had become directly involved in the destruction process.

Confirming intentionalist arguments that Hitler's Nazi ideology determined all German politics and that his intent had always been the annihilation of the Jewish race in Europe, it is apparent that the war with the Soviet Union became a life-and-death struggle that was waged with utter disregard for international law and the basic principles of humanity. Hitler and his lieutenants identified that war with the center of the Jewish-Bolshevik conspiracy. The simultaneous Einsatzgruppen assault on Soviet Jewry, then, was the direct and logical consequence of Nazi ideology.

The unusually high ranks of the Einsatzgruppen officers offer another proof for the importance of the campaign to eliminate the Jews. The leadership of an Einsatzgruppe with the personnel strength of a battalion was entrusted to generals only, and the commanding officers of the no more than company-strength Einsatzkommandos and Sonderkommandos were at least colonels. Even lowly drivers, interpreters, and other specialists in headquarters held officers' ranks.

Furthermore, after a short planning phase in the Reich Security Main Office, Heydrich gave clear and unambiguous directives to the leaders of the Einsatzgruppen and thereby set in motion a machine that eliminated millions of people. His directives were not piecemeal measures but a carefully drawn blueprint for mass murder, and there was a direct connection between the Gestapo and Security Service activities in Czechoslovakia, Poland, and the Soviet Union.

On the other hand, the Einsatzgruppen and their activities also corroborate many functionalist theories. Most important, the emergence of the Reich Security Main Office as the front-runner in the competition for power, influence, and recognition between the Wehrmacht, the Reich Ministry for the Occupied Eastern Territories, other government and Nazi Party organizations, and even within the SS proves that the radicalization of anti-Jewish policy was a function, or direct result, of the anarchistic power struggles within the Nazi system. As control organs of the Reich Security Main Office, the Einsatzgruppen were only temporary solutions until a permanent SS administration had been established. Subsequently, renewed competition between the Higher SS and Police Leaders, the Einsatzgruppen, and the civil administration ensued and led to further radicalization of anti-Jewish policies. In 1943, the Einsatzgruppen completely merged into the stationary SS apparatus, and SS officers were appointed as both Einsatzkommando leaders and local Security Service commanders (BdS or KdS) in personal union. The latter points additionally underscore this key functionalist argument.

Moreover, the conception of the Einsatzgruppen was certainly also a short-term solution to new and self-imposed problems. The Polish campaign had shown that the German bureaucracy, engaged in conceiving a Final Solution to the Jewish Question, did not know how to react to the masses of Polish Jews that came under German jurisdiction; the crimes committed by the Security Service after the military operations were completed could not be kept secret and caused protests from the Wehrmacht and the German population. Thus, the Einsatzgruppen activities in Poland indeed were a learning experience. To avoid similar complications during the invasion of the Soviet Union, the operations of the German armies and the Einsatzgruppen were conducted simultaneously and served as a cover—admittedly insufficient—for the massacres. And, at the same time, the Einsatzgruppen made certain that the other potential problem, the masses of Soviet Jews, would not become an actual problem.

Apart from Reinhardt Heydrich's directives, the Einsatzgruppen and their subordinated Einsatzkommandos and Sonderkommandos operated independently and with much leeway—a necessity because the vast Russian spaces, weather conditions, and lack of usable roads made communications and maintaining a direct chain of command difficult. The independence of the killing squads, however, certainly offered a classic potential for "working towards the Führer." Most commanding officers had come from the Reich Security Main Office, where they had been exposed to the increasingly radical solutions to the Jewish problem entertained by their superiors. Once the Einsatzgruppen had crossed into the Soviet Union, these officers knew that their goals coincided with the intentions of the Führer and the SS leadership, and commanders consequently initiated progressively more extensive extermination operations. Therefore, apart from the briefing these officers received before the invasion, no further and precise orders were required to ensure that each independently operating killing unit would eliminate as many Jews as possible.[100]

Yet, despite its deadly effectiveness, the mobile and traditional killing method of the Einsatzgruppen ultimately proved unsuitable to eliminate the large numbers of people. From a logistical point of view, there were simply not enough executioners. And psychologically for the perpetrators, and perhaps even more their superiors, it became increasingly difficult to deal with the repercussions of the mass executions. Despite their speeches and efforts to the contrary, even Himmler and other senior SS officers could not deal with the consequences; like their subordinates, they sometimes became ill, vomiting after witnessing their first mass executions. Moreover, the war in the east that appeared won after only a few months had turned into an almost four-year titanic struggle that prevented further organized measures against the Jewish population. It was therefore necessary to find a more suitable location—the General Government—in addition to a more effective method to solve the Jewish problem once and forever.

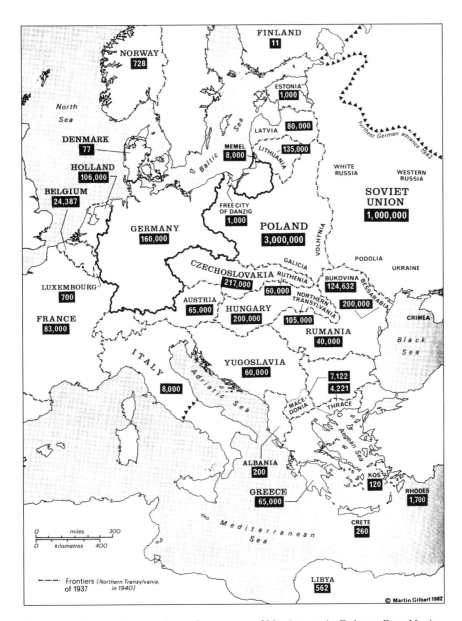

Map 4. Jews Murdered between September 1, 1939, and May 8, 1945: An Estimate. From Martin Gilbert, *Atlas of the Holocaust* (London: Routledge, 1993). Used with permission from Taylor & Francis Books.

Map 5. Survivors, and Those Who Returned, 1945. From Martin Gilbert, *Atlas of the Holocaust* (London: Routledge, 1993). Used with permission from Taylor & Francis Books.

2. THE CONFIRMED KILLERS

I have killed your fathers, your
mothers, or your sisters. I still need you
for work. But you too will be killed.

SS Technical Sergeant Martin Weiss

NE OF the most horrific massacres in history occurred in late September 1941 when units of Einsatzgruppe C and other police and military forces killed 33,771 civilians in the Babi Yar ravine near Kiev. Regarding these gruesome days in the Ukraine, the Einsatzgruppen Operational Situation Report simply states:

> On September 29 and 30, 1941 Sonderkommando 4a, the Einsatzgruppen head-
> quarters and two detachments from the Police Regiment South executed 33,771
> Jews in Kiev. Money, valuables and clothing were secured. . . . The action itself
> proceeded smoothly. There were no extraordinary incidents. By all means the
> "resettlement action" of the Jews found approval by the local population.[1]

The emotionally detached and sometimes malicious tone of the report does not convey the unspeakable horrors and the endless agony of the victims.[2] But then the officers who were in charge of this and similar operations had long been conditioned to perpetrate the killing of tens of thousands as "historical necessity" and "business as usual." They were the confirmed killers among the men who served in the Einsatzgruppen.

These brutal and vicious murderers stand out among their comrades because they always went far beyond the call of duty. They completely identified with the goals of the Nazi leadership, including the elimination of the Jews. More important, however, they wanted to leave their personal stamp on the realization of the Nazi plans. Therefore, they made certain that not a single Jew would escape. The executions were conducted efficiently, in a cruel and denigrating manner. The Einsatzgruppen officers killed for the basest reasons; persons who did not fall into the already far-reaching extermination program were murdered as well.

Apart from their behavior during the time they served in the Einsatzgruppen, all but one of the officers at the trials can be distinguished by several characteristics. These men had joined the SS and the Security Service organizations very early in the formation of those groups; and they had showed no emotions in front of the court, although they realized that in the eyes of the world they had committed heinous crimes for which they would be punished. Yet, their complete identification with Nazi ideology and acknowledging Hitler's will as binding law superseded all remaining moral considerations. In addition, after the war they categorically denied their SS activities to the Allied, and later the German, authorities.

During their trials these former Einsatzgruppen officers were uncooperative and often hostile to the courts—an attitude to be expected from mass murderers. The German district attorneys' offices charged these perpetrators with murder, and upon conviction they received the maximum sentence of life in prison. The only exception was SS Lt. Col. Dr. Otto Bradfisch, head of Einsatzkommando 8 operating in the Soviet Minsk region. Though Bradfisch had displayed the same general behavior as the other defendants in this category, the District Attorney's office in Munich followed the intentionalist arguments and charged and convicted him only of accessory to murder. He received a sentence of ten years in prison. One wonders whether the prosecutors considered that it was Bradfisch who in August of 1941 had questioned Reich Leader SS and Chief of German Police Himmler regarding who would bear the responsibility for the mass extermination of the Jews. Himmler had told the members of Einsatzkommando 8, and other members of the Security Police present, that the orders had been given by Hitler. As Bradfisch recalls, "It was a question, then, of a Führer-order, which had the force of the law, and . . . Hitler alone bore the responsibility for these orders."[3]

Although this category of confirmed killers represents only a very small fraction of Einsatzgruppen officers, they possessed certain characteristics that made them representative of the whole: some were educated intellectuals who became the commanding officers of Einsatzkommandos or Sonderkommandos; some were social outcasts and "misfits" whose careers in the Nazi organizations were their sole accomplishment; and others had been valued members of their communities, who might never have committed a crime if Nazism had not provided the opportunity to exercise almost unlimited power over a group of defenseless human beings.

The Commanding Officers

The early careers of the commanders of the Einsatzkommandos and Sonderkommandos were very similar. They all came from a lower middle-class background; their fathers were shopkeepers, white-collar employees, or non-commissioned officers in the Reichswehr, the German military during 1919–33, the time of the Weimar Republic. All were born between 1900 and 1910, which means they were in their early to late thirties when they took their positions in the Einsatzgruppen. Four of the future commanding officers had finished law studies shortly before or after the Nazis came to power, and if they had not already been active in right-wing and militant organizations before entering a university, they joined either the Nazi Party, the Storm Troopers (SA), or the SS during their studies. All but Dr. Bradfisch, who became a member of the Gestapo in 1937, had joined the Security Service by 1936. After they took their first assignments in the Security Service, most of the men met or worked under high-ranking SS officers who they followed into the Reich Security Main Office or its predecessors, and the different incarnations of the Einsatzgruppen, throughout their career.

SS Major Paul Zapp, in 1934, as an economics and philosophy student, had been one of the promising thinkers in the German Faith Movement, an organization that sought to find a synthesis between Christian and Nazi ideas (however ironic that might seem). Dr. Werner Best, the SS lawyer then in charge of personnel in the Security Police, had been impressed with Zapp's writings and invited him to join the SS. (It was Best who later formulated the 1935 Nuremberg Laws—the group of proclamations that delineated the citizenship requisites of the Third Reich and the status of Jews within the Reich.)[4] Best's interest convinced Zapp that the SS was indeed the organization that stood for the ideals of the new intellectual and religious elite in Germany. Zapp became a SS member and in 1936 joined the Security Service. At first he worked in Department III of the Reich Security Main Office, where he analyzed the incoming reports on religion and ideology. He then served in the same functions in the Security Service Sections at Breslau and Vienna. In 1940, Zapp was made an instructor of ideology at the Security Service Leadership School. After that, he briefly returned to the Reich Security Main Office, and at the time the Einsatzgruppen were assembled in Pretzsch in May 1941, he took over command of the Security Service Section Kassel. At this point, Zapp was already designated for a term in the Einsatzgruppen. In the summer of 1942 he was detached to headquarters of Einsatzgruppe D to become familiar with his new task, and soon thereafter he took the post as leader of Einsatzkommando 11a.[5]

True to Zapp's image of the SS as a physical and spiritual elite, he not only fulfilled his job with dedication, he also produced several articles, books, poems, and radio plays in which he set forth his philosophy. In a work published in 1935, he was still very much concerned with the issue of Christianity and racial inequality. He wrote:

> The officials of Christianity, especially the Catholic Church, and the doctrine of transcendence have facilitated the degeneration of peoples and thereby begun a racial decline that can only be stopped with the greatest difficulty and human hardship. Invoking the equality of all human beings consequently led to the destruction of the values and contents of faith, which are different in every race. But losing such race specific ideals means that a people is condemned to die because it loses its creative spirit. Thus the reign of Christianity brought with it the decline of all valuable racial forces. Of course, the Catholic Church did everything possible to maintain this condition and continues to do so until today because that way it could secure its own survival.[6]

When writing these lines, Zapp probably only thought about a solution to keep a pure and distinctly German form of Christianity free from Catholic and foreign influences. There is yet no indication of his sentiments against the Jews, and as late as 1936 Zapp was known to criticize Nazi racial policies. On the other hand, his concern about the decline of races, the negative practices of the Catholic Church with its transcendent doctrine of equality, and the use of terms such as "difficulty" and "human hardship" might also indicate more radical inclinations. Two years later, none of the relative restraint or criticism remained. In a poem dedicated to his new "God," published in 1938, Zapp revealed his conversion:

> You, our Führer, gave us our flag—
> Raised it in the midst of our enemies
> And gave us the order to protect it.
> We saw your eyes shine and knew:
> To follow you means a race
> for its [the flag's] honor and the survival of the people!
> You were not a ruler, not a despot,
> You were der Führer! That gave you the right
> To ask for the ultimate sacrifice: to give
> What men can only give once—life!

And thereby you distinguished free man from servant
and set the price for honor: victory or death!
Thus they stepped up, man after man,
And the struggle for the flag began.
Your troops were all equal,
Because your flag was the new Reich![7]

Such a zealous man must have made a quite an impression on the Nazi leadership, and it is no surprise that Zapp was later appointed to a significant position in the Einsatzgruppen. It is as important to note, however, that he certainly also brought his ideological fervor to his job at the Security Service Leadership School, where he must have influenced numerous other future Einsatzgruppen and SS officers.

Doctor Alfred Karl Filbert, SS Lieutenant Colonel and leader of Einsatzkommando 9, was another officer who had met his future superior in the Einsatzgruppen rather early. The subsequent leader of Einsatzgruppe A, SS. Brig. Gen. Heinz Jost, was Filbert's superior during his four years (1935–39) in the Security Service Main Office's desk for foreign countries. The future leader of Sonderkommando 1b, SS Lt. Col. Dr. Erich Ehrlinger, was also transferred to the Security Service Main Office in 1935, where he soon became deputy leader of Department II 1, the office monitoring the activities of the "Jews, Churches, and Enemies." His superior was SS Col. Franz Six, the later leader of the Advance Command (Vorkommando) Moscow, a special unit within Einsatzgruppe B designed for securing the Soviet capital after its fall. And finally, the later leader of Sonderkommando 7a, SS Lt. Col. Albert Rapp, joined the Security Service together with his student friends. (Eight officers from that group reached upper-level positions in the Security Police). Rapp soon came to the Security Service Section East in Berlin, which was supervised by the later leader of Einsatzgruppe B, SS Oberführer Erich Naumann. (The SS had no German army equivalent ranking for "Oberführer," and thus no U.S. Army comparable rank.) These four Einsatzgruppen commanders were thus members of what was called "Seilschaften"—closely knit groups.[8]

In their evaluations, superior officers described the future Einsatzkommando commanders as "extraordinarily diligent, well experienced, good organizational talents" and "above average performances."[9] Dr. Ehrlinger's evaluations are particularly telling. They are full of positive judgments: "He was an important help in a difficult position; he did an enormous amount of work [gewaltiges Arbeitspensum] with great dedication; I regret to lose such a valuable worker;" and, "He is the type of the imperturbable, convinced, and always pushing national socialist fighter and able leader who does not make compromises."[10]

It is thus no surprise that this group of officers quickly rose to relatively high ranks and offices.

By 1938 at the latest, the future Einsatzkommando commanders had reached the rank of SS captain and worked in upper-level positions within the German police apparatus. Their quick promotions, however, also mean that they had ample opportunities to recognize the true character of the Nazi regime. Ehrlinger definitely was directly involved in the organization of Kristallnacht, the Night of Broken Glass in November 1938, when Nazi mobs smashed the windows of Jewish-owned homes, stores, and schools, and set fire to synagogues throughout the country, thereby perpetrating the first violent and large-scale pogrom against the Jewish population in Germany. Kristallnacht was also a turning point in Nazi Jewish policy and a sign that Hitler's anti-Semitism was potentially different from previous forms of German anti-Semitism.

If the future Einsatzgruppen officers still did not know then the nature of the Nazi regime, they soon had other chances. Even Dr. Bradfisch, from his relatively remote position as leader of the State Police (Stapo) Office in Neustadt, must have gained clear insights, if not into the activities of the Einsatzgruppen, then into the functioning of the Secret State Police and the treatment of potential enemies. Ehrlinger also had been involved in the establishment of the Security Service offices in Vienna and Prague, and was then drafted to an Einsatzgruppe in Poland. And Albert Rapp had also been part of the Einsatzgruppen in Poland, where he was responsible for the expulsion of more than 100,000 Jews from the incorporated territories. He subsequently stayed as leader of the Security Service Section in Poznan.

Dr. Filbert, on the other hand, became, as the court in Berlin noted, "One of the highest officials in the Reich Security Main Office and especially in its political intelligence branch,"[11] and certainly must have known about the perverse Security Service activities in Austria, Czechoslovakia, and Poland. During his time at the Reich Security Main Office, Filbert, however, also experienced the downside of his loyalty to his superior, Heinz Jost. Due to a power struggle between Jost and the notorious Gestapo Chief Müller, Filbert drew Müller's wrath. To make matters worse, Filbert's brother had made unfavorable comments about a failed attempt on the life of Hitler and was arrested, at the orders of Himmler, and brought into a concentration camp. The incident essentially stalled Filbert's once promising SS career, and he asked for his resignation from the Reich Security Main Office. His request, however, was denied because of his knowledge of confidential material in foreign intelligence, and he remained in his position. He received no more promotions, but continued to be a convinced Nazi. Filbert then enthusiastically followed the draft call to the Einsatzgruppen because it presented him with a new beginning.

Three of the commanding officers became members of the initial Einsatz-gruppen in the Soviet Union. The three others attained their command later in 1941 or 1942. Ehrlinger had the longest tenure in the Security Police forces in the occupied territories. He began as leader of Sonderkommando 1b, was then appointed commanding officer of the Security Police in Kiev, and finally became the leader of Einsatzgruppe B until April 1944.

The executions and the other Security Police work in the occupied territories were very similar, and all Einsatzgruppen members participated in the shootings one way or another. But certain factors distinguish the commanding officers from the rest of the Einsatzgruppen officers. As leaders of their respective units it is of course to be expected that the commanding officers ordered, planned, organized, and occasionally supervised the executions. Beyond these normal command functions, however, the men set themselves apart because of their behavior on the crime scene, their attitude toward the victims and their subordinates, and their complete identification with Nazi extermination policy.

Karl Albert Filbert's successor as leader of Einsatzkommando 9, SS Lt. Col. Wilhelm Wiebens, and the other commanding officers took charge of their units with the explicit aim to execute the order (Vernichtungsbefehl) to kill the Jews as efficiently as possible.[12] Therefore, as the court in Berlin appropriately expressed it, they were the "engines of their units" and "nothing happened without them or their knowledge."[13] They were present at the execution sites, even for the killing of a small number of people. And like Ehrlinger, they "stood broad-legged at the edge of the pit and supervised the proceedings with submachine gun hung over their shoulders, the arms resting on the hips,"[14] or they restlessly ran up and down the trenches. They set examples for their men by conducting the first large-scale executions themselves, often selecting the personnel for the firing squads and making certain that everything proceeded as effectively as possible. With motivational speeches and neutral comments regarding the victims such as "these figures,"[15] which denied the very humanity of the victims, they attempted to ease their subordinates into the tasks. Moreover, they often gave the firing commands, and they participated in the shooting with their pistols or submachine guns. At one execution, Dr. Ehrlinger was so eager to begin that he pulled his gun and started firing before the Jewish victims had time to lie down in the grave.

According to the witnesses testifying in the German court, the officers had never showed any human sentiments or emotions toward their victims, but rather had caused them pain and suffering far beyond what would have been necessary for the killings. The commanding officers organized the executions so that the victims had to wait their turn in front of the mass graves, fully aware of their destiny, witnessing the murder of their relatives and friends and listening to the screams of their loved ones and the sounds of the bullets. Sometimes the victims had to dig their own graves. They were further denigrated through beatings and humiliations, and the undressing. Then, when their turn finally came, they had to stand or lie down on top of a mass of bloody bodies. Often no determinations were made whether or not the victims were dead when a day's work was finished. And when the Einsatzkommando leaders occasionally spared individual Jews, they did so only because they wanted to utilize their labor. Clearly, the Einsatzkommando leaders were the masters over life and death and they relished that role.

The Einsatzkommando leaders had no mercy for their victims, but, similarly, according to their junior officers, they cared little for their subordinates, except that these men should become effective tools in order to implement their will— the elimination of the Jews. The commanding officers harnessed the entire man-power of their units, even drivers, interpreters, and other specialists in their heinous tasks. Otto Bradfisch, for example, told one of his men who was nor-mally responsible for administrative and organizational duties, "Today is going to be a busy day; today it is your turn, too."[16] Another officer, Albert Rapp, had ordered the cooks and the exhausted men who had just stood night guard duty to participate in the execution that day. Rapp always made the drivers of his unit take part in the shootings. In addition, the Einsatzkommando leaders constantly pressed their subordinates for higher body counts, which they called *Abschuss-ziffern,* a term that usually referred to hunting practices and again underscoring the depraved indifference of these officers.

The leaders remained distant and shunned social contacts with their subor-dinates, ridiculing those who proved to be "too weak." When a young officer who had participated in the shooting of children for the first time started scream-ing for his mother, his fellow officers tried to console him, but Dr. Filbert causti-cally remarked, "And he wants to be an SS leader? One should send him back home with an appropriate evaluation immediately."[17] The commanding of-ficers always gave explicit orders that they expected to be fulfilled without hesi-tation and without mistakes. They did not tolerate objections regarding the mas-sacres—often threatening the protestor with court-martial—and they blocked all attempts to leave the Einsatzgruppen for an assignment at the front. In short, then, the Einsatzgruppen were trained to fear their commanders.

From these general behavioral patterns it is clear that the Einsatzkommando leaders—even Filbert, whose brother and whose career had suffered severely and gave him reason to hate and undermine Nazi policies—wholeheartedly agreed with the extermination program. Their actions were clearly guided by ambition and hatred of the Jews. Albert Rapp repeatedly preached to his men, during February to April 1942 that "the Jews and the Gypsies are lowly, down-

trodden, anti-social, disease-ridden, dirty people who deserve to be extermi-
nated. The Germans . . . are the master race, and the SS is the elite of the Führer.
Therefore, [his men] owe him blind obedience."[18]

Filbert forbade his men to talk to the Jews who cleaned their quarters, and he
objected when the men offered them coffee and tea. He was even more indignant
when his men let these Jews drink from the same cups that good Germans used.[19]
From such behavior it is evident that the Jews were nothing more than vermin to
the Einsatzkommando leaders. And that attitude was little better for other targeted victim groups such as the gypsies, who with the Jews were at the bottom of
the racial hierarchy. Wilhelm Wiebens had told a witness regarding a gypsy, "It's
better to kill one who is not guilty than to let a guilty one get away."[20]

Although these attitudes and motivations are more than enough reason to
identify the Einsatzkommando leaders as "confirmed killers," their individual
deeds further corroborate the judgment. The actions of these men played a primary role in convincing the courts in Berlin, Karlsruhe, Munich, and Essen that
they were not mere accomplices, but that they had committed murder on their
own initiative.

The Einsatzkommando leaders in the Soviet Union did their best to make
unnecessary a subsequent intermediary stage and a second sweep (as Raul
Hilberg termed them) in their search for Jews. They intended to destroy the Jews
as completely and as soon as possible. Therefore, neither single scattered Jewish
families living far off the prescribed routes of the Einsatzkommandos, hardships
of the Russian winter, nor even complaints of superior officers and fellow commanders could prevent these men from exceeding the limits of their orders.

Dr. Bradfisch's constant demand for higher numbers, particularly in 1942,
was indicative of the attitude of these officers for whom the killing of Jews had become a competition. One trial witness noted that "Einsatzkommando 9 was far
ahead of the other commands in the race for the highest numbers."[21] To achieve
his success, Filbert had divided his unit into several small squads and sent them
out on search-and-destroy missions. Such "Jew hunts," as they were called by
the perpetrators, were also practiced in Zapp's and many other killing units.[22]
Filbert's co-defendant and former deputy, SS Maj. Wilhelm Greiffenberger,
testified that in a conversation with Filbert he brought up the advice of their superior, Arthur Nebe, that Filbert should exercise more restraint in his ferocity
against the Jews. Filbert responded with irritation, stating that he received his orders directly from Berlin and that he would execute them as he saw fit. On another occasion, Greiffenberger reminded Filbert that the leader of Sonderkommando 7a, SS Lt. Col. Walter Blume, usually avoided the executions by keeping
his unit away from the cities with a larger Jewish population. Again, Filbert only
remarked, "Blume will certainly be punished for that."[23]

In striking contrast to Blume's apparently lackluster attitude, Albert Rapp, one of his successors, drove his unit to the utmost in order to kill every Jew he could find. When he took over Sonderkommando 7a in February of 1942, the unit was recuperating, on Oberführer Naumann's explicit orders, in Gomel, from the exhausting fall advance of 1941. However, Rapp not only scolded his predecessor for letting the men remain idle, he immediately mobilized the unit and moved on to Klincy, the center of a small territorial administrative unit (a Rayon, a district within a city) with some 50,000 inhabitants. Klincy was situated on the rail line between Gomel and Briansk and had not been destroyed during the German advance. Rapp had heard that numerous Jewish communities in the vicinity of the city also had not been touched by the first Einsatzgruppen attack. As Filbert had done with his unit, Rapp divided his men into multiple smaller killing squads and sent them on search-and-destroy missions. In his extraordinary zeal, he did not hesitate to cross into the territory designated for other Einsatzkommandos.

Rapp's determination and recklessness is best illustrated in the episode told by SS 1st Lt. Kurt Matschke, the officer Rapp had succeeded in the command of Sonderkommando 7a. Matschke related that shortly after Rapp's arrival in Klincy, Rapp and a detachment of at least fifty men set out to execute the inmates of a mental asylum in the little town of Trubtchevsk. Located more than 62 miles to the south of Klincy, and outside Rapp's area of operation, at that time Trubtchevsk was under attack from strong partisan forces. The responsible army rear area headquarters noted in its war diary: "Trubtchevsk requires at least a fully mobile battalion on sleds and snowshoes. Mission advisable only for the evacuation of the place and the transport of the supplies."[24]

In the story, Matschke then complained and asked why Rapp unnecessarily exposed the men to the extreme winter conditions. Rapp replied laconically, "Are you in charge here or am I?"[25] He and the men then left Klincy and, after an arduous and long journey on horse-drawn sleds, reached another town halfway to their destination. Again they were warned by the local military commander who said that because of the partisans, tank support was absolutely essential. Matschke also objected once more, telling Rapp, "I did not save the men during the retreat so that you can sacrifice them now for no reason."[26] Yet Rapp pressed on to Trubtchesvk with fifteen volunteers, where they committed the brutal massacre of forty mentally disabled persons.[27]

Trial records show that between February 21 and April 20, 1942, Rapp's Sonderkommando 7a had conducted "at least twenty-four mass shootings of Jews, gypsies, civilians suspected of partisan activities, Communists, POWs and mentally disabled, who had succeeded previously to escape from the Einsatzkommando 8, which roamed Klincy and its surrounding areas."[28]

Whereas Rapp could not be stopped by extreme climatic conditions and partisan attacks, Paul Zapp refused to listen to medical advice. Although he had fallen ill with a grave disease that required hospitalization, he chose to stay in the killing fields. The court in Munich found that "Zapp was as cold as ice toward the Jews," and he had organized and executed multiple large-scale massacres such as those in Nikolayev (3,500 victims), Kherson (4,000 victims), and Simferopol (5,000 victims). He had taken care of the small details as well. In Nikolayev, he noticed a single Jew who had tried to hide under the bodies, and immediately pulled his gun to shoot the man. The gun failed, but other executioners became aware of the Jew and quickly killed him.[29]

Dr. Ehrlinger displayed similar extraordinary zeal, especially after his appointment as commanding officer of Sonderkommando 1b in Minsk. In April and May 1942 he had established a so-called work-education camp (Abeitserziehungslager). One day in August 1943, a prisoner had escaped from the camp. According to witnesses among the camp prisoners and Ehrlinger's subordinates, Ehrlinger was visibly upset and immediately appeared. The prisoners had to line up and through an interpreter Ehrlinger announced that some of them would be shot as a deterrent for future escapes. During his address he stood over the "chosen" prisoners who were lying face down on the ground, so that they could not immediately see what he was doing. Ehrlinger then randomly determined who was to be shot. When this stirred a commotion among the lines of prisoners, he suddenly pulled his gun and fired into their ranks. Ehrlinger only stopped when his magazine was empty and multiple victims, none of whom had been selected previously for execution, were hit and fell to the ground.[30]

A look at the disciplinary action taken against these officers during their time in the Einsatzgruppen adds to the image of their personalities and human qualities—or rather, the lack thereof. On October 20, 1941, Dr. Filbert was recalled from the Einsatzgruppen and accused of having violated his duties during his time at the Reich Security Main Office—a result of the earlier power struggle between Jost and Müller. Filbert was relieved of his duties and held under house arrest for two years. Nevertheless, when the investigation was suspended in 1943, he willingly rejoined the Reich Security Main Office and its Criminal Police department. Still anxious to work for the accomplishment of the aims of his former accusers, he diligently organized and ran the office dealing with crimes against the economy.

Commanding Officer Albert Rapp also had to deal with an SS investigation and punishment. In the summer of 1943, while under the influence of alcohol, he had shot at the barracks of his unit, causing many of his subordinates to take cover. Rapp first received a letter of reprimand, then, after Himmler's personal intervention, he was confined to his quarters for fourteen days.

Like their wartime actions, the postwar behavior of these perpetrators also reveals their lack of human sensitivities as well as no capacity for understanding a need for redemption. These men never intended to be held responsible for their deeds. When it became apparent that Germany would be overrun by the Allies, all but Wilhelm Wiebens, Filbert's successor at Einsatzkommando 9, had changed their names and assumed the identity of common German soldiers. (Wiebens had been sentenced by the British to fifteen years for executing two Royal Air Force pilots, but he was released in 1955 for good behavior.)[31]

Because these commanding officers had used their expertise and their connections with the Reich Security Main Office and the Secret Police—and also because of the chaotic conditions in the aftermath of the war—they had no problems hiding their true identities. In order not to be discovered, Rapp even broke off all contacts with his family. These formerly high-ranking SS officers then took on jobs as manual laborers, far below their qualifications. However, as early as 1950 they re-emerged under their actual names and quickly reached highly respected positions in West German society. Bradfisch and Zapp became insurance brokers, Filbert a banker, Ehrlinger a sales manager for Volkswagen, and Rapp edited and published magazines. It appeared as if their service in the Nazi organizations had never happened. When they had participated in the de-Nazification efforts of the Western Allies, they nonchalantly lied about their war activities and categorically denied membership in the SS.

And this overall attitude did not change after the German police finally caught up with these men. Although they could no longer deny membership in the SS and the Einsatzgruppen, they diminished their involvement in the massacres. Only after multiple witnesses had definitively linked them to certain events, did they gradually admit their participation. But the picture they drew of the events still differed greatly from the truth. They conceded that they had never undertaken efforts to withdraw themselves from their obligations, but they insisted that they had never played major roles in the executions. They claimed to have never fired a gun themselves and blamed all responsibility on other SS leaders. Interestingly, Albert Rapp tried to escape any ultimate retribution by pushing a spring from his bed into his heart immediately after his arrest.

The attitude and the bearing before, during, and after their service in the Einsatzgruppen, and in particular their hostility toward the authorities who finally held them accountable for their deeds, was exemplified in Otto Bradfisch's complaint about the legitimacy of the court in Munich: "It is an absurdity [ein Unding] to be prosecuted for obeying the orders of a legitimate state leadership,"[32] His statement categorizes the commanding officers as convinced followers of Nazi racial policies and confirmed killers.

Ideology and Character Intersect: Franz Stark

The career of SS Capt. Franz Stark offers a contrast to the commanding officers in this study—Bradfisch, Ehrlinger, Filbert, Rapp, Wiebens, and Zapp. Stark came from a different social background. He owed his ascendancy from unskilled laborer to the position of an SS leader not to his education, intelligence, or other qualities, but solely to the Nazi Party. A little older than these six officers, Stark was born to an unwed mother on October 7, 1901, in St. Louis, Missouri. He was the only Einsatzgruppen officer prosecuted by the West German courts who was not from Germany or the formerly German territories. Stark and his mother had returned to Germany in 1903, where at the age of five he was taken from her because she had beaten and injured him repeatedly. He was given to foster care, and after eight years of schooling, he began an apprenticeship as a mechanic; however, he never qualified as a journeyman. Too young to participate in World War I, Stark volunteered for Youth Movement leader Gerhard Rossbach's Freikorps (Free Corps) in 1919. Without having seen action, he was discharged soon thereafter. Stark then moved to Munich where he worked as a messenger for various enterprises. On January 1, 1920, he joined the NSDAP—National Socialist German Workers' Party. In 1921, he volunteered for another Freikorps and participated in the suppression of Communist uprisings in the Ruhr area and Upper Silesia. He was involved in the failed March 1920 Kapp Putsch, the attempt to overthrow the Weimar government by Gen. Walther von Lüttwitz's antirepublican forces and Wolfgang Kapp, a nationalist politician who had helped found the German Fatherland Party in 1917. Kapp's attempt to form a new nationalist government failed after only four days, however, when the civil servants refused to take his orders and a general strike of the workers paralyzed the country. After the Kapp collapse, Franz Stark returned to Munich, where he remained at times unemployed or worked short-term jobs.

Since 1920, Stark had been a loyal follower of the Nazi Party. He had joined the Storm Troopers on the day of its foundation in 1921, then in November 1923 had marched with Hitler and 2,000–3,000 followers in the Beer Hall Putsch, another failed effort to overthrow the Weimar government. Stark subsequently served as a messenger for the Nazi Party, after it was banned. For his bravery in numerous beer hall and street brawls, he was awarded the Nazi Blood Medal (Blutorden). In 1933, Stark had the major breakthrough of his career when Reinhardt Heydrich hired him as a house servant. Stark also joined the SS and the Security Service within the SS, and was given a job as a registration clerk within the Security Service Section South. He had reached the rank of captain when the Reich Security Main Office drafted him for service in Sonderkommando 1b in October 1941. Two months later, the mobile Sonderkommando was transformed into the stationary Office of the Commander of the Security Police and Security Service (KdS) Weissruthenien—White Ruthenia—at Minsk.[33] It was there that Stark committed his crimes.[34]

Like the six officers mentioned, Stark participated in several executions in a supervising position and his activities went beyond organization and conduct of the massacres. On one occasion he was ordered to shoot the Jews in the city of Rakov. When events did not proceed quickly enough, Stark began to fire at the helpless victims even before they had reached the execution site. Then, on the first day of a large operation against the Jews of the Minsk ghetto, from March 1–3, 1942, he was in charge of loading Jews into railroad cars that transported them to the execution site. Stark patrolled the street leading from the ghetto to the trains, constantly using his whip to accelerate the proceedings. On the following days he was part of the execution command and single-handedly shot at least thirty people.

Stark, however, was more than a follower of orders. An incident that occurred in the night after the first day of the March operation illustrates that he killed for the basest reasons. On March 1, 1942, when Stark drove the Jews to the cattle cars with his whip, the head of the civil administration, (the Gebietskommissar—territorial commissioner or governor) Wilhelm Kube, inspected the ghetto clearing and repeatedly objected to the unnecessary brutality of the Einsatzgruppen. According to witnesses, harsh confrontations developed between Kube and various Security Service officers. The commanding officer of the Einsatzkommando, SS Lt. Col. Eduard Strauch, complained about this interference in SS matters in a special report to SS Lt. Gen. Erich von dem Bach-Zelewski, the Higher SS and Police Leader-Center.[35] The altercation was part of an ongoing struggle between the territorial governor, Kube, who was known to be "weak on the Jews," and the Security Service leadership within the district.[36] Among the SS men with whom Kube had a run-in that particular day was Franz Stark. Kube witnessed how Stark mercilessly whipped Jews who were herded toward the loading platform. He stopped and scolded Stark: "One does not use whips against human beings."[37] But Stark ignored Kube and continued. Kube then tried to wrestle the whip away from Stark, but he failed, and eventually left the scene.

Stark was so agitated about the scandalous interference from what he believed to be a "party bigwig" that he looked for immediate revenge. It was known that Kube employed a number of Jews in his office, among them three barbers who had been deported from Vienna and regularly cut the hair of the territorial governor and that of his German personnel. Stark thus decided to kill Kube's barbers, as an act of retribution for the insult. With an unknown SS subordinate,

Stark abducted the barbers from their quarters and shot them. When the bodies were found and the German authorities looked for the murderer, Stark proudly reported to Strauch and admitted his deed.[38] In this case it is evident that although the victims were Jewish, racial motivations only played a subordinate part in Stark's behavior. At the time, he knew that the western Jews were not yet included in the elimination program, and he picked the barbers only for his private revenge with Territorial Governor Kube. Stark thus committed the crime on his own initiative and not because he wanted to be an accomplice in the Nazis extermination campaign. Coincidentally, the development of German anti-Jewish policies gave Stark the opportunity to easily complete his personal vendetta. Considering the above circumstances, the court charged and convicted him of murder.

Stark, like other Einsatzgruppen officers, hid under an assumed identity immediately after the war. But he began using his real name too soon and was subsequently interned by the American occupation forces in September 1945. He was released in 1948 and worked several jobs in construction and as a driver. As the commanding officers had done, he reverted to his original social status once the Nazi years had passed.

But a striking contrast is evident in the postwar behavior of the commanding officers and Stark. Stark was not well educated, but during the trial he admitted that what he had done was wrong and that it was not justifiable under any circumstances. As the court writes in its sentencing, "He admitted his crimes in frank and relentless openness [geradezu schonungsloser Offenheit]."[39] It is also noteworthy that Stark was a simple man who had only eight years of schooling. He was exposed to right-wing propaganda when he was only eighteen years old, and in the Freikorps he had learned that violence and brutality were legitimate means to achieve objectives. He had joined the Nazi movement when it was still an almost unknown political splinter party, and because of his lack of education he absorbed the philosophies of the party, and they soon had a dominating influence over him. The Nazi Party furthermore offered him the chance to achieve an officer's rank that usually required the German secondary school diploma (Abitur) or its equivalent. With this background, it is no surprise that Stark became one of the most loyal, blind, and stubborn followers of Nazi orders. Yet, even these considerations do not excuse his actions, in particular the excessive cruelty and murders committed of his own choosing.

Stark and the six other officers were no "ordinary men" under any definition of the term. Bradfisch, Ehrlinger, Filbert, Rapp, Wiebens, and Zapp constituted an elite even within the Nazi system, and their rise to social prominence after the war proves that they would have been successful under other political conditions as well. And Stark most likely would have been considered a failure, destined to

remain within the lower social strata in every other society. But another perpetrator, SS T. Sgt. Martin Weiss, perhaps comes closest to Christopher Browning's definition of an "ordinary man."

The "Exemplary Murderer": Martin Weiss

Martin Weiss was one of eight children in a well-respected Protestant Christian
family in Karlsruhe. His father was a master plumber and heating installer and
owned his own business. Martin was born on February 21, 1903. After eight
years of schooling, he became an apprentice in his father's shop and passed
the journeymen's exam specializing in heating installation. During this time
he belonged to a non-political youth movement called Wandervogel—literally
"migratory birds." These youth groups met on weekends and during the summer for hiking and camping trips.

From 1923 to 1927, Martin Weiss helped his brother establish a farm in South
America. Upon his return to Germany, Weiss studied for the master's exam
specializing in installation of heating systems, and he successfully passed. When
his father died in 1928, Martin took over the business. Under his leadership, the
shop flourished and Martin's reputation in the community grew. He married in
1930 and had three children. Because of his passion as an equestrian, in 1934
Weiss joined the Reiter SS, the organization within the SS that emphasized
horsemanship, with the rank of Private First Class. Weiss then joined the Nazi
Party in 1937, as a result of his Reiter SS participation, though heedless of the
party's political activities.

On September 6, 1939, Weiss was drafted into the Wehrmacht, and because
he was already an SS member he was assigned to the Waffen SS, the military
branch of the SS. After boot camp he was sent to a mechanical supply unit and
participated in the Nazi's French campaign. In August 1940, he was released
from the army and returned to his business in Karlsruhe. During this time Weiss
was a model citizen. He never committed a crime, and witnesses from his hometown testified that he was known for his decency, hard work, diligence, helpful-
ness, good judgment, and "a sense for everything noble and good."[40] His life
showed no trace of violence, brutality, or even political fanaticism. In the spring
of 1941, however, he was again drafted to the Waffen SS and sent to the Einsatzgruppen in Bad Düben. There, or sometime during his service in Russia, a complete personality change occurred.

Weiss first belonged to Einsatzkommando 3, and then from October 1941
to July 1944 to the Office of the Commander of the Security Police and Security Service for Lithuania, in Vilnius, where he worked at the Jewish desk.

Weiss was the liaison officer to the Lithuanian Sonderkommando and responsible for the organization and execution of all measures against the Jewish population in the ghetto and the inmates of the local Lukishki prison. Although superior officers occasionally supervised his work, Weiss was the de facto commander of the ghetto. He held only an SS rank of technical sergeant, but he enjoyed the commanding officer's undivided confidence and the Jewish inmates recognized him as "their master over life and death."[41] At times, Weiss also served in other departments of the commander's office, and he joined in raids against local partisans.

Weiss's routine schedule is of interest. Three to four times per week he inspected the Jewish ghetto police and the Lithuanian guards at the gate of the ghetto. He always made certain that the Jewish work crews could not smuggle in extra food rations or other items. Always vigilant and suspicious of illegal activities, he carefully checked working permits. In addition, Weiss and another Security Service member, his co-defendant at the trial, SS T. Sgt. August Hering, commanded the SS Sonderkommando during searches of the ghetto. Most importantly, however, Weiss was in charge of the selection of victims for the executions. At the execution site near Ponary, a village eight miles south of Vilnius, it was Weiss who gave the necessary orders to the auxiliaries; after the execution, he reported the number of victims to his superiors. In his function as an executioner, he occasionally also led excursions to the smaller ghettos in the vicinity.

From his "job description" it is understood that Weiss could exercise restraint or cruelty. Weiss chose the cruel path. During the thirteen to fifteen executions he supervised at Ponary, he always made certain that the victims had to walk through a gauntlet of Lithuanian auxiliary troops before they were killed. As in many other executions, the victims had to lay down on top of their previously murdered brethren and often had to wait hours—sometimes days—before they were finally shot. As to the controls at the gate, which could have been conducted in a relatively humane manner, Weiss turned them into a horror for the inmates. Witnesses described how he beat Jewish men, women, and children with various tools if they had not attached their Star of David, or if they had carried with them the smallest amounts of food—and sometimes for no particular reason. On his orders, all persons found in possession of food had to be brought into the office of the Jewish police where the victims were stripped completely, and then given up to fifty lashes. Weiss always participated in these beatings. Overall, the court established that Martin Weiss killed at least six people just because they did not "behave properly" in his presence, as he deemed it.

The inspections of the prison and selections of victims offered Weiss even more opportunities to exercise his cruelties. As the court in Würzburg irrevocably established, Weiss always wore a club or whip and mercilessly separated families and tore children from their mothers' arms. During the liquidation of the Vilnius ghetto in September 1943, he severely beat a Jewish woman who would not leave her relatives destined for execution. And during inspection tours to the tailor shop within the ghetto, the workers had to stand at attention immediately and, upon his orders, perform knee-bends, jump over tables, or crawl under furniture until they collapsed from exhaustion.

Weiss's behavior during other inspection tours was recounted by a witness, Szynom, who told how, during the controls at the gate, Weiss once found a man with a few potatoes and a bit of fish. Weiss shouted, "You dog! You may starve to death, but you cannot bring anything with you!"[42] He shot the man on the spot. Another ghetto inmate witnessed the search for work permits, the "Action of the Yellow Permits (Aktion der gelben Scheine)," when Weiss discovered forty to fifty people hiding in a house. Yelling, "Out with you, you damned," he drew his pistol and fired into the group. At least one person was hit. Later, during the Children's Action (Kinderaktion), when all children under the age of eighteen were to be selected for execution, Weiss asked the witness G. about his age. When G. responded that he was already twenty years old, Weiss responded, "Then we will get you later." To another group of Jewish witnesses who had the task of disposing of the bodies of the victims shot during transport to Ponary, Weiss commented, "If I would not see blood every day, I would be thirsty for it." On another occasion, when Weiss returned from an excursion to a neighboring ghetto where he had just conducted the execution of the elderly and the sick, he told his Jewish policemen, "You should be grateful that I cleaned up such a mess for you." During another selection, he told an old Jewish dentist, "If you are still able to walk, then you can walk to your execution," and made him travel on foot the eight miles to Ponary.[43]

Not surprisingly, Weiss was the most feared Security Service member in Vilnius and its vicinity. Witnesses noticed that the streets of the ghetto emptied immediately when Weiss arrived and people started shouting, "Death is coming."[44] The chairman of the Jewish Council, Jacob Gens, gave Weiss the sinister title of "exemplary murderer."[45] Even his superiors were afraid of his extraordinary brutality and ruthlessness. The officer in charge of the local Security Service branch office waited until Weiss was on leave before he dared to release a prisoner from Lukishki prison into the ghetto, and he warned the prisoner to look out for Weiss. When other Security Service members asked another officer what would happen to the Jews when the Germans had to retreat from Vilnius, the officer replied that if it would be up to him, he would let the Jews go, but he was afraid of what Weiss would do.

One wonders how such a formerly valuable member of the community could so quickly turn into a sadistic, brutal, and remorseless mass murderer who made the elimination of the Jews not only his own goal but exceeded the standard set by the Nazi regime. Was he not a well-respected family man and artisan in his hometown? He had never been motivated politically, and had joined the SS and the Nazi Party only because of his interest in horsemanship. When he had been drafted into the army and participated in the war in the west, he did not stand out in any way. He had never shown signs of brutality and anti-Semitism. Up to that point in his life he did not differ much from many other Germans. But when Weiss was drafted into the Einsatzgruppen and put into a position to decide the fate of tens of thousands, another personality trait came to the forefront.

From the description of Weiss's activities in Vilnius, it is safe to assume that he relished his new role. The Nazis had given him control over the Jews there, and he performed like an absolute sovereign in that domain. This is further underscored by his attitude during selections for execution from Lukishi prison. Weiss decided on a whim whether an inmate would be executed at Ponary or whether he would accept a bribe from the prisoners' Jewish Council and have the individual released to the ghetto. Yet even at this point, Weiss sometimes seemed to recognize the possible repercussions of his deeds. When on leave, he again reverted to his former personality. He told his friends that he would rather fight against the enemy at the front than against the civilian population behind the front. Moreover, he added, he would not want to carry the responsibility for what his superiors were obligated to carry, acknowledging that although he was forced to be inconceivably harsh, fears for the well being of his family made him oblige. Weiss's duplicitous nature was also evident when he stated that the Jewish question could not be solved by shooting innocent women and children.[46]

Here one might initially assume a hint of questioning of the orders and policies of the Nazi regime, but that such remarks were more likely nothing more than a deceit and justification to placate his conscience is evident from Weiss's subsequent behavior. As soon as he returned to his Einsatzkommando kingdom in Vilnius, he became even more cruel. In fact, Weiss committed some of the most heinous acts after he came back from leave.

The most probable explanation for Weiss's utter disregard for the human rights of the people in his charge then remains a combination of factors. The demoralizing focus of the war and the unscrupulous anti-Semitic propaganda of the Nazi regime, combined with the state-sponsored organization and group sanctioning of the horrors, turned Weiss into a mass murderer. The reversal of moral norms, as was practiced in the eastern territories, brought his hidden criminal and sadistic disposition to the surface.

"Hitler's Willing Executioners"?

It is abundantly clear that these eight individuals—Bradfisch, Ehrlinger, Filbert, Rapp, Stark, Weiss, Wiebens, and Zapp—were indeed confirmed killers. Not only did they make the mass extermination of the Jewish population their own goal, they used the destruction of the Jews to channel their murderous instincts. It is also obvious that with the exception of Martin Weiss, these men were not Christopher Browning's quintessential "ordinary" Germans. The question then remains whether they fulfill Daniel Goldhagen's criteria: Were they "Hitler's willing executioners"?

Goldhagen concludes his book with the following statement:

> That the perpetrators approved of the mass slaughter, that they willingly gave assent to their participation in the slaughter, is certain. That their approval derived in the main from their own conception of the Jews [i.e., eliminationist anti-Semitism] is all but certain, for no other source of motivation can plausibly account for their actions.[47]

At the same time, however, Goldhagen qualifies his statements and points out that eliminationist anti-Semitism was not in the forefront of motivations among all perpetrators because different mechanisms and varying degrees of eliminationist anti-Semitism were at work within these individuals.

Part 6 of Goldhagen's work, however, dismisses the alternative explanations for the behavior of the perpetrators such as peer pressure, wartime brutalization, or obedience to authority, because they do not sufficiently explain four essential questions: (1) Why did the perpetrators display so much initiative? (2) Why did the perpetrators readily follow orders they did not philosophically agree with and could have avoided? (3) Why were the killing institutions, such as the Reserve Police Battalions and the Einsatzgruppen, so cruel? and (4) Why were the individual perpetrators so cruel?

The answer to these questions, according to Goldhagen, is always the same: because of "eliminationist anti-Semitism." Goldhagen's answer, however, does not always apply to the confirmed-killer officers, who were certainly the most likely material out of which to recruit "willing executioners." Therefore, it is necessary to take a closer look at his arguments.

The reader will at least partially agree with Goldhagen's answer to the first questions because this chapter has shown that the confirmed killers took the initiative in the extermination program although they had opportunities to extract themselves from the killing fields. Their behavior not only warranted the murder charges in the German courts, it also explains that they must have been influenced by motives other than obedience or conformity to the group. Whether or not this other motive was eliminationist anti-Semitism cannot be clearly deduced from the evidence.

The trial judgments from the District Courts in Berlin, Essen, Karlsruhe, Koblenz, München, and Würzburg substantiate Goldhagen's observation that "Many men from the Einsatzkommandos, including commanders, deny . . . that they ever knew of genocidal intent or that they killed Jews."[48] But such claims, made by the commanding officers' defense lawyers, were ridiculous. The Einsatzgruppen commanders had advanced to positions in the German police that allowed them to recognize the brutality and the anti-Semitic character of the Nazi regime well before the beginning of the war with the Soviet Union. The court evidence furthermore shows that these men, with their proven intellectual abilities, leadership skills, and determination, definitely understood the genocidal intent when they were first appointed to their commands in the Einsatzgruppen. At times, they even accepted the possible consequences. As Dr. Ehrlinger told his deputy and co-defendant, Dr. Hans Karl Schumacher, in a grave tone after an execution, ". . . If the war is lost, the victors will justly hang us all from the next lantern pole."[49]

The reader will perhaps also partially agree with Goldhagen's eliminationist anti-Semitism answer to the third question: Why were the killing institutions so cruel? The horrors of the seemingly endless mass executions conducted by the Einsatzgruppen have been described. They definitely were extraordinarily callous, systematically degrading and brutally killing defenseless men, women, and children. Nevertheless, other instances of genocide have shown that governments or people do not necessarily have to be anti-Semitic to create institutions that commit such cruel massacres; other factors are at work.

The evidence regarding the confirmed killers, perhaps the worst category of officers even within the Einsatzgruppen, is less ambiguous on Goldhagen's remaining questions. These officers' behavior clearly challenges Goldhagen's notion that the perpetrators followed the order to kill Jews only because of their eliminationist anti-Semitism. If not for this anti-Semitism, Goldhagen suggests that some Einsatzgruppen officers actually would have asked to be relieved of their horrible duties, without consequences for their lives and careers; the superior officers he cites granted transfers to other units rather easily.[50]

But this was not always true. Circumventing orders and extracting oneself from the executions were not always as easy as Goldhagen claims. On the contrary, it was often extremely difficult, especially for the men serving under one of the commanding officers discussed in this chapter. The reader remembers how these men had insisted that the order to kill the Jews was to be fulfilled in their units. They proscribed every minute detail of even the smallest execution and left nothing to the initiative of their subordinates, which might have allowed loopholes for non-compliance and evasion. In addition, these eight confirmed killers made certain that everyone participated in the executions, even after previous strenuous duties. When approached by their subordinates about the legitimacy of the executions, these officers reacted brusquely and categorically denied all requests for transfers. They threatened the officers who tried to object with an appearance before the SS courts, with the death penalty, and with consequences for their families.

Yet, to the contrary, as demonstrated by the material the German prosecutors compiled at the Central Office of the State Justice Administrations for the Investigation of National Socialist Homicide Crimes, as well as the research of scholars like Helmut Krausnick, Christopher Browning, and Daniel Goldhagen, among others, refusal to follow an order to shoot Jews or Communists did not constitute an imminent danger for a single Einsatzgruppen member, Reserve Police officer, Wehrmacht soldier, or any other German who did not follow such an order.[51] Despite a popular myth, and the threats of these eight Einsatzgruppen officers, not one case is documented of someone being charged in a court or summarily shot for refusing to execute Jews. In most circumstances, negative consequences seldom occurred. At the worst, such objectors were no longer promoted, were demoted in rank or position, or were transferred to the eastern front. Considering the brutal character of the war in the Soviet Union, however, especially after its first year, transfer to the front was definitely a form of punishment. SS officers who transferred usually were sent to a Waffen SS unit, where their chances to survive in battle were almost equal to those of the other soldiers. But casualties within Waffen SS units were higher than in regular Wehrmacht units because Waffen SS men often did not have military training and experience equivalent to army soldiers.

The title of the Central Office—Central Office of the State Justice Administration for the Investigation of National Socialist Homicide Crimes—indicates that its purpose was to prosecute Nazi crimes and, therefore, the evidence compiled by its investigators perhaps could be considered biased. Nevertheless, we have to accept the assumption that the Nazis did not severely punish any refusal to kill a civilian, as did the juries in the German courts, because no other reliable sources exist to prove the opposite.[52] All but one of the courts followed the lead of the prosecution and decided that the Einsatzgruppen members should have known that there were no extreme forms of punishment for disobedience.

On the other hand, the court records do confirm that to achieve a transfer from the units under the leadership of the confirmed killers was not as easy as Goldhagen and Browning would have their readers believe. If there was indeed a theoretical opportunity to leave these units, it was met with ridicule and most likely social exclusion. Dr. Filbert's derogatory remark about the young officer's emotional reaction after his first execution of women and children no doubt was a severe humiliation. In an organization such as the SS, which was based on elitist, masculine values that prized both physical and emotional strength as well as unconditional loyalty, a superior's comment about a subordinate's emotional weakness must have been a devastating punishment.[53] For this reason, the court in Berlin believed that Filbert's co-defendant, SS 1st Lt. Schneider, attempted to keep secret his own efforts to be relieved of his duties, in order not to lose his reputation as an exemplary, tough SS officer.

And, thus, one must question as well why Goldhagen's work dismisses the influence of peer pressure, claiming that it could not have functioned for larger groups. In this assessment he clearly disregards an important principle in the selection process for the Einsatzgruppen, a principle that worked in particular for Bradfisch, Ehrlinger, Filbert, Rapp, Stark, and Zapp. They had come from closely knit groups of officers, bound together through successive stages of their careers—the practice used by the Reich Security Main Office to ensure unconditional loyalty and force potentially uncooperative officers to fit in. Conformity to the group was a strong element in their motivation.

Regarding Goldhagen's fourth question, the cause for the individual cruelty, no one can deny that the confirmed killers displayed brutality far beyond what was already inherent in the Einsatzgruppen. Goldhagen argues that the close contact between the Reserves of Police Battalion 101 and their victims gave the perpetrators the opportunity to be especially cruel. His observation certainly also applies to the Einsatzgruppen. Nevertheless, it seems as if Goldhagen fails to recognize the implications of his own statement. Looking at Franz Stark and Martin Weiss, in particular, is it not possible that their cruel character traits had been brought forth not by anti-Semitism alone, but also by the opportunity and the daily exercise of power? Stark most likely would have killed regardless of the ethnic group of his victims, as long as he could get even with the territorial governor. But the political and military situation made the Jewish barbers the easiest available target for his revenge. For Weiss, too, this was the first time that the lives of a large number of people were put into his hands. He might have reacted similarly if it had been any other group of people. If, for example, in France during 1940 Weiss had been in charge of French prisoners of war instead of serving in a supply unit, it is conceivable that his brutal character traits might have emerged. But Weiss's position in Vilnius was the only opportunity of this kind in his career.

The evidence regarding the confirmed killers does prove, indeed, that many

Einsatzgruppen members were anti-Semites and believed that every means was justified in the elimination of the Jews. They agreed that there was a "Jewish Question" and that it had to be solved one way or another. However, there were many levels of anti-Semitism, and Goldhagen's eliminationist form was only the most extreme. Even the confirmed killers sometimes wondered whether physical elimination was the correct solution, as Martin Weiss had told the witness during his leave. Weiss's case especially seems to indicate that he adopted anti-Semitism to justify his actions to himself, for he always made his derogatory remarks about the Jews right after he had directed an execution. And that his anti-Semitism was not a deeply rooted form can be seen in his prewar life, when he had been known for his good judgment with no involvement in political fanaticism.

For the other officers in this group, it is important to emphasize once again their extraordinary Nazi indoctrination. Goldhagen's comment regarding SS Major General von dem Bach-Zelewski's actions applies to these eight Einsatzgruppen officers: "If for years, for decades, one preaches that the Slavic race is an inferior race, that the Jews are not human beings at all, then the inevitable end result must be such an explosion."[54]

These eight officers had indeed undergone a unique and extensive practical and ideological conditioning and training program, in which they had participated in or at least monitored the increasingly radical anti-Jewish policies of the Nazi regime for years. They had been members, in Ian Kershaw's words, of "an ideologically driven police force with its own agenda, on the look-out for racial target groups, searching for fresh possibilities of 'solving the Jewish Question.'"[55]

Because these officers did not come from all levels of German society, they cannot be representative of the German population. Their extraordinary careers would not have been possible outside the realm of the SS. Dr. Ehrlinger stated in his trial, that these men "saw the SS as their career for life, and this wish determined their unconditional devotion to the Führer and National Socialism. . . ."[56] Only in this narrow sense and with the reservations as noted is it thus possible to speak of "Hitler's willing executioners."

Goldhagen does recognize the significance of the Einsatzgruppen and their murderous activities in the extermination of the European Jews, as do other Holocaust scholars. Yet it is, therefore, remarkable that Goldhagen keeps his coverage on the Einsatzgruppen restricted to only some ten pages.[57] It is even more surprising that Goldhagen admits—albeit in a small footnote—that he would have liked to elaborate on the subject, however it would not have fit into the overall framework of his book.[58] But there might be another explanation.

Perhaps a closer analysis of the Einsatzgruppen members, as it is presented in this study, would have revealed that even the worst group of perpetrators in the Einsatzgruppen, the confirmed killers, displayed somewhat different character traits and attitudes toward their tasks than Goldhagen outlines in his book.

The following chapters will demonstrate how other types of officers reacted to the elimination campaign.

3. THE OFFICERS FROM
THE EASTERN BORDERLANDS

Damn it! One generation has
to go through this so that our children
will have it better.

First Lieutenant Alfred Krumbach

N JUNE 24, 1941, SS Maj. Hans-Joachim Böhme, commanding officer of the Tilsit State Police, briefed his junior officers on their latest assignment. On orders of the leader of Einsatzgruppe A, various local police agencies were to form the Tilsit Einsatzkommando and liquidate the Jews and hard-core Communists living on a strip of land some sixteen miles wide along the former German-Lithuanian border. Four particular Einsatzgruppen officers—Lukys, Carsten, Behrend, and Sakuth—became members of the Tilsit Einsatzkommando not only because they had grown up in the region, but because they had worked in one of the local police organizations. The other officers in this group also either were from the region of the ethnically diverse German border areas of eastern Prussia and Upper Silesia, or they were ethnic Germans.

Because of the violent history of the area, most of these officers had been victims of major wars, civil wars, or forms of ethnic conflict before they were drafted to the Einsatzgruppen. Such a chaotic, disruptive background resulted in several important consequences. Many of these men came from families that were torn apart; they had been forced to relocate several times during their youth; they often lost their homes, farms, and other belongings in the disruption; and they had to live under different political and social systems and under the sovereignty of different states.

On the other hand, growing up outside the borders of Germany before September 1939 also gave nine future Einsatzgruppen officers the luxury to watch the development of the Nazi state and its racial policies from a distance and from the perspective of outside observers. However, these nine—Kroeger, von Krell*, Greiffenberger, Hering, von Toll, Lukys, von der Rohde*, Behrend, and K.— came from such contested and ethnically heterogeneous lands that often they and their families had suffered injustice from foreign neighbors. In addition, the Baltic region contained many Jewish communities, and most of these officers had long been exposed to various forms of anti-Semitism. In short, they had ideological and political reasons to blame the misfortunes of their unusually harsh and turbulent youth on their neighboring peoples. Not coincidentally, these were the same peoples the Nazis targeted for subjugation or complete eradication: Slavs, Poles, Communists, and Jews. One would, therefore, expect that hatred of the Jews and Communism played a significant role in these officers' motivation to participate in the Nazi extermination schemes.

Background

Because upbringing in the eastern borderlands was the primary selection principle for this group of officers, they do not share many other characteristics. The two oldest, SS Maj. Wilhelm Greiffenberger and Police Chief of Krottingen Pranas Lukys, were already forty-one years old when they were drafted into the Einsatzgruppen. Lukys was not a German citizen, but he was trained in Germany and received his directives from the German occupation forces. Thus, he could be tried by German courts under Paragraph 7, Section (2)2 of the penal code, which stipulates:

> The German criminal law is likewise applicable to crimes committed abroad if
> such conduct is punishable by the law of the place where it occurred, or if no
> criminal law enforcement existed at the place where the crime was committed,
> and if the perpetrator . . . was a foreigner at the time of the crime, and if he was
> apprehended in Germany. . . .[1]

Greiffenberger and Lukys both were strongly influenced by the experience of the Great War and the Russian Revolution with its aftermath. By contrast, the youngest officer from the eastern borderlands, SS 2d Lt. Wilhelm Döring, was just born in 1917. Lukys, SS Maj. Anton von Krell*, SS 2d Lt. Eberhard von Toll, and SS Sgt. Lukas von der Rohde* came from landowning families; SS Oberführer Dr. Erhard Kroeger, SS Major K., SS 1st Lt. Kurt Matschke,[2] SS T. Sgt. August Hering, and SS Major Greiffenberger had middle-class origins; and the fathers of the others were soldiers, policemen, railroad employees, or civil servants.

SS First Lieutenant Klaus Winter*, Kroeger, von Krell*, Matschke, Greiffenberger, K., von Toll, Lukys, and Döring had graduated from the secondary school (Gymnasium), but only six immediately went on to university studies. Kroeger was the highest educated among those. He had studied history, philosophy, and law, receiving his doctorate in jurisprudence in 1928. Matschke and von Krell* also began to study law, but they left the university before graduation. K. studied shipbuilding, and thereafter became a materials inspector for the German maritime firm Lloyd. Von Toll attended two semesters of agricultural studies and went on to manage his father's estate. And Lukys prepared to become a teacher. That also was Winter*'s plan, but economic difficulties forced him to work in a machine factory. The others finished eight to ten years of schooling and then entered apprenticeships in agriculture, sales, and technical professions, or they became police officers.

Obviously the officers not born on German soil—Kroeger, von Krell*, Greiffenberger, Hering, von Toll, Lukys, von der Rohde*, Behrend, and K.—could not join German Nazi organizations before they moved to German-controlled territory. That was no problem for Greiffenberger, whose family had been in Germany since being expelled from Russia during the First World War; but the others did not arrive before 1939, when they became part of the vast Nazi resettlement schemes after the defeat of Poland. Nevertheless, all but Hering and K. had been active in right-wing formations or in the military and police forces of their native countries, where they at least received some weapons and leadership training. Von Toll and Behrend served two years in the Lithuanian army, von der Rohde* was drafted to the Latvian military, and Lukys became a Lithuanian police and intelligence officer.

Erhard Kroeger, on the other hand, was a Nazi Old Fighter. He was the leader of the ethnic German Nazi movement of his native Latvia. As such, he had been in steady contact with Himmler and Heydrich since 1936, and they had put him in charge of the resettlement of ethnic Germans from Latvia and Lithuania after the division of the region by Hitler and Stalin in 1939. One of his most reliable aids in this task was von Krell*, who had made a name for himself in Latvian ethnic German youth organizations since 1932.

After the division of Poland, the other ethnic German officers also joined different Nazi and police organizations. K., for example, worked in the Volksdeutsche Mittelstelle (VoMi), the agency responsible for the reintegration of ethnic Germans into the Reich, where Himmler in his function as Reich Commissioner (Reichskommisar) for the Strengthening of Germandom became his superior. Von Toll and von der Rohde* managed newly established German farms in the Wartheland, the Reich's newly acquired Polish territory, and

Behrend became an interpreter at the Border Police outpost in Memel (now Klaipeda).

Of the longtime German citizens—Sakuth, Carsten, Döring, Greiffenberger, and Matschke—Greiffenberger first briefly served in the German army on the eastern front in 1918, joined the Freikorps "Grenzschutz Litauen" (Border Patrol Lithuania) thereafter, and was then transferred into the German military. Together with SS Capt. Edwin Sakuth, SS T. Sgt. Gerhard Carsten, and Döring, Greiffenberger became a member of Nazi organizations long before Hitler came to power. For Greiffenberger and Döring, the economic crisis had played a role in that decision. Greiffenberger lost his electronics business in 1931, could not find other employment, and his family had to live in poverty as a consequence. To him, Hitler appeared to be a welcome savior, and he joined the Nazi Party in 1931 and the SS the following year. Having been a Security Service informer since 1932, Greiffenberger accepted a full-time position as the administrative manager of the Security Service Section at Dresden in 1935. From Dresden, he then went on to become a personnel officer in the Reich Security Main Office.

According to court documents, Wilhelm Döring grew up as Wilheln No. (the first two letters of his Polish-sounding name, which he later changed) in Ratibor, a town in the three-country corner of Germany, Poland, and Czechoslovakia. In 1939 he took on his mother's more Germanic maiden name, Döring, on the advice of his superior. Two years later, Döring was separated from his father, who had to flee because of problems with the Polish minority. To compound the ethnic animosities, Ratibor had been cut off from its natural hinterland by the new borders drawn in Versailles following the First World War, and the town thus struggled economically. In the early 1930s, the economic depression hit Ratibor even harder than in the rest of Germany. Döring thus grew up in a city of economic misery and deep ethnic divisions. Raised in an authoritarian, nationalist, and militarist household, he joined the National Socialist Pupils League (Schülerbund), which was merged into the Hitler Youth (Hitlerjugend, or HJ) in 1933. At the same time, Döring became a member of the Border Patrol (Grenzschutz), an illegal para-military organization run by the Reichswehr, and received training as a non-commissioned officer. When the Border Patrol was merged into the Nazi Storm Troopers soon thereafter, he was accepted as a staff sergeant, although he was only sixteen years old.

In the years before the war, Döring had two distinct opportunities to learn about the injustices and the character of the political movement he had joined at such a young age. In 1934, his father informed him that one of his school comrades had been shot during the Röhm Putsch. This violent event briefly disturbed Döring's image of the Nazis, but like so many other German conservatives, he consoled himself thinking that these were just the necessary early excesses of a regime that had to clean up after the disastrous liberal and democratic governments of the Weimar Republic.

Four years later, when he was in training for a police career, he naively could not believe that the police had orders not to interfere with the measures against the Jews during Kristallnacht. He was upset again for a short period, especially because his family had always maintained good relations with individual Jews, despite its misfortunes. As the judges in Bonn point out, the Döring family shopped in Jewish stores, rented a vacation room to a Jewish couple every summer, and a Jewish pediatrician had cared for Wilhelm as a child. Only during his advanced training at Security Police Leadership School in Charlottenburg in 1939–40 did Döring finally learn to accept the Nazi image of the Jews and their destructive influence in politics and the economy. In what he considered mere formalities, he joined the Nazi Party and the SS during his training.

As was the case in many Silesian families, Kurt Matschke also grew up in a German nationalist household. The experience of a brief Polish occupation after the First World War and a plebiscite, determining that his hometown of Heueberg would remain German, only reinforced Matschke's nationalist convictions. To him, therefore, the Nazis offered hope for the restoration of a powerful German nation state. Although Matschke was raised as a Catholic, he spontaneously "converted" to Nazism, as he put it, after attending a Josef Goebbels speech in 1932. Matschke joined the SS in the same year because he wanted to actively contribute to the Nazi goals. Through his temporary job as estate adviser who, according to the Nazi agricultural program divided and sold the estates of large landowners, Matschke often worked with local SS leaders. When he once criticized the police president of Breslau, a Storm Trooper member, one of the present SS officers suggested that Matschke joined the Security Service.

He did so only a few days before the Röhm Putsch. Under the command of SS Lt. Gen. Udo von Woyrsch, who later led the notorious Einsatzgruppe zbV in Poland, Matschke participated in the arrest and execution of the local police president. At this point he believed that Ernst Röhm and the Storm Troopers had indeed attempted a coup, and that the execution of the ringleaders was justified. The newly appointed police president, the SS Oberführer Wilhelm Dunckern, then convinced Matschke to give up his law studies and embark on a full-time Gestapo career. Matschke complied again and began working at the Gestapo office in Liegnitz.

After the Saar plebiscite in 1935—the vote by the people of the region to once again become part of Germany—Dunckern was transferred to the Gestapo office in Saarbrücken and brought with him his loyal follower, Matschke. Matschke was assigned to the Department for the Fight against Communism and Marxism.

During this time and in his advanced training in Charlottenburg, Matschke learned Gestapo methods. The two most important techniques were "protective custody," a process that allowed the Gestapo to arrest people and send them to concentration camps without legal due process, and "enforced interrogation," the use of torture to achieve confessions. Promoted to Second Lieutenant the day before Kristallnacht, in which he did not participate, Matschke subsequently took over the anti-Communist/Marxist desk with the beginning of the war. Like most future Einsatzgruppen officers, he therefore had ample opportunities to recognize the true character of the regime he supported so enthusiastically long before he was drafted to Sonderkommando 7a in September 1941.

Like Greiffenberger, Sakuth became a Nazi Party member in 1931. He came to the Tilsit Security Service Section in 1937. In July 1939, he was appointed commanding officer of its Memel branch office. Gerhard Carsten, on the other hand, became a police officer after two years of military service. He joined the Nazi Party in 1937, but his simultaneous application for the SS was rejected because he could not establish the required Aryan descent. Nevertheless, Carsten continued to believe in National Socialism. He took the required classes at the Security Service Leadership School in Charlottenburg in 1938 and subsequently was assigned to the Border Patrol outpost at Schmalleningken in 1939. He had permission to wear an SS uniform with the equivalent rank of technical sergeant.

Like Carsten, Winter* also volunteered for the German military. His goal was to become an explosives specialist. Unhappy with his training, however, he resigned in October 1935 and decided to become a teacher. He then worked as a piano player in a bar to finance his studies. On the recommendation of a school official, Winter* soon joined the SS and the Security Service, where he first worked in the Cultural Department of the local branch. In March 1940, he was transferred to the Reich Security Main Office. As were all officers designated for future leadership positions, he was required to study law. His classes were interrupted, however, by the call to the Einsatzgruppen in May 1941.[3]

A closer look at the remarkable career of Pranas Lukys demonstrates even more lucidly what this group of officers had to endure before they found their way to the Einsatzgruppen. Although Lukys was not a German citizen, his early life reflects best the ethnic turmoil and the political upheaval prevalent in the Baltic States and the East German borderlands in the time between the First World War, the Russian Revolution, and the German invasion of the Soviet Union.

Lukys was born in the Lithuanian town of Raseiniai where his father owned a large agricultural estate. With the German troops advancing into northwestern Russia in 1915, he was brought to St. Petersburg on orders of the Czarist government, as were all boys over the age of fourteen. There he was forced to work in a tannery until he was sent to a Lithuanian school in Voronesh. In December 1918 he returned to his hometown and volunteered for the Lithuanian army. In his four years of service, he primarily fought against the Red Army and later the Poles. In 1920 he was wounded and captured by the Poles; he was, however, able to escape to Germany in 1921. In the same year, he returned to Lithuania, where he attended the military academy for six months. After his training, he joined the military intelligence branch of the Lithuanian General Staff, for which he continued to work after his official resignation from the military. As an intelligence officer, he helped to plan the occupation of the Memel area by the Lithuanian forces.

Following the German model, Lithuania had organized a strong political police. Lukys was transferred to this branch in 1923. He began his job in Kovno and then in Schaulen (Siaulai), and was finally appointed Security Police commander in Krottingen, a border town between eastern Prussia and Lithuania, with a population of about 5,000. As a known anti-Communist, Lukys was dismissed when elections briefly brought a new leftist government to power in 1926. Nurturing his old connections to the Lithuanian military, however, he began to secretly prepare volunteer brigades for a military takeover. The coup succeeded and ended the brief liberal-socialist interlude in Lithuanian history. On December 17, 1926, the country's new leaders immediately reinstated Lukys as Security Police chief in Krottingen, an office he held until the Russian occupation of Lithuania. Lukys's tasks remained the protection of his country against Polish espionage and Communist infiltration.

On the night of the Soviet invasion, Lukys fled to the German part of town. The Germans transported him and other Lithuanian policemen to a work camp in eastern Prussia that was run by two future members of the Tilsit Einsatzkommando. After three weeks of confinement, Lukys was allowed to leave the camp and settle with his family—whose flight he had arranged in the meantime—in the nearby border town of Bajohren. There he had to report twice every week to the local Border Police post. At this time he established contact with the officer in charge, SS 1st Lt. Dr. Erwin Frohwann, one of the main perpetrators of the massacres later committed in the Memel area.[4]

In December 1940, the German authorities sent Lukys to Lublin in the General Government, where he reported for duty in the German Criminal Police. After a short time there, he was allowed to join his family in Memel and worked in a local textile factory. As before, he had to register with the German Border Police. Then, in June 1941, on the day before the German invasion of the Soviet Union, Wehrmacht officials enlisted Lukys, with his intimate knowledge of the local area, for the liberation of his native country. He was to accompany the German forces, help locate Russian partisans, win over the Lithuanian people for the Nazis, and assist with the destruction of the Bolshevik government. On June 24,

1941, Lukys returned to his home with the victorious German army. As before 1939, the new Lithuanian puppet government installed him as Security Police chief of Krottingen. However, with his third reinstatement as chief, Lukys's odyssey was far from over. In December 1942 he was arrested on murder, rape, and corruption (in particular, he was suspected of not returning the valuables taken from the Jews to the proper SS offices)—charges by his latest master, the commanding officer of the Security Police and the Security Service in Kovno. But as before, in July 1944 Lukys was able to flee and find his way back to his family in Memel. They left the area and went to the Austrian city of Linz. Yet, driven by his greed, Lukys returned one more time to look after his misappropriated valuables in Memel. He was promptly recognized and arrested by the SS, but managed to escape again and fight his way back to Linz. From Linz, the approach of the Red Army finally forced him to move his family to Passau in December 1944.

After the German defeat, Lukys worked for the American occupation forces until his family emigrated to the United States in 1949. His own application for emigration was denied in 1952, and he became an accountant until his arrest by the German police on February 21, 1957. He was tried in the court at Ulm for the crimes he committed during his third time of service as police chief.[5]

Service in the Einsatzgruppen

Although every officer in this group from the eastern borderlands had participated in at least one execution, they displayed a wide spectrum of conduct and attitude toward the extermination campaign. Men such as von der Rohde*, Hering, Lukys, Matschke, Behrend, and, to a somewhat lesser degree, Sakuth, did not differ much from the confirmed killers of the previous chapter. They had also volunteered for activities that went beyond the extermination program and the orders of their superiors. On the other hand, officers such as K., Greiffenberger, Kroeger, von Krell*, and Döring can be described as relatively "decent" men who did not completely lose their sense of justice while serving in the Einsatzgruppen. They soon recognized that they were committing heinous crimes against humanity and attempted to get away from their units. Their requests for transfers were granted, and consequently their tenure in the Einsatzgruppen was rather short. The remaining officers, those not among the "confirmed killers" or these relatively "decent" men, fit somewhere in the middle.

On the sliding scale of cruelty and human depravity, August Hering was perhaps the worst perpetrator in this group. Like his comrade in crime, confirmed killer Martin Weiss, Hering had received a proper upbringing and had not been politically active before he came to Germany in February 1941. While still living in a resettlement camp, he was called up and sent to the Einsatzgruppen only three months later. Hering first belonged to Einsatzkommando 3, and subsequently to the Lithuanian Office of the Commander of the Security Police and the Security Service (KdS) in Vilnius, where he had the same tasks and responsibilities as the "exemplary murderer," Martin Weiss. Hering not only supervised multiple selections and executions in Ponary, he used his club or whip—albeit on a lesser scale than Weiss—on the inmates of the ghetto during its establishment, for controls at the gate and execution selections. Multiple witnesses testified regarding one unforgettable event when he single-handedly removed the mentally ill patients from the ghetto hospital, loaded them on a truck, and brought them to the execution site in Ponary. Exceeding his orders, he also took their warden, a man named Kamper.

Relishing his role as the unlimited sovereign of the Vilnius ghetto, Hering furthermore committed other acts of purposeless cruelty. In October 1942, he tore apart the work permit of the father of the witness Zippa for no apparent reason, and thereby subjected the man to the next execution. Moreover, according to another witness, Hering callously shot a Jewish woman in front of her friends and calmly stated, "There you have an example."[6] In contrast to Weiss, however, Hering attempted to get away from his tasks in Vilnius, and in May 1942 he was indeed transferred to a Wehrmacht unit. But this remained his only redeeming action.

Lukas von der Rohde*, of this eastern borderlands group, was familiar with living among Jews from his upbringing in Riga, Latvia, and he was not known for anti-Semitism during his youth. His political conviction changed, however, when he joined the SS in 1941. Once he was drafted to Sonderkommando 11a in January 1942, he definitely thought of himself as a member of the Master Race (Herrenmensch). He carried the insignia, a whip or club, to enforce his new status whenever he participated in actions against the Jews, and that was often. Although he was supposed to be an interpreter, his comrades called him their "Specialist for Jewish Questions" and he distinguished himself as extraordinarily cruel and depraved during the earliest actions of Sonderkommando 11a.

Von der Rohde*'s lack of positive human qualities is evident in incidents that happened shortly after his unit arrived in Barlad, a small town in southern Russia. One day the members of the unit had ordered the local Jews to clean the unit's barracks. The Jews were to fetch the water from a well some 165 feet from the buildings. The Security Service men, including von der Rohde*, lined up on both sides of the path and beat the Jews with wooden clubs as they moved along toward the well. To the delight of his comrades, von der Rohde* also made some Jews kneel down and pray. When one of the unit's vehicles returned from an errand, the SS men forced another Jew to lay under the truck, open the oil plug, and let the hot motor oil run over his body. To round out the "festivities" of the day, the Einsatzgruppen members finally organized competitions in which the Jews had to pull heavy horse-drawn wagons across the courtyard.[7]

A subsequent massacre in Nikolayev gave von der Rohde* another occasion to display his savage cruelty. This time he was responsible for preventing escape attempts during transport to the execution site. When some Jews managed to flee, von der Rohde* took charge of the situation. An excellent marksman, he initially let the Jews run away, giving them a glimmer of hope. Then, shortly before they escaped the range of his rifle, he calmly aimed his weapon and killed each one, as if he were shooting targets at a county fair.[8] To him, this exercise must have been a welcome diversion from the boredom of his usual duties, and certainly also a most welcome opportunity to prove his skills.

Pranas Lukys was not much better. He had an advisory role in the executions in Krottingen and Polangen. Moreover, he coordinated the measures between the Security Service and the native auxiliaries and, most revealing about his motivations, he did not shy away from hands-on participation.[9] As the court in Ulm clearly established, however, Lukys directed his wrath more against Communists than Jews.

His strong anti-Communist conviction is apparent in all his actions, but in particular during the first execution on June 26, 1941. Immediately after the German invasion, the Tilsit Einsatzkommando began to arrest the Jewish population and alleged Communists. The prisoners were held in the local synagogue. Lukys, who had been cooperating with the German authorities and the Security Service since his return to Krottingen, was not yet officially reinstated as Security Police chief, but because of his expertise, the Einsatzkommando consulted him in the selection of the Communist prisoners. However, after the first selection was over, the number of prisoners destined for execution seemed to be too high to the officer in charge, Böhme, and he ordered a repeat of the process. That time, Lukys's co-defendant, SS Maj. Werner Hersmann, was officially in charge of the selection. However, Hersmann relied to a large degree on Lukys's police files and recommendations. Lukys was thus put in a position where he could decide over life and death of the prisoners and, of course, he had the opportunity to make the Communists pay for the injustices he had suffered. He relished the chance to finally get even so much that he singled out for execution almost everyone presented to him. Fortunately, his reasoning often appeared "too threadbare," even for the Security Service man, Major Hersmann, who released more prisoners than Lukys would have liked—a total of twenty.[10]

Two other events are even more telling about Lukys's personality. In the first case, he had prepared the execution of sixty Communists with his old acquaintance, Dr. Frohwann. The killing was supposed to take place in the sandy beach area near the Baltic resort town of Polangen. Lukys was responsible for the transport of the victims from the work camp Dimitrava to the execution site. Upon Lukys's warning that these were very dangerous Lithuanian Communists, Frohwann advised Lukys to make certain that the victims could not escape. As if waiting for this opportunity, Lukys produced electric wire and tied the victims together in twos for transport. They would remain tied to each other during the execution as well.[11]

The eyewitness Motzkus, a member of the Memel Border Police, told of the second incident. Motzkus had visited Lukys on a day at the end of September 1941 when Lukys reported that he had arrested a Lithuanian couple who he suspected of Communist activities; he was holding them in the Polangen jail. Both Lukys, the witness, and another Lithuanian Hiwi then took the prisoners from the jail and drove them to a prepared grave in the dunes near Polangen. At the execution site, Lukys told the couple that they were going to be shot and that they should say good-bye to each other. The couple did not comply. Lukys had them kneel next to the grave and shot them.[12] In both cases it is evident that his conduct was directed primarily against Communists and that he closely cooperated with the German invaders. Moreover, it is also obvious that Lukys displayed a talent for organization and cruelty, and that he enjoyed his power over the people at his mercy.

The same applies to the next perpetrator, Franz Behrend. Witnesses describe him as a young, active, and overly zealous Gestapo officer. As fit his subaltern rank in the Einsatzgruppen, he was mostly assigned tasks such as guard duty, house searches, and escorting the next group of victims from the waiting area to the execution site. But while performing these duties, he had the opportunity to do whatever he liked with the people in his charge. As the court in Ulm clearly established, Behrend always made the Jews run to their execution, like cattle to the slaughter, and spurred them on with loud commands preceding at least two executions. Unfortunately, the court could not clarify whether Behrend or another SS officer had commanded the Jews to move "Faster! Faster! The more you hurry, the earlier we are done for today!" Nor could the court clarify whether or not it was Behrend who had beat the running Jews with a club during the first execution in Garsden. Nevertheless, the court record shows that considering Behrend's overall character, most likely he was the person responsible.[13]

Behrend also did not shy away from the "dirty" work. Without hesitation, he followed Dr. Frohwann's order to shoot a former Lithuanian detective by the name of Gewildis. Together with Criminal Police 2d Lt. Motzkus, the witness from the Lukys case, he brought Gewildis to a quarry he had selected in advance. There both policemen dug a grave, had the victim lie face down, and shot him in the back of the head.[14]

But Behrend was more than a follower of orders and an eager underling. He completely identified with the general elimination order and made it his goal that everyone else complied as well. By early August 1941, the German occupation forces had anticipated that jurisdiction over Lithuania would soon be transferred from the military to the civil administration of the Reich Ministry for the Occupied Eastern Territories (RmBO). Therefore, various civilian agencies scheduled a meeting for a day in August (the court was unable to establish the exact date). On the agenda were topics such as logistics, food supplies, the Jewish Question, the number of victims, and the cooperation between Lithuanian and German authorities. The invited participants were the county supervisor (Landrat) and the mayor of Krottingen, a delegate from the territorial governor, Lukys and another Lithuanian police officer, a former Lithuanian partisan leader, and a Nazi agricultural expert. Conspicuously, no SS officer was invited.

The always alert Behrend, however, learned of the meeting and decided to attend. The court records do not specify why an interloper with the lowly rank of corporal was granted permission to stay, in particular because the people at the meeting felt visibly uneasy during his presence. Perhaps the officials thought that if they must tolerate the SS at their meeting, they would rather deal with this subordinate than with a higher-ranking officer. Regardless, Behrend remained.

When the issue of feeding the population was discussed, the problem arose of how to deal with the Jewish women and children currently held prisoner at various locations in the county. Here Behrend interjected and forcefully reminded the officials that on Böhme's explicit orders, all women and children were to be included in the executions. He further explained, "The Jewish women and children do not work anyway; therefore these useless eaters must be eliminated." When the county supervisor and the Lithuanian police officer objected that their superior officers had not approved such measures yet, Behrend flatly stated, "Only the Gestapo is responsible for this area, and my superiors wish that the women and children be liquidated. The 'Regierungsrat' [the Major Böhme] has decided." In the following days, Behrend repeatedly visited both the county supervisor and Lukys to remind them of the liquidation of the women and children. As a result of his persistence, the Tilsit Einsatzkommando and its Lithuanian auxiliaries commenced with such executions earlier than planned.[15]

Apart from Behrend's anti-Semitism, this episode sheds light on two additional themes. First, because the meeting initially excluded all SS officials, it seems as if the officials present did not want the SS to meddle in what they considered their own affairs. Thus, the meeting appears to be another instance of animosities between different Nazi and government offices, a notion that further corroborates the functionalist interpretation of the interior workings of the Nazi state. Second, and typical for Behrend's motivation, the meeting demonstrates that he also used the elimination of the Jews to further his career and to show his importance.

Careerism and personal aggrandizement were also the main reasons that brought another Tilsit Einsatzkommando officer, Edwin Sakuth, to the execution sites. Although it did not fall directly under his tasks as commander of the Memel branch office of the Security Service Section at Tilsit, Sakuth thought it was imperative that he should be present at three separate executions. As the court in Ulm correctly observes, the presence of an officer of his rank, as a captain, at the executions signaled to the rank-and-file that the proper legal procedure was being followed and that the victims actually had been sentenced to death. With his appearance alone, Sakuth thus significantly supported the executions. Yet, he easily could have avoided at least two of them.

On the other hand, he could not extricate himself from the action in Polangen on June 30, 1941, because Polangen was located just under seventeen miles from his office in Memel, and the Einsatzkommando needed his local knowledge. Instead of merely rendering the requested logistical support, however, Sakuth made sure that everyone noticed he was the right-hand man of the officer in charge, SS Major Hersmann. Moreover, Sakuth on his own negotiated with a Luftwaffe unit, the 6.Fluganwärterkompanie,[16] and, telling them that a number of partisans had to be executed, he arranged for one platoon of that unit to serve as shooters. During the execution, Sakuth informed Hersmann that they were missing a Jewish pediatrician who worked in the Memel hospital. Hersmann immediately had the physician dragged from the hospital and shot with his brethren. With his insider knowledge, Sakuth then also organized the subsequent celebration, the Sakuska.[17] Such parties were usually held after all executions in Lithuania. The consumption of alcohol that most often had already started during the executions continued through the revelry. The cynical executioners even paid for their festivities with the money collected from the victims.

Even Security Service officers such as Gerhard Carsten, who once had been rejected by the SS on racial grounds and had been forced to join the Gestapo against his wishes (he wanted to be a simple detective), were not free from anti-Semitism and individual acts that went beyond their normal duties. Carsten shot, on the spot, a Jew he had apprehended close to Schmalleningken.[18] Later, when Carsten was in charge of the execution at Georgenburg, Böhme, who was observing the procedures, not only harshly criticized Carsten's lack of organization, he intervened and took over effective command of the operation. Being publicly accused of failure by a superior is probably one of the worst insults for the honor of any military or police officer, yet despite this humiliation Carsten later bragged about the massacre, announcing, "This morning the Jews of Georgenburg were put to the sword."[19]

Yet, Kurt Matschke's behavior is perhaps even more ambiguous. On the one hand, he followed the general elimination order enthusiastically; on the other hand, he had tried to restrain his even more ardent superior, Albert Rapp, during a bitter Russian winter that would have been dangerous for their own men. Two other incidents, however, show that Matschke's behavior was not too different from that of the confirmed killers. The first happened during the German retreat in January 1942. Sonderkommando 7a was then under Matschke's command. The unit had arrived in the town of Welish, which was about to be encircled by Russian troops, when Matschke received Erich Naumann's order to eliminate the 200 Jews held in a camp there. Matschke immediately visited the responsible military officer in charge, a Colonel Sinzinger. Of this meeting, the witness Giehl, who had been a battalion commander under Sinzinger, told the jury, "Matschke acted utterly disrespectful [daring to make demands of a colonel]." Matschke informed Colonel Sinzinger that he had to liquidate the Jewish camp and demanded that Sinzinger give his consent. Sinzinger refused. Matschke then threatened that the elimination of the Jews was a Führer order, and if Sinzinger continued to defy it, he must accept responsibility. Sinzinger remained adamant and suggested that Matschke and his men instead help with the defense of the city. Soon thereafter, Matschke's direct superior, Naumann, also managed to reach the city. Nonetheless, he merely acknowledged Sinzinger's refusal and ordered Matschke to withdraw his men altogether.[20]

The other event happened in the early summer of 1942 when Matschke was in charge of the men left behind in Klincy. As the former members of Matschke's unit recalled, one day an extended gypsy family arrived, consisting of ten to fifteen persons. Matschke had them shot immediately. Although it is feasible that a wandering gypsy band was an ideal medium for the gathering of intelligence, the court in Essen established that Matschke never bothered to interrogate the gypsies and murdered them because the general elimination order included gypsies and other "undesirables." This situation moreover proves that Matschke acted of his own will. If, as he claimed in court, he really did not agree with the Nazi annihilation scheme, he could have let the gypsies go without consequences as no superior officer had been present on the scene.[21]

And finally, among the ethnic German officers, Eberhard von Toll, a shooter in a number of executions, would not have stood out from the others if not for two reasons. First, he was one of the few officers drafted under the Emergency Decree to Secure Manpower for Tasks of Special State-Political Significance. Second, he was injured during an incident of Jewish resistance at the execution site. During an action of the Minsk Office of the Commander of the Security Police and the Security Service, in the spring of 1942, von Toll was part of the execution squad. Shortly after the execution began, the Jews tried to fight their murderers and wild shooting ensued. While standing at the edge of the grave, a stray bullet grazed von Toll's head, causing him to fall into the pit. He landed on top of the bloody mess of bodies. His comrades quickly pulled him out and saw that his wound was cared for in a nearby hospital.[22]

A Contested Issue: Jewish Resistance

A brief digression is necessary here because the previous incident seems to contradict what many historians have usually thought about the perpetration of the Holocaust in general. Scholars such as Yehuda Bauer and Lucy Dawidowicz argue that the Jewish efforts to maintain a sense of organization and a civilized society—as they did with the Jewish Councils—are remarkable manifestations of resistance. Raul Hilberg and others, however, contend that the such compliance—essentially passivity—of the Jews during all stages of the Holocaust facilitated German measures. Some Jewish ghetto communities, for example, had even selected the next group of deportees, those to be executed, *before* the Nazis made the actual demand. Therefore, the destruction of the European Jews, though initiated and planned by the Germans, was indirectly facilitated by the victims; Jewish submission played a part in their own annihilation.[23]

With regard to the Einsatzgruppen massacres and the behavior of the victims specifically, Hilberg further writes, "In almost every major action the victims outnumbered their captors 10 to 1, 20 to 1, or even 50 to 1; but the Jews could never turn their numbers into an advantage."[24] Hilberg then emphasizes, "It is significant that the Jews allowed themselves to be shot without resistance."[25] Hilberg must have come to his conclusion relying on the Nuremberg documents, and especially on the Ereignismeldungen, which understandably avoid mentioning accidents or acknowledging mistakes, disturbances, or worse.[26]

The study of the German court records, however, reveals a number of cases when the victims fought back courageously. Certainly, such individual acts of bravery and defiance did not stop a single massacre and, as Hilberg correctly affirms, no German executioner was ever killed; but because the victims were completely helpless and had to overcome considerable odds, these cases warrant reporting. According to witnesses, the incidents usually included attempts to escape during transport or execution, sometimes even from the grave.[27] At times, these efforts were accompanied by attacks on the guards or executioners.[28] In one outstanding example, visiting officers from a nearby Order Police battalion saw a Jew, who had been decorated with Germany's Iron Cross in the First World War, lunge at the leader of the execution, Hans-Joachim Böhme; other Jews meanwhile attacked officers of the Tilsit Einsatzkommando, and still others tried to escape. Yet in the end, all the Jews were shot, and only one Security Service member was injured by an errant bullet.[29] During another execution in Gorodok, the defendant Klaus Winter*, who was in charge of the guards, noticed that a Jew was trying to escape from the execution site, but the man was killed by a shot in the head even before Winter* could act.[30]

The Remaining Officers: Duty, Loyalty, and Conscience

Among the ethnic German Einsatzgruppen officers who acted—at least at times—in a more decent manner, if that term is at all appropriate in connection with the Einsatzgruppen, K. leaves the best impression, but also the shortest. As a member of Einsatzkommando 3, and since July 1941 Sonderkommando 1b, he stayed with his unit until August 1942. During these fifteen months he received orders to observe two executions that were conducted by Latvian auxiliaries; at one massacre he fired at a victim who was still moving in the grave.[31] However, for more than a year in the Einsatzgruppen he stayed away from other killings, despite his high rank of captain. The court documents in Karlsruhe do not specify how he managed to do so, but because he was a shipbuilding engineer and had no military or police training, one might assume that his superiors, among them Lieutenant Colonel Ehrlinger, thought that he was not sufficiently qualified. K., nonetheless, was promoted for bravery at the front soon after he left Sonderkommando 1b. In summary, K. appears to have been an effective organizer who consciously avoided participation in the massacres.

In contrast, the records of the remaining officers are much more ambiguous. Greiffenberger, for example, acted as an informal liaison between the younger officers of his unit and their haughty and unapproachable commander, Dr. Alfred Karl Filbert. When Filbert had openly humiliated his officer with sarcastic remarks regarding the man's performance and behavior at the execution, witnesses saw Greiffenberger put his arm around the shoulders of the young officer to console him.[32] In addition, Greiffenberger always expressed his reservations about their infamous tasks, and in general tried to rein in Filberts' genocidal zeal. Greiffenberger was particularly pleased that he was trusted by the head of the Criminal Police, Arthur Nebe, to transmit to Filbert the orders to exercise more restraint.[33] Unfortunately, Filbert responded negatively. Greiffenberger subsequently used his connections to the Reich Security Main Office to be relieved of his duties in the Einsatzgruppen after only five months.

However, Greiffenberger also had a reputation as a reliable officer who followed orders once he had voiced his scruples. Therefore, Filbert had put him in charge of several executions, which Greiffenberger ran effectively. It is more important to note that Greiffenberger could easily have removed himself from the massacres, if it were not for his sense of self-importance. Though initially

dispatched to Einsatzkommando 9 as an interpreter, Greiffenberger insisted
that the position was below the duties of a major, and, thus, Filbert made him
his deputy. Greiffenberger's work with the Security Sevice since 1932 also
speaks against him. From his prewar positions as a personnel officer in various
Security Service offices and finally the Reich Security Main Office, he knew
about the criminal activities and possibly the genocidal intent from early on.
Yet, he never thought about resignation from the Security Service or non-
compliance with his orders.[34]

Non-compliance or open disobedience also was not an option for the leader
of Einsatzkommando 6, Erhard Kroeger, nor for his subordinate, Anton von
Krell*. Nevertheless, they at least attempted to have some mitigating impact on
the executions. Shortly after the German occupation of the small town of Do-
bromil, the Security Service discovered the bodies of some denizens of the town
that had been shot by the Soviets. The responsible Higher SS and Police Leader
Friedrich Jeckeln and the leader of Einsatzgruppe C, Otto Rasch, immediately
after their occupation ordered the execution of 307 Jewish "hostages." They
were to be shot by Kroeger's unit in the same abandoned mine where the town
citizens' bodies had been found. On Kroeger's intervention, Rasch agreed to
reduce the number of victims to one hundred. Kroeger and von Krell* then
briefed their troops and remained present during the selection and execution.[35]

In this particular group, Wilhelm Döring was not only the youngest officer,
but his career in the Einsatzgruppen was exemplary. Furthermore, because his
behavior was so ambiguous and therefore the most disturbing, it is imperative to
review his career. During his youth in Ratibor, he had begun to affiliate with nationalist and military organizations. Not surprisingly, Döring had volunteered
for military duty with the outbreak of the Second World War. He could not bear
seeing his friends participate in the glorious military campaigns without ever
having the chance to contribute himself. But his superiors in the Security Police
did not let him go, and instead of getting a front assignment, Döring was first sent
to the Reich Security Main Office and subsequently to Einsatzkommando 8,
where he served from June 1941 to April 1943.

Döring's tasks in this unit reflect a process that Daniel Goldhagen appropriately deems "habituation to the killings." At first Döring was used as a liaison
officer between his unit and the headquarters of Einsatzgruppe B. His duties exposed him to reports about the massacres, but he believed that the victims were
Russian partisans and saboteurs who deserved to die for resisting the advancing
Wehrmacht. Döring convincingly demonstrated to the court in Bonn that at this
time he really did not know that the victims were innocent and helpless Jews.
Called back to Einsatzkommando 8 in August 1941, Döring received orders to
prepare the transfer of staff headquarters from Minsk to Mogilev. He became ill

with jaundice, however, and spent the next five weeks in a hospital and on re-
covery leave at home.

After Döring's return to the unit on October 26, 1941, his commanding
officer, Lt. Col. Otto Bradfisch, put him in charge of a platoon consisting of
sixteen men. Bradfisch then told him to eliminate all active and potential enemies, and explained that these enemies were primarily Jews. In the ensuing conversation between the officers, Döring objected to such a terrible assignment,
but again Bradfisch responded that these were Hitler's orders. Still, Döring remained hesitant until Bradfisch finally threatened: "The task equals an assignment at the front. Therefore anyone who does not follow the order is guilty of
cowardice. Anyone who does not follow the order will be squashed like a bug; a
battalion more or less does not matter."[36]

Döring immediately obeyed, assumed his duties as platoon leader, and conducted several executions.

In November 1941, Döring's platoon was ordered to kill sixteen children
from a mental institution in Shumjatchi. These children were about ten years
old, could not walk or speak, and were found crawling on the floor of the only
room, which was filthy with urine, feces, and decayed food. The nearly naked
children were dirty and covered with purulent discharge. Their only caretakers
were a Russian woman and a fourteen-year-old boy who was also mentally ill, but
at least he was able to walk and beg for food in the nearby village. The sign at the
door left by a passing German army unit read: "Off Limits! Infectious Disease!"

According to Döring's statement, he did not like the order to eliminate the
children and phoned his friends at Einsatzkommando headquarters. They referred him to the Einsatzgruppe. There, an unknown officer explained to him
that the liquidation was necessary because the children constituted a serious
threat to the health of the population and the German troops in the area. Satisfied
with the justification, Döring complied and proceeded with the execution. But
fearful of being exposed to a dangerous disease, the platoon refused to touch the
children and made the caretakers load them onto the vehicles. At the execution
site, a deep shaft in an old brickyard, the men took shovels to remove the children
from the trucks, shot them, and dumped the bodies into the shaft.[37]

From the court records in Bonn, it seems as if from this point on Döring tried
to avoid further executions by becoming more active in combating partisans.
Regardless, however, when his platoon apprehended Jews during such partisan
operations, he still complied with his general orders and had them shot. In the
long run, however, the steady exposure to the grizzly life of the Einsatzgruppen
must have caused a change in Döring's behavior. The court records state that
Döring "lost his faith in National Socialism"[38] and almost reversed his previous
convictions, recognizing that, in his words, "Human beings who have the same

right to live as anybody else were murdered for no reason."[39] Döring achieved a transfer from Einsatzkommando 8 in May 1942.

Witnesses testified that in his subsequent positions Döring helped Jews and other Eastern European people on several occasions. As a police officer in Klincy, he released three Jewish tailors and a Russian peasant without punishment, although he had found a hand grenade in their possession. Later, in Lodz, Döring repeatedly intervened on behalf of Poles, despite the fact that Polish rebels had forced his father to abandon the family when Wilhelm was a child in 1921. Döring apparently put the animosities of his youth behind him and also helped to liberate a young Pole who had been found to be buying food on the black market. On another occasion, he prevented the severe punishment of a Polish woman who had fled from work conscription to Germany, by placing her as a maid with a local German family. And in yet another case he vouched for a woman who had participated in the Warsaw ghetto uprising without personally knowing her.[40]

In contrast to Döring's benevolent behavior, which was certainly also an effort to atone for past crimes, other Einsatzgruppen officers did not change. Kurt Matschke, for example, knew about the terrible fate of the Jews in the Soviet Union, but back in Germany he had organized four transports with more than a thousand Jews from Cologne to Theresienstadt, which was located in the Reichsprotektorat. In order to avoid interventions on behalf of individuals, Heydrich had conceived of Theresienstadt as a camp for the old and decorated Jewish war heroes. Yet in the end, 88,202 of 140,937 of these "favored" Jews were further deported to Auschwitz, and 33,456 died there. Only 16,832 remained alive on May 9, 1945.[41]

Later, during 1943, when the fortunes of the war were clearly going against Germany, concerns about either making amends for previous crimes or noncompliance might have crossed the minds of many perpetrators. Indeed, other officers in Matschke's department at the Gestapo office in Cologne occasionally showed leniency and exempted older or weaker Jews from deportation. Matschke, however, categorically refused to make exceptions. As a loyal follower of Nazi doctrines until the end of the war, he told his colleagues when they urged him to also exercise some restraint, "I execute every order exactly as it is given to me."[42]

Consequently, Matschke refused to give in to the plea of a Cologne citizen, the witness M.-S., who had asked him to release her half-Jewish sons, arrested for hiding a Jew and his German girlfriend. Perhaps in this case Matschke had no other choice than to deny the request because the witness's sons had openly broken the Nuremberg Laws; yet, before the witness could leave his office, Matschke commented, "If it would be up to me, all half-Jews would be sent to a concentration camp without further bother."[43] His racial convictions were thus more extreme than the official Nazi policies toward individuals of mixed Jewish blood.

Concerning the non-Aryans, the Reich Citizenship Law of November 14, 1935, a subsequent ordinance to the Nuremberg Laws, had distinguished between these Mischlinge—Jews and individuals of mixed Jewish blood. Among them, all persons with one Jewish parent (half-Jews) were classified as "Mischlinge of the first degree." All persons descending from one Jewish grandparent were classified as "Mischlinge of the second degree." However, the Mischlinge remained a problem for the Nazi bureaucracy. Long discussions were held during the January 20, 1942, Wannsee Conference, originally set up to coordinate the implementation of the Final Solution. And the discussion continued as well thereafter.

The Reich had intended to deport or sterilize the Mischlinge of the first degree, and assimilate the Mischlinge of the second degree into the German nation. But no definitive policy was established for those of the first degree, for fear of repercussions from the German relatives. These Mischlinge, however, were eventually conscripted into forced labor during the winter of 1944–45.[44]

The Aftermath: Postwar Careers and Behavior in Court

It is remarkable how easily these and most other Einsatzgruppen officers could go undetected by the authorities in the postwar newly founded West German republic. It is perhaps even more astonishing that many of these former SS officers and mass murderers soon emerged in respected professions, in government agencies, and in law enforcement, an occupation whose very purpose they had led *ad absurdum* in the Third Reich. This general observation also applies to the officers from the eastern borderlands. Among them only seven—Kroeger, von Krell*, Sakuth, Matschke, Winter*, von Toll, and Greiffenberger—were captured by the Allies. Some revealed their true identities and were sentenced for belonging to an organization deemed criminal by the International Military Tribunal. Sakuth and Matschke received two years in prison, von Toll eight months. Winter* was classified as a Mitläufer, literally a "fellow traveler," or minor accessory, and he was fined one hundred German Marks! Matschke was additionally charged with the deportations to Theresienstadt and sentenced to another two years. Greiffenberger received the most severe judgment because he fell into Soviet hands. The Russian court never learned of his membership in Einsatzkommando 9, but sentenced him to death for espionage. However, this was commuted to twenty-five years of hard labor, and subsequently he was released, in a frail physical condition, in 1953.[45]

The other officers in this group were able to flee from the advancing Red

Army, and most took an escape route over the Baltic Sea and Denmark. Usually after remaining in obscurity for a couple of months, or after their relatively mild sentences had expired, they accepted temporary jobs. Soon thereafter, however, these former officers emerged in professions suited to their education and prewar occupations. By 1959, six of the fourteen officers in this group again reached positions they were well qualified for but should never have achieved given their history in the Einsatzgruppen. Thus, K. became chair of the German-Baltic Ethnic Organization (Deutsch-Baltische Landsmannschaft) in the state of Nordrhein Westfalen, and ironically the German Red Cross's General Office in Bonn hired the former mass murderer von Toll.[46]

After working for the American occupation authorities in Sennelager, Edwin Sakuth first became an agent for refugees and subsequently an administrative clerk in the Compensation Agency for Refugees from formerly German Territories in Northeim County.[47] And Gerhard Carsten became a detective with the Criminal Police in Arnsberg.[48] Ultimately, many more former Einsatzgruppen officers who had been tried in the West German courts (twenty-four), at one point in time returned or attempted to return to serve in the police force before they were discovered.[49] And almost all Einsatzgruppen officers soon resurfaced after the war in well-paying and respected jobs.

Differences in the attitudes of these officers toward the crimes, and their behavior once they had been apprehended, often had a significant influence on the sentencing. Some, such as K., Greiffenberger, Döring, and unexpectedly also Behrend, admitted their guilt, showed signs of remorse, openly cooperated with the investigations, and accepted their penalties as retribution. Their court behavior is appropriately summarized in Wilhelm Greiffenberger's statement during his main trial: "We finally have to say what happened, and take the responsibility for it."[50]

Other officers, however, could not accept that they were to be held accountable for their deeds. The postwar lives of Kroeger and von Krell* are most telling in this respect. After short periods as American or French POWs, where they did not reveal their SS background, and following a few years in temporary jobs, both emerged as leaders in a West German youth welfare organization (Jugendsozialwerk). When suspicions about possible activities in the Einsatzgruppen arose, Kroeger fled to Switzerland, then to Austria, and to Italy, where he was captured in 1962. Nevertheless, the Italian authorities denied the German request for extradition and released him in 1963. Subsequently, Kroeger was caught again in Switzerland and finally extradited to Germany in 1966.

Von Krell* did not stay too long in his position with the Jugendsozialwerk. Monitoring the ongoing investigations into former Nazi criminals, he took on a position with a German company in Cyprus. When the German authorities requested his return to stand trial, however, he escaped to South America. The local police found and arrested him in Curacao (then a Dutch protectorate) and returned him to Germany.

Once charged in court, Kroeger and von Krell* responded with unconvincing and incredible excuses. Both stated that they had believed the executions were legal according to the rules of war at the time. Obviously, the court rejected their ridiculous claims.[51]

The remaining officers resolutely denied their participation in the massacres, and when that did not work, tried to show that they had served only in subordinate and inconsequential functions. August Hering, for example, stated that he had only been an interpreter; Eberhard von Toll claimed that he had never been a shooter; and Lukas von der Rohde* tried to present himself as a lowly link in the chain of command who was unable to act differently. Of course, their crimes belied their cowardly testimony.[52] Overall, as the courts found, these men left "not a believable impression" during the trial.

This negative image was particularly evident in the behavior of Pranas Lukys. The court in Ulm described him as a "clever, experienced, yet at the same time extremely cunning human being with a good memory who never lacked an excuse, especially when others implicated him."[53] His defense strategy was characteristic. He first always denied the deed, then requested that witnesses who now lived in the United States (or other distant countries) be invited to corroborate his statements. If such witnesses indeed appeared and did not produce results satisfactory to Lukys, he challenged their credibility.[54] When the prosecution presented the testimony of two witnesses who had emigrated to Canada and the United States, respectively, Lukys immediately accused one, a man named Us., of being the former mayor of Vevirzeniai, who had impregnated his Jewish maid and later killed her in a nearby forest. Of the other witness, a woman named Sin., Lukys said that she had worked for the Communists in Lithuania and after 1945 in Germany, and should not be trusted. Fortunately, the court challenged Lukys in both cases.[55]

The differences in behavior predictably are reflected in the judgments of the German courts. Among other factors, such as position in the Einsatzgruppen and during the executions, number of victims, time served in Nazi organizations, previous sentences, and other hardships, an uncooperative demeanor often combined with unwillingness to recognize the magnitude of the crimes led to prison sentences of between twenty-one months and five years. Hering and von der Rohde*, the only perpetrators charged with murder, received life and thirteen-year sentences, respectively. Of the more cooperative and remorseful group, K. was acquitted, Greiffenberger received three years in prison, Döring four, and Behrend five years and three months.

Conclusions

It has been established that all officers in this group from the eastern borderlands immediately realized that the order to eliminate the Jews constituted a crime against humanity and was against international law and all accepted rules of warfare. Von Toll had even called the order a "criminal madness."[56] Nevertheless, all officers complied without much hesitation, in part because they were reared in authoritarian families and because they had previously served in the military, the Freikorps, the police, and various Nazi organizations that demanded strict obedience. In addition, exposure to Nazi propaganda and political education had imbedded the principle that the Führer was the highest executive, legislative, and judiciary authority. Therefore, his commands, no matter how criminal or unjust, were always binding law. That is how the courts characterize the behavior and the attitudes of these Einsatzgruppen officers.

However, this seems insufficient and contradictory, considering that the courts also emphasize that these men could distinguish between good and evil and that they clearly recognized their crimes. Moreover, these SS officers were not always as subservient as the courts found. Matschke, for example, had no problems confronting a much higher-ranking officer if he agreed with the issue at stake. He had found it more important to kill the 200 Jews of Welish than to respect and obey a colonel. And, thus, in order to understand the behavioral ambiguities, it is necessary to reflect on their social, educational, and political background, as well as the attitudes displayed in the killing fields. For although obedience to authority and following orders were powerful motives, a number of equally important additional factors were at work.

The epigraph to this chapter has been chosen because it was so typical of these and other officers in the Einsatzgruppen: "Damn it! One generation has to go through this so that our children will have it better."[57] On one level, it is evident that no one was particularly pleased with the order to kill the Jews. If, however, they did not like their duty and recognized it as a gross infraction of the most fundamental human rights, why did they follow? And were there, as Daniel Goldhagen alleges, ways to circumvent the order?

Definitely, there were. As noted, K. avoided all but one execution, although he served under the command of a cold-hearted Nazi fanatic. Another witness, O., explained that it was relatively easy to shirk from the massacres; interpreters and other specialists in the Einsatzgruppen usually learned well in advance about planned executions and could pretend to be sick or busy with other tasks on the day an action was scheduled. O. had been an SS captain and became a weapons specialist at the Minsk Office of the Commander of the Security Police and Security Service. He left for extensive inspection tours every time an execution was scheduled. On other occasions, he simply remained in his quarters.

Other officers, such as the "devout" Christian believer von Toll, could have used religious and moral arguments to be relieved of shooting duties.[58] Sakuth, the only Security Service member at the Memel Border Police station, could have found pretenses to stay at his post. And because no superior would have known about the gypsy family, Matschke could have let them go as well.

Pranas Lukys, as the only non-German perpetrator, did not work for a German agency at all; he was a Lithuanian citizen. Therefore, he did not have to accept any German orders. In his position as police chief of Krottingen he did have to respect the wishes and requests of the occupation power and could not act entirely independently; yet although the court believed that the Gestapo was all-powerful, it also established that the clever Lukys found ways to disregard German decrees time and again. In cases when the Border Police told him to arrest his friends, Lukys always warned them in advance and helped them to escape.[59] Furthermore, knowing that Lukys worked against the Gestapo when he withheld from them the Jewish valuables, one might safely assume that this was not his only instance of disobedience. Thus it is clear that a superior order was not a sufficient reason for participation in the massacres.

On another level, the chapter epigraph contains a pseudo-justification for the elimination of the Jews, namely that future generations no longer have to deal with their influences in the world. Of course, such arguments are only valid if one believes in the Nazi images of the evil, all-powerful, all-controlling, behind-the-scenes manipulating Jew, as these officers did. Most officers in this group were indeed anti-Semites, but their form of anti-Semitism differed from Goldhagen's deeply rooted eliminationist brand. In fact, with the exception of Lukys, no one thought about using the excuse of having suffered from Jews and Communism to justify their deeds. A look at Wilhelm Döring's career proves Goldhagen wrong. This Saul-turned–St. Paul was a young and enthusiastic Nazi follower since his teens. He was not anti-Semitic during his youth, however; only later did he accept what he had learned during his police training. In the Einsatzgruppen, Döring had been exposed to the massacres only gradually and had repeatedly expressed his doubts during the Röhm affair in 1934, during Kristallnacht in 1938, before his first execution in 1941, and again before the execution of the mentally ill children in 1942. If he had always been a dedicated eliminationist anti-Semite, he would not have needed this habituation or bothered to confirm his orders.

Moreover, he would not have changed and entirely lost his faith in National Socialism.

Both Behrend and von der Rohde*, as well, had peacefully coexisted with Jews for a long time and therefore must have acquired their anti-Semitism during their careers. Even in Matschke's case it is possible to argue that he adopted his hard-line stance toward the Jews in Cologne as a response to the horrifying experience in the Einsatzgruppen. Had he not hunted and killed Jews in the Soviet Union, he would not have needed to justify his deeds to himself.

On yet another level, inherent in the epigraph is the implication that conformity to the group was a strong motive. The officers of the Tilsit Einsatzkommando huddled together to cheer each other on when one of them uttered those words. Certainly no one wanted to be a coward, and each found consolation in the fact that they were all engaged in the same criminal activity. This strong feeling of belonging to the same group even influenced officers with ample reason to disobey or leave their units. Carsten, for instance, had followed the elimination order and was proud that "the Jews were put to the sword," although he had been detached to the State Police in Tilsit against his wishes and despite Böhme's humiliation in front of his comrades. Von Toll, too, continued to be a shooter despite the mishap of falling into the grave and finding himself among the bloody bodies of the victims, a circumstance that not only must have sickened him but most likely also made him the laughingstock of his comrades.

In addition, as the court in Koblenz found, "Refusal to participate in the killing of Jews constituted a character weakness and a human failure in the honor codes of the SS." Yet, at the same time, disobeying the order and being regarded as a weakling had no consequences for the perpetrators, even if commanders such as Bradfisch or Zapp threatened with court-martial and the death penalty. Therefore, the decision not to participate in the massacres only required the courage to live with the consequences of being shunned by one's comrades.[60] That no officers in this group, and in only a few others, took such a decisive step only underscores that peer pressure was an extremely potent motivation for the perpetrators.

Several other factors, however, also were part of the decisions of the officers from the eastern borderlands. Lukys had admitted that he hated Communism and tried to exact his revenge; and the other officers, as well, had been exposed to virulent hatred of Communism. With their right-wing, traditional, and conservative background and their training in Nazi organizations, it is feasible that they saw the war against the Soviet Union as a struggle of two opposing religions, Nazism and Communism. This is evident from the choice of words of the officers in court. Matschke spoke of his "conversion" to Nazism, and Döring told how he lost his "faith" in National Socialism. The officers from the eastern bor-

derlands therefore seem to have absorbed the myths disseminated by Nazi propaganda, and the perpetration of the killings certainly took on a pseudo-spiritual
component.

Yet, we should not forget another important incentive. Officers such as von
der Rohde*, Hering, Matschke, Lukys, and Behrend were put into positions of
absolute and unrestrained power over a group of people who had been systematically denigrated for years. Von der Rohde* was the acknowledged "Jewish
expert" in Sonderkommando 11a, and the very act of having the Jews kneel in
front of him exemplified the difference in status and power. Hering "ruled," together with Martin Weiss, over the Vilnius ghetto. Matschke was in charge of his
detachment; and Behrend determined how the next group of victims reached
the execution site. In one case, he and a comrade alone decided over life and
death of the Lithuanian police officer. Of course, Lukys was in just that position
for almost his entire career, but in particular during the execution selections.
Therefore, elements such as the specific tasks of the perpetrators, opportunity,
and circumstances that put them into a position of power are necessary and determining explanations for the behavior of these men.

Greed, aggrandizement, and career concerns are other explanations. They
are evident primarily in Lukys's actions, but also in the motivations of Behrend,
Carsten, Greiffenberger, and the others. Lukys became too greedy even for his
German masters, who eventually arrested him. And after his escape from an SS
prison, it was his greed that drove Lukys back to the crime scene to recover
the Jewish valuables he had hidden from the German authorities. Behrend, too,
crashed the meeting of local officials to make sure that the Jewish problem was
solved according to his liking. And Carsten was proud to tell others about the
ongoing massacres, although he was not accepted into the SS. Even Greiffenberger could have remained an interpreter and used the opportunities this
position offered to dodge the executions.

In addition, the obligatory Sakuskas, the victory parties after the killings, not
only show the cynicism, but also the camaraderie and the sense of belonging together in the killing units. The perpetrators cemented their bonds with alcohol,
bragged about their deeds, and brought "cowards" and other outsiders back into
line. At the same time, the alcohol served to help the perpetrators wash down
remaining doubts, overcome scruples, and forget the horrors of their chosen
profession.

Goldhagen's conclusions about the perpetrators and their motivations are
confirmed, for there indeed existed a high degree of indifference, cynicism,
human depravity, and anti-Semitism among the ethnic German Einsatzgruppen
officers. However, the behavior of the ethnic Germans in the Einsatzgruppen,
does not prove the two key aspects of Goldhagen's argument. First, by definition

and because of their training and habituation in right-wing and Nazi organizations, these men were not ordinary Germans. Second, the anti-Jewish feelings in these officers were not deeply rooted; rather, they were acquired during their careers.

Yet, since the evidence from the Einsatzgruppen officers from the eastern borderlands does not sufficiently bear out Goldhagen's claims, we must now consider a category of killers for whom anti-Semitism might have been a principal motivation because they did not take advantage of the chances to extricate themselves from the massacres their special positions offered.

4. THE SPECIALISTS

When one of my subordinated drivers
who participated in the execution got sick,
I led him aside and used the opportunity
to sneak away.

SS First Lieutenant Friedrich Merbach

URING A night in early August of 1942, Einsatzkommando 8 and other killing units held their gas vans ready to asphyxiate a trainload of Jews from Germany. SS Technical Sergeant Thomas Gevatter* was driving one of these newly devised mobile gas chambers. After the van was loaded with approximately fifty Jews, he and an accompanying SS officer left the railroad station and headed to the execution site. But before they reached their destination, Gevatter*'s van got stuck in mud and water. Angry about Gevatter*'s clumsy driving, the SS officer ordered him to immediately begin with the gassing. Gevatter* refused. The SS officer then brandished his submachine gun. Gevatter* complied and gassed the Jews. Afterward, Gevatter* was never punished for his initial disobedience; however, his superiors thought that he could not be trusted with further actions against the Jews and he was sent back to his former position as a driver with the State Police outpost in the Moravian city of Brünn (today's Brno in the Czech Republic).[1]

Gevatter* was one of the men who served as drivers, communications and weapons specialists, personnel officers, or interpreters in the Einsatzgruppen. These specialist officers had a unique status in their units.[2] They enjoyed certain privileges because their job was crucial for the proper functioning of the Einsatzgruppen. Knowing that their commanding officers depended on their technical and administrative expertise, in addition to having risen through the ranks, gave the specialists a sense of pride. Nevertheless, being a specialist in the Einsatzgruppen also had a downside. Fellow officers often viewed them with jealousy, suspicion, and at times contempt because the specialists' knowledge was limited to a narrow and "secondary" function.

Rarely, however, had the other specialists acted as bravely as Gevatter*. They usually did not use the special advantages of their position to extricate themselves from the killing of the Jews. On the contrary, driven by feelings of inferiority and finally given the opportunity to prove themselves in front of their comrades, they often contributed to the massacres far beyond their assigned tasks. The motives that may have influenced such behavior are of interest.

Background

Six of the specialist officers were already in their late thirties and early forties when they served in the Einsatzgruppen because it usually took a combination of ambition, time, and patience to rise through the ranks. SS Captain Helmut Reil*, SS 1st Lts. Karl Kretschmer, Friedrich Merbach, Kl., SS Technical Sergeant Gevatter*, SS S. Sgts. Werner Wachholz*, and Walter Fahnemann* were slightly younger. But in general the specialist officers were somewhat older than the rest of the Einsatzgruppen officers. Contrary to many of their comrades who had middle- and upper-class backgrounds, the specialists were the sons of artisans and lower-level civil servants. Wachholz*, whose father owned a vineyard, and Reil*, whose father was a senior civil servant, were the exception.

Only Reil* and Kl. had finished their education at a Gymnasium. The others either had finished only eight years of schooling, or had left their Gymnasium early to become apprentices in various trades, as was common for young men of their social origin. Seven officers in this group, immediately after their schooling, had learned a skill closely related to their later special function in the Einsatzgruppen. SS Second Lieutenant Hans Wiechert, Gevatter*, and Merbach became car mechanics; SS 1st Lt. Jacob Herbert Oswald became an electronics technician; Wilhelm Kaul, who had been put into the SS rank structure as an SS first lieutenant, became a clerk in the personnel department of the cultural office in Recklinghausen; Reil* became an accountant; and Kl. found a job with the government health insurance service.

The specialists' low level of education in comparison to many other Einsatzgruppen officers does not mean, however, that they were not ambitious. On the contrary, they worked diligently to better their status and eventually all but Gevatter*, Wachholz*, and Fahnemann* reached officer ranks. Long before that, however, Wiechert had studied six semesters of engineering, Oswald had taken evening classes to prepare for his studies in electronics and engineering, and SS 2d Lt. Bruno Schulz had studied on his own to become an engineer.

Another officer, SS Second Lieutenant P., could not find a job as a car mechanic and was thus obligated to temporarily take on work as a musician before he was placed as an administrative assistant in the local government health insurance office. Seeing no chances for further advancement, he quit and joined the police force, where he advanced to Criminal Police detective (Obersekretär) within a year. Like Kl., P., and Kaul, who had to leave their Gymnasiums early to earn money, Wiechert and Oswald also had to give up their ambitious career plans and settle for work in their field of training. Given this failure to complete their education because of economic pressure in the early 1930s, it is perhaps understandable that these officers looked to the Nazis who promised a better future.

Not surprisingly then, most officers in this group had already joined the Nazi Party or the SS—sometimes both—before Hitler came to power, or by 1933 at the latest. Apart from hopes for a better economy, most specialists cited Hitler's heavily propagandized anti-Communism and efforts to restore Germany's position in the world among the main incentives leading to their decision. As did so many other Germans at the time, they uncritically revered the Nazis as long-awaited saviors. In his interrogation, Hans Wiechert succinctly summed up their motivations: "I had been a convinced opponent of Communism for a long time and hoped that Nazism would fight Communism as well as eliminate the consequences of the Versailles Treaty and overcome the economic problems in Germany."[3] Two other specialists, Helmut Reil* and Werner Wachholz*, joined the SS primarily because it promoted sports and physical fitness.

On the other hand, Wilhem Kaul, Karl Kretschmer and Bruno Schulz did not become members in Nazi organizations from their first opportunities in 1933. After finishing two apprenticeships as a drugstore clerk and a salesman, respectively, Kretschmer found a permanent job with the Berlin Order Police in 1928. Ten years later, he passed the required training for police officers in senior administrative positions and was transferred to the State Police Section in Karlsruhe. According to his training, he worked there in purely administrative functions. In 1940, Kretschmer passed another qualifying exam at the Reich Security Main Office. At this time he also chose to apply for Nazi Party and SS membership. As he stated, he did so because he wanted to fit in and not jeopardize his by then promising career. Nevertheless, in March of 1941 he failed the required ideological training, and the SS refused to accept him. Kretschmer then decided to leave the Security Police altogether and requested a transfer to the air force (Luftwaffe). But his failure had put him in disgrace with the SS, and his Luftwaffe application was rejected. The SS, however, offered him a chance to redeem himself by serving a term in the Einsatzgruppen. In August of 1942,

Kretschmer assumed his duties as head administrative officer of Sonderkommando 4a. His early career thus proves it was not easy to leave the Security Police service.

Bruno Schulz also finished two apprenticeships, in the mechanics and metal-
worker trades. In 1923, he decided to become a policeman and was accepted into
the Order Police. After attending the required training classes, he was assigned
to Königsberg (today's Kaliningrad). In 1935, he resigned after twelve years of
service.[4] However, because his family could not live on his meager pension,
Schulz reapplied for police service, as he stated in his application, "Preferably
as a county sheriff [Gendarm] or temporarily as a detective in other police organizations."[5]

At the time, the Gestapo had a shortage of manpower, and the agency
charged with the job placement of former soldiers and policemen suggested
Schulz. Schulz accepted the Gestapo offer on March 1, 1936. He initially trained
as a radio and telegraph operator, then was assigned to the Tilsit State Police and
its department responsible for Memel-German affairs. Schulz's duties included
the gathering and reporting of information for the Security Police Main Office
(the predecessor of the Reich Security Main Office). In addition to his techno-
logical training, Schulz also received instruction in Criminal Police procedure.
When the Memel area was returned to German control in March 1939, Schulz
was appointed leader of the Border Police post in the small town of Laubszargen.
Because his family could not make the move to this town, he requested a return
to the State Police office in Tilsit, which was granted in 1940. Both economic and
family considerations influenced Schulz's decision to abandon the pursuit of a
career as a sheriff, and he became part of the Security Police. He also joined the
SS and the Nazi Party.

Another specialist, Helmut Reil*, had a rather typical career for an administrator. He became a clerk with the Berlin city administration when his schooling ended in 1929. Six years later, he was finally promoted to city inspector. On
August 1, 1938, he was transferred to the Security Police Main Office. At this
agency and its successor, the Reich Security Main Office, Reil* worked in the
controller's office, where he was responsible for salaries. From June 1941 to April
1944, he served with Einsatzkommando 2 in Riga. Because he had never received
police-specific or military training, his tasks included financial administration,
building maintenance, organization of food supplies, and field mail.

Wilhelm Kaul similarly had served a long time (ten years) in the Order Police
before he was transferred to the Gestapo during the restructuring of the German
police organizations in the mid-1930s. He never applied for SS membership, but
joined the Nazi Party in 1937. According to his training at the cultural office, Kaul
always served in administrative and, in particular, personnel functions. In March

1939, Kaul was again transferred, this time to the personnel department of the Security Police Main Office, where he worked until his delegation to the Office of the Commander of the Security Police and the Security Service (Kds) in Minsk in July 1942.

The remaining officers in this group became Nazi Party and SS members even earlier. SS Second Lieutenant P. chose a Gestapo career because he did not see a chance for advancement as a health-insurance accountant. Kl. had an almost identical early career; he even transferred to the Gestapo in the same year, 1937. From then on both worked exclusively in their specialties, accounting and finance, until they were send to the Office of the Commander of the Security Police and the Security Service in Kiev. Kl. arrived there in August 1942; P. arrived five months later, in January 1943. From their interrogations it appears that neither became a member of the Gestapo because of his identification with the future goals of this organization, but simply because the expanding Nazi police branches offered career opportunities. Because they continued to work in exclusively administrative functions—albeit for an organization with entirely different and radical goals—they did not know yet that they would become part of the Einsatzgruppen and their criminal activities.

The same observation applies to the three future transportation specialists and drivers. They had also joined the Security Service and the State Police primarily because openings were available when they needed jobs. Merbach had been unemployed from 1931 to 1933 and, being a journeyman car mechanic, it seemed logical that he should join the Security Service when it offered him a position as a driver in 1934. He proved to be effective, reliable, and trustworthy, and was put in charge of the Security Service Main Office vehicle park only two years later. In October 1941 he took over the same duties when he was transferred to Sonderkommando 1b and its successor, the stationary Office of the Commander of the Security Police and the Security Service at Minsk, in White Ruthenia (today's Belarus).

Merbach's colleague, Hans Wiechert, became a driving instructor after he quit his engineering studies, but his poorly financed business failed in 1935. He then took the chance to work for the State Police office in Tilsit, which was looking for drivers. After a short time, his new employer sent him to Technical Police School in order to qualify him for taking over the vehicle pool of the organization. Wiechert passed his classes and took on his new duties; his additional tasks included archival work and investigation of political crimes. After 1938, his job was again restricted to vehicles, weapons, and ammunition; he was also charged with the organization of shooting exercises and physical education of the unit. In October of the same year, Wiechert was dispatched to the predecessors of the Einsatzgruppen in the Sudetenland (the German settlement area in the Czechoslovakian border region of Bohemia, Moravia, and Silesia) and again later in Poland. Contrary to the other officers, Wiechert therefore had ample opportunities to learn about the practices of the Einsatzgruppen, especially because he was in charge of three essential tools—transportation, weapons, and ammunition. Upon his return from Poland, Wiechert was appointed personal driver of the former Lithuanian president. And shortly after the German invasion of the Soviet Union, the leader of Einsatzgruppe A enlisted him together with his old unit, the Tilsit State Police, to help with the elimination of the Lithuanian Jews.

SS Technical Sergeant Thomas Gevatter*, after an incomplete apprenticeship as a car mechanic, also lost his job as a truck driver in 1931. He then started his own transportation business and joined the Nazi Party and the SS. Gevatter* had calculated that membership in Nazi organizations would help him establish a solid professional foundation. He did not know much about the Nazi program and its racial components; he was attracted to the SS because of its elite status and the appealing black uniform. Regardless, his new business soon faltered.

After January 30, 1933, however, Gevatter*'s fortunes seemed to change for the better. The Nazis commissioned him as an auxiliary police officer in the struggle against Communists, Social Democrats, and other enemies of the new regime, and then gave him a permanent job as a driver with the State Police in Dresden. Subsequently, Gevatter* served in the Reich Protectorate, where he stayed with the State Police in Brünn until he was drafted to the Einsatzgruppen in 1941 and became a driver with headquarters of Einsatzgruppe B. As such, he participated in several actions as a guard or shooter. In June 1942 he was transferred to Einsatzkommando 8, where he took over the operation of the newly arrived gas van.

The other gas van driver, Walter Fahnemann*, had worked as a driver, newspaper deliverer, and oil factory worker since he had ceased his apprenticeship as a designer in 1923. He gladly became a member of the Storm Troopers when the organization offered him a job as a driver. After the Nazi seizure of power, Fahnemann* obtained a permanent position as a driver with the police president in Berlin. He was thus one of the few Storm Trooper members who succeeded in securing a government job after 1933.[6] However, Fahnemann* soon threw in his fate with the SS and the Security Service because of the better salary. He was accepted and served with the predecessors of the Einsatzgruppen in Austria and Czechoslovakia.

On November 9, 1939, Fahnemann* helped with the arrest of two English spies who were alleged to have committed the unsuccessful attempt on Hitler in the Bürgerbräukeller. On this sixteenth anniversary of his failed attempt to overthrow the Weimar government, Hitler appeared for a speech in the Munich Bürgerbräukeller. Acting on his own, the Swabian carpenter Johann Georg Elser planted a bomb in one of the pillars of the building. Unfortunately, Hitler left early and remained unharmed when Elser's bomb exploded (for similar reasons, Hitler later escaped a series of other attempts on his life that culminated in the bomb exploded by Colonel Stauffenberg in Hitler's quarters on July 20, 1944). The Nazis blamed the incident on the activities of foreign agents but apprehended and executed Elser.[7]

As a reward for Fahnemann*'s contributions in the capture of the English agents, Hitler personally decorated him with the Iron Cross (Second Class) and promoted him to Heydrich's personal chauffeur. However, despite his new fame, Fahnemann* quickly lost his position because of his habitual drinking. Heydrich had noticed that Fahnemann* smelled of alcohol, obviously drinking on the job, and therefore decided to teach him a lesson. With the intent of sobering Fahnemann*, Heydrich drove him back to his quarters and commanded him to walk several miles through the cold winter night and then report to his office. Fahnemann soon appeared in Heydrich's headquarters, much too early to have walked the distance and still visibly showing the effects of alcohol. Upon Heydrich's interrogation, Fahnemann* admitted without hesitation that he had called another car to give him a ride. Heydrich immediately sentenced him to ten days arrest and then sent him back to his previous position in the Reich Security Main Office. In November 1941, however, Fahnemann's* superiors offered him another chance; he was given top-secret instructions in the operation of the new gas vans and then transferred to Sonderkommando 4a, which was still stationed in Kiev.

Much like Hans Wiechert, Thomas Gevatter*, and Walter Fahnemann*, SS 2d Lt. Bruno Schulz had the unique opportunity to witness and participate in the anti-Jewish measures of the Nazi regime long before he served in the Einsatzgruppen. In fact, Schulz is the only officer in this group to have expressed publicly that he endorsed the measures taken against the Jews. Schulz's predecessor as Border Police post leader in Laubszargen, the witness Ka., testified that upon taking command, Schulz's first concern was the situation of the Jews. Schulz disclosed to Ka. that he regarded the Jews as a foreign element within the German people and that he would treat them accordingly. Even after the war, Schulz bragged that he had been a Security Police officer, which would indicate that he had very likely been involved in the persecution of the Jews.

When he returned to the Tilsit State Police in 1939, Schulz took over its Jewish desk. His routine duties included monitoring the valuables of the Jews who had emigrated and surveillance of the villages near the Führer's new headquarters, "Wolf's Lair," near Rastenburg in eastern Prussia. Schulz fulfilled his tasks with zeal and dedication. Shortly before the invasion of the Soviet Union, he received the order to remove the remaining Jews from Tilsit. Schulz com-

plied and divided the Jews of the city into two railroad transports. He personally accompanied the transports to Königsberg, where he turned them over to
another SS officer. In court, Schulz claimed that at the time he did not know
what happened to the deportees, but from his work at the Jewish desk he must
have learned that they were probably shipped to the ghettos or labor camps in
the General Government.

His colleague, Hans Wiechert, on the other hand, clearly sympathized with
many Nazi goals, but anti-Semitism was definitely not one of them. He maintained his friendship with a Jew even after 1933. Although it might have jeopardized his career in the SS, Wiechert also continued to visit the house of his friend
regularly. Yet his support for the friend went even farther. When all Jews from
Tilsit were arrested during Kristallnacht, Wiechert asked his commanding officer Dr. Gräfe (at the time, Böhme's predecessor), for permission to look after
his friend. Gräfe reluctantly gave his consent, but also warned that the action
might have negative consequences for Wiechert's position. Undaunted, Wiechert arranged to have his friend transferred from the state prison to the police fa-
cility, where he could better watch over him. Soon thereafter, Wiechert succeeded in having his friend released and helped him to emigrate to the United
States. This Jewish friend, Le., flew in for the trial in Tübingen from his new
home in Chicago to testify on Wiechert's behalf. Although this is certainly an
unusual and rare case, it demonstrates that in 1938 friendship and humanitarian care for an individual Jew was still occasionally possible to combine with a
successful career in the SS and police forces, even with the acquiescence of
one's superior.

Finally, Werner Wachholz* and Jacob Oswald had perhaps the most extraordinary careers prior to their detachment to the Einsatzgruppen. Wachholz*
was an ethnic German from the Soviet Republic of Georgia whose family had established a successful vineyard on the sunny slopes of the Caucasus Mountains.
Wachholz* could have been discussed with the other ethnic Germans in Chapter 3, but his function and behavior in the Einsatzgruppen clearly qualify him as
a specialist.

Wachholz*'s father had lost the winery during the implementation of Stalin's first Five-Year Plan in 1929. Deemed an enemy of the people and persecuted
by the Soviet authorities, Wachholz* managed to cross the mountains to Iran.
Passing through Turkey, he finally reached Germany, where he found a job in
viticulture. In 1932 he joined the Reiter SS because he was interested in horsemanship. Five years later, he also became a Nazi Party member and volunteered
for the labor service. There the Security Police approached him because of his
knowledge of the Russian language. He accepted a position with that organi-

zation in 1939, passed the necessary training program, and subsequently worked with the Border Police in Danzig (the Polish Gdansk). In 1941, he was drafted to Einsatzkommando 12 and served as an interpreter.

Wachholz* had joined Nazi groups in 1932, but Jacob Oswald had already sympathized with the Nazi movement in the early 1920s. He was involved in Hitler's Beer Hall Putsch in 1923 and subsequently fled to Austria, where he lived until 1934. Despite his emigration, Oswald became a German Nazi Party member in 1930 and joined the SS in 1932. For his participation in the Putsch and for the wounds he received in a political brawl in Austria, the NSDAP recognized him as an Old Fighter (alter Kämpfer) and decorated him with its Blutorden (Blood Medal). Yet because of his political activity for the Nazis, Oswald was expelled from Austria in 1934. Upon his return to Germany, he embarked on a full-time career within the SS.

Oswald received his basic training under the then SS Oberführer Theodor Eicke in Dachau, the first concentration camp run by the SS. The camp had been established on the orders of Himmler, the then Deputy Police Commissioner of Munich and Reichsführer SS, on March 20, 1933. Its purpose was to "concentrate all Communists and Social Democratic officials who cannot be allowed to remain free as they continue to agitate and to cause unrest." Local police, Storm Troopers, and other SS authorities soon built their own camps for the rising numbers of Communists and Social Democrats taken into custody. Only later were Jews included among the prisoners. Himmler also appointed Eicke as inspector of the concentration camps. Eicke's Death Heads Squads subsequently became the guards of the increasingly widening concentration camp system.[8]

After Oswald's promotion to second lieutenant, he took charge of an SS guard company at the Dachau camp. He also attended several SS leadership classes and worked in an SS-run camp for Austrian refugees. After a short period of unemployment in 1937–38, the SS placed him as security chief and deputy Security Service delegate in a Lübeck machine factory. In the same position he switched to a Kiel electronics firm in 1940 and worked there until the local police president drafted him for the Security Police under the Emergency Decree to Secure Manpower for Tasks of Special State-Political Significance. Oswald began his tour of duty with the Office of the Commander of the Security Police and the Security Service in Minsk in February 1943.

This was the information that Oswald had volunteered to the German authorities. Otherwise, he categorically denied all participation in the massacres. The court in Koblenz could link him irrevocably to the murder of only one Jew during the elimination of the Minsk ghetto. For lack of information, it is therefore impossible to determine his motivations; but from his long career in the SS, it is very likely that he was trained to completely identify with all Nazi measures and follow orders without hesitation. His silence in front of the new German authorities only corroborates this assumption. The other cases, however, offer more tangible evidence.[9]

Participation in the Final Solution

Each specialist position contained characteristic duties and responsibilities that either forced the pertinent officers to contribute or allowed them to extricate themselves from the executions. How much these officers made use of their opportunities and how deeply they became involved in the criminal activities, however, was a matter of the situation and individual choice. The following investigation starts with the drivers, then turns to the interpreter, and concludes with the officers in administrative functions.

Drivers Hans Wiechert and Friedrich Merbach both had participated in multiple shootings. Their primary responsibility was the organization of vehicles and drivers for the transport of the executioners, and sometimes the victims, as well as issuing weapons and ammunition, which made their presence necessary at the executions. In their rendering of these basic services, the men must have realized that they were helping to kill innocent human beings, a fact they already should have known from their previous career in the SS, and obviously they should have objected. Nevertheless, Wiechert and Merbach not only did not make enough use of the chances to leave the scene once the firing began, but they remained and committed acts that went far beyond their basic duties and elementary notions of justice and human conduct.

During Wiechert's first execution, near Polangen on June 30, 1941, his men had to establish a semi-circle approximately 100 to 130 feet wide on one side of the mass grave to prevent unauthorized access and possible escape attempts. Wiechert was thus positioned close to the crime scene and witnessed the execution in all its gruesome details. A cadet who was in charge of the execution squad from a Luftwaffe training unit testified that the victims first had to dig their own grave. Due to the sandy soil, that was an extremely challenging endeavor as the walls kept caving in. In order to accelerate the process, Security Service guards beat the Jews with wooden clubs and berated their unfortunate victims with cruel sarcasm: "Work faster, Isidor, soon you will be with your God."[10]

During the execution, the eighteen- and nineteen-year-old Luftwaffe soldiers shot poorly because they were nervous; some even closed their eyes. Many victims did not die instantly and had to suffer until they received their "mercy shots." One victim turned around and shouted at his executioners, "You Germans are such barbarians!"[11]

The walls of the grave continued to cave in during the shooting, and the bodies of the victims did not neatly fall on top of each other as planned. Therefore, the Security Service members forced a Jewish gynecologist to neatly layer the bodies. Constantly mocked with taunts—"You violator of women, now you have the chance to do some real work"—the doctor was finally shot with the last group of victims. He did not die instantly, however, and continued to crawl over his dead brethren, blood gushing from a wound in his back, until he was finally dispatched with additional bullets.[12] At one time during the day, a transport plane from the Luftwaffe had circled low over the execution site, presumably taking photos. The leader of the execution, SS Major Hersmann, cursed as he became furious about this indiscretion: "This [pilot's behavior] is a big mess [grosse Schweinerei]."[13]

Subsequently, to specifically avoid the added post-execution work of layering bodies (and to maximize a grave's capacity), Higher SS and Police Leader Jeckeln had conceived of the "Sardinenpackung" method of executions—like sardines in a can. Victims had to lie face down in the grave and on top of the previous group of victims; they were then shot in the back of the head.

At the horrific Polangen site, Wiechert should have had considerable doubts about the legitimacy and necessity of the operation because of the pre-execution secrecy and the behavior of the policemen. Yet, Bruno Schulz had to secure the execution site, and from his position he had an even better view of the events. Nevertheless, both never questioned their orders and continued with their work. To the contrary, in what can be seen as another case of habituation to mass murder, Wiechert took on increasingly more tasks.

On July 3, 1941, when "the Jews of Georgenburg were put to the sword,"[14] as SS Technical Sergeant Carsten who was in charge of this execution had put it so nonchalantly afterward, Wiechert had fulfilled his transportation duties and was free to leave the scene. But Böhme, who was unhappy with Carsten's poor organization, noticed the by then idle Wiechert still present. Böhme assigned him a group of Jewish prisoners and their Security Service guards and had the prisoners dig another mass grave. As at Polangen, the work in the sandy ground progressed only slowly. In addition, the working space within the grave was too small for the Jewish workers, who understandably were extremely nervous and constantly obstructed each other. Wiechert yelled at them and beat them with a wooden club. When two Jews turned their spades against each other, Wiechert should have interfered, but he and his men rather enjoyed the spectacle. When the grave was finally dug, the execution continued under Carsten's command. Wiechert's new task then was to administer "mercy shots," which he did in at least two instances.[15]

Subsequently, on another day in July or August of 1941, Wiechert's opportunity to be in the spotlight had finally arrived. He was put in charge of an execution. It took place in a former Soviet military base at a place called Wilkowischken. As one might expect from Wiechert's previous behavior, his promotion also made him reach a new level of cruelty. As during the other massacres, Wiechert had initially been ordered to supply vehicles, weapons, and ammunition, but the situation changed when the execution squad arrived in the barracks, with some Lithuanian Hiwis under SS Major Hersmann's leadership.

Before the execution began, Hersmann and Wiechert went to the arsenal, where they discovered new Russian rifles and ammunition. Hersmann then changed the plan. He ordered Wiechert to conduct the execution with the Russian weapons because allegedly the Hiwi auxiliaries present had volunteered for the job and were more familiar with the Russian arms. Left in charge of the killing, Wiechert issued the rifles to the Lithuanians. As he admitted, he then gave explicit orders to make certain that everything proceeded quickly and smoothly. The Hiwi executioners had to line up in groups of three along the mass grave, the first of these kneeling, the other two standing to the left and right. Each group of three shot at one victim, the kneeling group aiming at the head, the other two at the chest. Before he gave the firing command, Wiechert announced to the victims, "You are executed on orders of the Reichsführer SS for hostile actions against the Wehrmacht."[16] This statement was supposed to be a justification, and it was the standard procedure for most executions conducted by Einsatzkommando Tilsit. Yet from their ages, dress, and general appearance, it must have been obvious to the executioners that the large majority of the victims were innocent Jewish civilians who had nothing to do with the conduct of the war.

In addition to the Russian rifles, Wiechert had the executioners use a special type of ammunition. The newly discovered Russian cartridges contained projectiles that had a severe explosive impact on the target. The victims were killed instantly as the bodies were ripped apart. Sometimes the victims' heads were completely torn apart by the impact.[17] The image that emerges from the testimony on this particular instance is extremely grim; and it appears as if both Hersmann and Wiechert deliberately contributed to making it so. Both knew that the explosive bullets had devastating effects on the bodies, effects perhaps even too harrowing for German personnel to witness. This, then, might be the real reason for the use of the Lithuanians. Hersmann also calculated that Wiechert, as a weapons expert, would like to oversee a "live" demonstration of this ammunition. And Wiechert, in turn, did not want to disappoint his superior; therefore he organized the execution, in particular the positioning of the shooters and the clearly proscribed target areas, virtually guaranteeing the maximum outcome. Clearly, Hersmann and Wiechert satisfied their desire to demonstrate that they could do with the Jews whatever they wanted.

Merbach did not get as deeply involved in the executions as did Wiechert, but he rendered logistical and other support on several occasions. Merbach had arrived in Minsk as the leader of an advance command for Sonderkommando 1b, then stayed in the newly created Office of the Commander of the Security Police and Security Service and took over its vehicle pool. He was in charge of all vehicles except the gas vans, which remained under the personal control of the commanding officer, SS Lieutenant Colonel Strauch.[18] As had Wiechert, Merbach supplied the vehicles, weapons, and ammunition for the executions. Moreover, he organized at least five transports of thousands of Jews from the ghetto to the execution site in Trostinez.

During the execution operations, Merbach was free to be anywhere he wanted, including the execution site, but he chose to remain there more often than his duties required. He did not even hesitate to jump in as a shooter when another executioner fainted, and he killed at least one person, even though he had no reason to serve as a shooter. He was only responsible for the "friction-free functioning" (reibungsloser Ablauf),[19] as it is so vividly expressed in German military jargon, of the victims' transport; thus, he should have been wherever he anticipated logistical problems and where he would be most needed. That certainly was not at the execution site. In fact, his participation in the shootings clearly interrupted his primary duties. In addition, as Merbach himself admitted, it would have been easy to avoid participation, as when one of his drivers, who was in the execution squad during the March action of 1942, became ill and Merbach simply drove him away and never returned. His superior did not even notice he had left the scene.

Overall, during his two years at his position in Minsk, Merbach was never ordered to directly participate in the shootings because, according to his statement, his "proven expertise" and "experience" as a vehicle organizer were more important than his services as a shooter. Merbach, therefore, must have had other motivations that made him overreach his orders.[20]

Thomas Gevatter*'s options, however, were more limited because he was the driver of the gas van in Einsatzkommando 8. Upon his arrival in Mogilev, an unidentifiable SS officer had told him to drive the vehicle, and an enlisted man then instructed him in its proper operation. Whenever a Gefängnisräumung was scheduled—a "prisoner evacuation," as the policemen euphemistically called the routine gassings of the inmates of the local jail—the commanding chief, SS T. Sgt. Walter Strothmann*, ordered Gevatter* to have the gas van ready around midnight. All gassings were conducted at night to keep them hidden from the population.

Gevatter* first drove the van into the courtyard of the jail. He opened the rear doors and backed the truck tightly against a ramp. The prisoners had to enter the truck through the rear door. Gevatter* did not participate in the loading. He usually waited outside until the van's chamber was full. Through the small gap between the back of the truck and the ramp, he occasionally caught a glimpse of the victims. They always included women and children. Gevatter* then moved the van forward so that the doors could be closed. At this point an armed escort officer entered the truck cab and ordered Gevatter* to leave the jail.

The trip to a trench on the outskirts of the city took about twenty to thirty minutes. Gevatter* always followed another truck, in which a special work detachment, a Sonderkommando made up of Jewish prisoners, rode with members of Einsatzkommando 8. Another SS officer was also present, in a separate car. At the execution site, Gevatter* backed up his van and pulled as close as possible to the designated grave. He and other police officers, or Russian Hiwis, then connected the hose that led from the exhaust system to the interior of the gas chamber. Gevatter* regulated the engine to the proper gassing speed and usually left the vehicle until the prisoners were dead. The procedure took about ten minutes. The Reich Security Main Office had been very much concerned about the quickest, most efficient method of gassing, and a report of a technical expert had noted:

> The gassing is usually conducted wrong. The drivers always have the engine run at full speed to finish as fast as possible [which is incorrect]. . . . My research reveals that with the proper positioning of the throttle [at a lower rpm] death occurs quicker while the victims fall asleep peacefully. Grotesquely torn faces and feces, as they were experienced before, no longer appear.[21]

The escort officer would order Gevatter* to disconnect the valve and let the engine run idle while the Jewish Sonderkommando opened the rear doors and unloaded the gas chamber. After that was finished, Gevatter* returned to the jail for the next group of victims. In general, it was possible to make at least three trips each night. At the end of the night, the Security Service members forced the Jewish workers to clean the gas chamber from feces and other excrement, then finally shot them.

On a day in early August of 1942, Gevatter* received orders to have the gas van ready for an action outside of Mogilev. After several hours of driving with the other vehicles of the unit, he arrived at a railroad station where cattle cars loaded with Jews from Germany, and several other gas vans were already waiting. The SS officer in charge of the operation gave a typical speech promising the Jews resettlement, and the victims were forced into the vans. Whenever two were filled, they left.

At Gevatter*'s turn to depart, an unknown SS second lieutenant from a different unit entered his truck cab and told him to follow the convoy. As he drove, Gevatter* noticed a large puddle of mud and decided to run through it. His van got stuck. The SS second lieutenant was furious, and told Gevatter* to begin with the gassing on the spot. Gevatter* refused the command, and instead he stopped a truck that was coming from the other direction. He asked its drivers, two Russian Hiwis, to help him pull the van out of the mud. In the meantime, the second lieutenant had also exited and had aimed his submachine gun at the Russians. He ordered them to connect the hose to the gas chamber, which they did. Gevatter* felt threatened as well and proceeded to restart the engine. After the prisoners were dead, the SS officer was still pointing his gun at Gevatter* and the Russians and forced them to remove the bodies from the gas chamber and load them onto the other truck. Gevatter*'s van remained mired in the mud; the operation was over for him, as was, soon thereafter, his service in the Einsatzgruppen.[22]

When he had become a gas van driver, Gevatter* had taken several measures to avoid participating in the massacres. Short of sabotaging his orders, he usually followed only hesitantly and did not care about approval from his superiors or promotions. He also requested leave whenever he learned in advance about a planned execution. Strothmann*, his roommate in Mogilev, testified that Gevatter* had to force himself to obey each time a Gefängnisräumung was ordered. Gevatter* claimed that he obeyed only because he feared for his life. That his fear was real—at least in one instance—is evident when the SS second lieutenant had pulled his gun. However, as Gevatter*'s transfer from Einsatzkommando 8 proves, even after his act of defiance, in general his worries were not based on a correct evaluation of the situation in his and other killing units.

Refusal to kill Jews was never punished harshly. One such instance involved Gevatter*'s colleague, Fahnemann*. According to witnesses, two other Security Service members, an unidentifiable SS officer had ordered them to execute a Jewish professor and his daughter. The three had refused in unison, and the SS officer had to shoot the victims himself. Perhaps the SS officer was afraid to challenge the three Security Service men alone, yet he apparently had never reported the incident, and thus the act of disobedience had no consequences for the men.[23]

Although Fahnemann* had learned that he did not need to follow such commands, he nevertheless later participated in multiple executions. Moreover, unlike Gevatter*, Fahnemann* had to clean the gas chamber of his vehicle at the end of each action, a grisly sight that should have given him a good cause not to comply. For some inexplicable reason, however, Fahnemann* always made certain that his vehicle was ready for its sinister purpose, even during the bitter cold of the winter, when he carefully nurtured a fire under the engine to prevent it from freezing.[24] That he was willing to go to such length to keep his van operational under all conditions certainly means that he agreed with his tasks. Although he could have easily feigned technical problems, he confessed that "an order is an order," implying that it must be obeyed at all cost.[25]

Specialist Werner Wachholz* was also put in a position that would have allowed him to easily extricate himself from the executions. His routine duties—coordination of the massacres with the local authorities and translation of commands to the victims—obviously required his presence on site, but Wachholz* was additionally responsible for the acquisition of fur clothing and other goods for his unit. Because he always learned about a pending action in advance, he could have, at least at times, used his additional duties as an excuse to be absent.[26]

Whereas the officers responsible for vehicles usually had to be with their trucks, and interpreters often had to translate commands at the execution site, the officers working in other technical and administrative positions had no reason to be present at the executions per se. It was understood in every military unit, however, that all officers, even personnel managers, accountants, and electronics specialists, had to be ready to lead the men in every task their superior assigned them. For this reason, the remaining officers included here were all selected to be in charge of at least one execution. P., for example, was the accounting officer for the Office of the Commander of the Security Police and the Security Service in Kiev. Nevertheless, as it was the practice under SS Lieutenant Colonel Ehrlinger, all officers of the unit had to participate in the massacres. To prepare P. for future tasks, Ehrlinger had him observe the proper conduct of an execution in April 1943. Then in August of the same year, Ehrlinger appointed him to supervise the next action.

Although it appears rather astonishing, the court in Karlsruhe established the following sequence of events. P. was unable to determine from the daily schedule that his execution duty would be a gassing. As he had learned from his previous experience, he went to the jail in order to, as he thought, accompany the victims to the execution site. When he arrived, the last victims had just been loaded into a large vehicle, which he did not recognize as a gas van. P. noticed, however, that among the persons loaded onto the truck were women and young children. He then climbed into his own car, which he had parked outside the jail, and waited for the driver of the van to pull out of the courtyard. The driver started the engine and let it run. After ten or fifteen minutes, P. went back to ask why the truck was not following him. The driver told him that he had gassed the victims. Only then, according to court records, did P. realize what had happened.[27]

From this episode, it would appear as if P. was an officer who kept himself so focused on his primary task, the financial matters of the unit, that he failed to see what was occurring around him. Yet, it also would seem that the culpability remains; he did know of the mass executions and had been preparing to direct one himself at that time.

Similar notions apply to the following two perpetrators. Helmut Reil* had not learned about the tasks of the Einsatzgruppen before he came to Riga to replace an older civil servant who had resigned. He was therefore completely surprised when Stahlecker told him that every SS leader had to shoot at least once. With no prior military training, Reil* was understandably nervous and had problems handling his rifle the first time he served as a shooter.[28]

Focusing on administrative duties initially also must have prevented Wilhelm Kaul from noticing that his unit was participating in large-scale murder. Hardly any other plausible explanation exists for his behavior on July 28, 1942, the final elimination of the ghetto in Minsk. Obviously such a major event needed detailed planning, and Kaul either chose not to know or he was not informed. He had come to the Minsk Office of the Commander of the Security Police and the Security Service in July 1942 and had taken over its department of personnel and economic affairs.

On the morning of the 28th, Kaul arrived late in his office and noticed that the building was empty and all his men were gone. As the defendant's own statement and other witnesses established, Kaul asked the only remaining officer, SS 1st Lt. Georg Heuser, what was going on. Heuser informed him that a massive action had begun and ordered him to participate. Kaul complied and immediately drove to the execution site in Trostinez, where he reported to the officer in charge, SS Capt. Artur Wilke. Wilke instructed Kaul to take his place in the row of shooters. At this time, hundreds of Jews had already been killed. Kaul pulled his pistol and shot at three victims. Because one victim had already been hit by another shooter, Wilke harshly reminded Kaul not to shoot at the same target twice. Thereafter, Kaul purposely fired his remaining bullets into the wall of the grave, pretending that he was finishing off still-living victims. He then used an appropriate moment to step away from the shooters and return to his office. During the excitement and confusion at the execution site, no one noticed his disappearance, and Kaul was never cited or punished for leaving the scene. Yet, despite his initial hesitancy, his apparent inability to shoot innocent victims, and the fact that he left the scene of his first mass murder, Kaul volunteered to supervise the guards during a gassing only one month later.[29]

From the beginning of Kaul's duties at the Minsk office, Heuser enjoyed tormenting him; he despised Kaul as a non-SS member and mere bureaucrat. According to other members of the unit, Kaul was known to be weak and "not soldierly," and he often had been the subject of ridicule. When Kaul had heard of his required involvement in the executions, he immediately used his connections to the Reich Security Main Office to attempt to transfer back to Germany; but his request was denied. Citing problems with his administrative tasks, Kaul then asked the commanding officer, Strauch, to at least exempt him from the killings, with the same negative result. Kaul remained in Minsk until April 1943, a period during which several large-scale executions took place.[30]

Considering the treatment Kaul received from his fellow officers and his behavior during the action of July 28, one can draw some general conclusions about the status of the specialists in their units. The operational officers often looked down on the specialists and dismissed them as useless bureaucratic "pencil pushers." It is, therefore, conceivable that Kaul was purposely kept in the dark about the July massacre. That Kaul did not count as a full officer can also be deduced from the fact that he accepted orders from another officer with the same rank, Heuser. And Wilke, the officer in charge of the Trostinez execution, probably silently excused Kaul's departure from the site because Wilke had observed that Kaul was an ineffective shooter.

Whatever reasons his superiors might have had for not punishing Kaul, he realized, as had Merbach and the other specialists, that leaving an execution resulted in no adverse consequences. And, yet, if killing innocent human beings was not their main duty, was easy to avoid, and held no consequences for failing to participate, why did they continue to kill?

The Aftermath

The postwar careers of the former specialists have an identical pattern. All but Merbach, Reil*, and Gevatter* were interned by the Allied occupation authorities and sentenced for belonging to an organization deemed criminal by the International Military Tribunal at Nuremberg. Nonetheless, the Allies never learned that these specialists—with the exception of Kretschmer—had served the Einsatzgruppen. After they were released, all but Oswald (who remained unemployed), worked briefly in unskilled occupations until they returned to jobs according to their education and training, usually in or close to their former hometown.

Many former Einsatzgruppen specialists, a percentage higher than from any other category, found employment in the bureaucratic apparatus of the new German republic. Kl. returned to the police forces and soon became a department head in the state Criminal Police office in Saarbrücken. Kaul and K. both returned to their prewar professions, the former as a customs official, and the latter as an accountant in the government-operated older citizens insurance organization. Schulz and Gevatter* were the only officers to find permanent employment outside their field of training; Schulz became a tax secretary, and a bank hired Gevatter*. Because accountants, personnel clerks, and other administrators are needed in every organization and under every political system, it seems only logical that these men re-entered their bureaucratic professions rather quickly. It is a dilemma of the West German state, however, that it allowed so many former Nazi criminals access into its corps of civil servants. Forty-four Einsatzgruppen members had become civil servants before they were indicted.

The career development of the former specialists had been uniform and rather predictable, but their attitude toward participation in the massacres and cooperation in the documenting of the circumstances remained distinctly different—as did their punishment, which often depended on the degree of cooperation, recognition of wrongdoing, and repentance. In general, one group, including Wiechert, Reil*, Gevatter*, Kl., P., and Kaul, openly cooperated with the German authorities—in Wiechert's case, even to the most intricate details.

With Wiechert, one might question, however, whether his cooperation was from a sense of remorse and honesty or whether he calculated that there had been already too many witnesses. Possibly his confession even included a degree of pride in his deeds. That is certainly the case with Bruno Schulz, who was proud to have been involved in the extermination of the Jews, and the other officers who, as the court in Tübingen stated, "were not too concerned about the full recognition of their guilt."[31] And Merbach always attempted to diminish his role in the executions or deny participation in the organization of the transports from the ghetto to the execution site. Of course, he caught himself in his web of lies because it is impossible that the officer in charge of the vehicle pool of a unit and proven transportation expert had played no part in the unit's major massacres. In the end, the court's sentences for these men also somewhat corresponded to their defensive attitude in court. Of the former group, Gevatter*, Reil*, Kl., and P. were acquitted; Wiechert and Kaul both received four years and six months in prison. The less cooperative officers were sentenced to prison terms between 3½ and 7 years.[32]

The Letters of Karl Kretschmer

Karl Kretschmer's alleged activities have not been discussed with those of the other specialists because the court in Darmstadt could not prove his involvement beyond reasonable doubt and thus had no choice than to acquit.[33] The letters that he wrote to his wife and family during his time with Sonderkommando 4a, however, reveal most motives of the specialist officers.

September 27, 1942

As I said before, I'm in a bad mood. At first, I still have to overcome my inner scruples. The sight of the bodies (including women and children) is not encouraging. My comrades are literally fighting for the survival of our people. They are only doing what the enemy would do to us. I believe that you understand. Since from our point of view this war is a Jewish war, the Jews now have to bear its consequences. There are no more Jews as far the German soldier stands in Russia. You can imagine that it took sometime before I got used to it.

October 15, 1942

I already told you about the shootings, that I could not fail in this respect either. They have told me more or less that they finally have a leading administrative officer who is a reliable fellow. My predecessor had been a coward. That is how people are judged here. Be assured, however, that you can rely on your father. He always thinks about you and doesn't shoot more than necessary.

October 19, 1942

If we spend the winter at this place, as an administrator I will only leave quarters for larger-scale executions and otherwise stay home. If not for the scruples I still have about our activities in this country, service would be really beautiful. Since I already wrote you that I positively supported the last action and its results, "scruples" is not really the correct expression. It rather is the weakness not to be able to see dead people. The best way to overcome it is to participate more often. Thus it becomes a habit.[34]

That Kretschmer did not destroy these letters, although he was under close scrutiny from Russian and German authorities and had even spent time in an East German jail, suggests that he was not afraid of discovery and never expected to be held responsible.[35] If he was not afraid of punishment after the war, however, he was not afraid of his superiors during the war either. He clearly states that it was his own decision to participate in the massacres.

The evidence in the cases of the other officers shows that they, too, had a choice during almost every action. Moreover, the specialists were known as otherwise well-trained officers who were not afraid to stand up to their superiors. As the witness Harm Willms Harms testified, "Wiechert once reported Böhme for using a duty car for private purposes."[36] We can also recall that Fahnemann* frankly admitted he had disregarded the intimidating and ice-cold

Heydrich's orders without hesitation and later refused to shoot the professor and his daughter.

Kretschmer's letters prove that killing human beings was not an easy task. He had to overcome considerable difficulties, and that his family must have supported his behavior certainly helped him to accept his horrible duty. It is clear that even officers long identified with Nazi organizations and ideology, such as the specialists, had to be habituated into their tasks. Kretschmer mentions it repeatedly and grapples with finding a proper explanation for his "weakness." Others such as Wiechert, Schulz, and P. were certainly also gradually prepared for these "greater" tasks.

Yet, if the specialists were correct civil servants, not blind followers of orders, and had to be gradually acclimated into killing Jews, why did they not speak up during their initiation to mass murder? Perhaps an explanation is that the circumstances simply were "right." This conclusion is consistent with psychologist Stanley Milgram's theory that all humans harbor aggressive instincts and they only wait for the appropriate circumstances to express them.[37] Exploration of almost every case proves that the situation and human weakness help to explain how the specialists could participate in the executions. For the first time, most were no longer in charge of inanimate objects such as trucks, ammunition, or files, but human beings. Had they not been sent to the Soviet Union, the infamous opportunity might not have occurred for most of these men.

Nonetheless, reflecting on the Einsatzgruppen officers, it is also clear that anti-Semitism must have been another important motivation for these men; otherwise, Kretschmer would not have classified his initial inability to shoot Jews as a weakness. More importantly, his letter of September 27, 1942, indicates that he had internalized the propaganda as it was expressed in Hitler's notorious prophecy, which in effect blamed the "international Jewish financiers" and "bolshevization" for "plunging the nations once more into a world war."[38]

Hitler, Goebbels, Himmler, and other senior Nazi leaders had used similar rhetoric regarding the struggle against a perceived Jewish-Bolshevik world conspiracy long before the Second World War. With the invasion of the Soviet Union, however, Nazi and military propaganda increasingly began to equate these political and racial enemies, the Bolsheviks and the Jews. A passage from an information bulletin (Mitteilungen für die Truppe) for the German army reads:

> We would be insulting the animals if we were to describe these men [the commissars], who are mostly Jewish, as beasts. They are the embodiment of the Satanic and insane hatred against the whole of noble humanity. The shape of these commissars reveals to us the rebellion of the *Untermenschen* [subhuman

individuals] against noble blood. The masses, whom they have sent to their deaths by making use of all means at their disposal such as ice-cold terror and insane incitement, would have brought an end to all meaningful life, had this eruption not been dammed at the last moment.[39]

It was expected of the soldiers to identify with these Nazi stereotypes, and that became even easier as the war went on because the increasingly brutal reality of the conflict actually began to resemble the horrible images perpetuated in Nazi propaganda.

Both Omer Bartov and Christian Streit have convincingly argued that indeed a majority of the German soldiers of all ranks truly believed in the equation of Jews and Bolsheviks, and many willingly participated in the destruction process. These soldiers and their superiors, however, all too conveniently forgot that it was the German behavior that had created the grim reality in the first place.[40]

If the soldiers at the eastern front accepted such dehumanization of the enemy, one must assume that the Einsatzgruppen members—who had gone through a much more intensive ideological training and had already participated in previous measures against political and racial enemies—also accepted Hitler's equation of Jews and Bolsheviks. One of the best indications of how far Nazi propaganda had penetrated into the minds of the specialists, however, is Karl Kretschmer's first letter. Despite the disappointment of failing his ideological training and his detachment to the Einsatzgruppen as a form of punishment, Kretschmer still believed that the war with the Soviet Union was a life and death struggle, and killing "the enemy"—the Jews—was as important as fighting against soldiers at the front.

In addition, SS officials and Einsatzgruppen commanders often tried to justify the killing of civilians with the alleged crimes World Jewry had committed by bombing the German cities, as the commander of Reserve Police Battalion 101 had briefed his men before their first massacre.[41] Moreover, one has to remember that Nazi propaganda and the attitude of the specialists coincided on another level. Most specialists had joined the Nazi movement because of its tough anti-Communist stand, and Nazi orators likened the war with the Soviet Union to a crusade against Bolshevism.

Apart from Kretschmer's letters, the sources are—perhaps understandably—silent on the issue of anti-Semitism.[42] Only Bruno Schulz was known to be an anti-Semite who embraced the measures of the regime from the beginning. Other specialists such as Hans Wiechert successfully pursued a career in the Gestapo, yet he maintained a friendship with a Jew, helping to save his friend's life. However, Wiechert's actions appear ambiguous and should be analyzed further. Just as other SS leaders knew their "one good Jew," which Himmler had noted in his 1943 Poznan speech, perhaps Hans Wiechert also thought of Le. as his good Jew.[43] This would explain how he could risk his career for his Jewish friend, yet mercilessly torture and brutally kill the Jews in Polangen and Wilkowischken.

But anti-Semitism alone is definitely an overly simplistic and insufficient explanation for Wiechert's and the other specialists' behavior. Wiechert also acted so savagely and brutally because he had just witnessed how Böhme had sharply scolded Carsten. When Böhme instructed Wiechert to dig another mass grave, Wiechert felt the eyes of his commanding officer on him. He thus wielded his club not only to torture the Jews, but also to showcase his dedication, reliability, and efficiency. Moreover, during the execution with the destructively explosive ammunition, Wiechert anticipated what Hersmann expected. Hersmann, on the other hand, concluded that allowing Wiechert to experiment with the Soviet matériel would appeal to Wiechert as a weapons specialist. And, thus, the circumstance of superior orders and pride in professional expertise corresponded and motivated Wiechert to plan the execution as cruelly as possible.

The need to fulfill the expectations of their comrades and to prove to themselves that they were capable of participating in the main duties of the unit was a very powerful incentive for the other specialists, with the exception of Thomas Gevatter*. Gevatter* did not care too much what "the pigs," as he referred to his superiors in private, or his peers thought of him.[44] For Kretschmer and the others, however, participating in the massacres meant that they had the chance to show the rest of the unit that they were indeed reliable fellows rather than cowards.

Wilhelm Kaul's case, in particular, proves the latter point. Kaul was even more an outsider because he was not an SS member. He was known as a weakling, and he acted like one. In a country proud of its Prussian military and punctual tradition, a "real" officer would have never been late for duty, especially on the day of a major action. Of course, a "real" officer would also always know the whereabouts of his men. Furthermore, a "real" officer would have been informed about the actions of his unit at all times and would have had no reason to ask another officer. Obviously, a "real" officer then would not have consented to the order of an officer with the same rank. And once at the execution site, a "real" officer would not have been nervous and have shot so badly that the supervising officer (Wilke) would be happy that Kaul had left surreptitiously, sparing the officer the indignity of dismissing a fellow officer in front of the enlisted men. Therefore, we can assume that Kaul was motivated to participate in the gassing a month later to make up for his previous failures.

To some specialists such as Kaul, Reil*, and P., the compartmentalization of tasks, an excuse that after the war was used by Adolf Eichmann and many other so-called "desk perpetrators," was another important exculpatory factor. In order to rationalize their behavior, these men claimed to have fulfilled only their limited duties. Yet, in reality, even their limited actions had far-reaching repercussions. Kaul, Reil*, and in particular P. had apparently focused so intently on their special functions that they did not notice that their units were participating in genocide. Kaul seemingly did not know about the major ghetto clearing action at Minsk in July 1942; Reil* apparently was unaware that his victims had never been legally condemned; and P. amazingly did not even realize that his unit was using a gas van. In fact, the court in Karlsruhe acquitted P. precisely because the driver of the gas van performed his job independently and did not require P.'s supervision.[45]

The specialists' feeling of being a small cog in a machine and their concentration on subsidiary tasks, however, also has a social-psychological explanation. As Stanley Milgram's research has demonstrated, the division of labor and the abandonment of individual control for the benefit of the whole are acquired behaviors in the functioning of human society. Milgram saw an even higher level of obedience in his control experiments that included the performance of subsidiary tasks.[46] Similarly, most Einsatzgruppen specialists complied all too willingly and, unfortunately, often went far beyond what was expected.

In addition to documenting the motivation of the specialists, their trials and judgments have shown that of all Einsatzgruppen officers, the specialists most resemble Christopher Browning's sample group of "ordinary men." Most specialists came from the lower middle class, were generally not highly educated, were old enough to have formed their world views before the Nazis became prominent, and did not volunteer for service in the killing fields. Yet Browning's group and the specialists are different in one important aspect. Apart from Thomas Gevatter*, who remained a technical sergeant throughout the war, the specialists had an extraordinary ambition and willingness to render their services to every master. In contrast to Browning's policemen who had signed up for the Reserve to dodge front-line duty in the Wehrmacht, the specialists deliberately joined Nazi organizations to further their careers. One even was an Old Fighter, whose affiliation with the Nazi Party went back to the party's origins. The other specialists became Nazis primarily because of the opportunities that the expanding Nazi organizations offered, the anti-Communist rhetoric, and economic pressure. Hitler's early successes then seemed to validate their decision to join the growing Nazi cause. And thereafter, the specialists—apart from Kretschmer—never considered leaving the Security Police.

In the end, the most important explanations to account for the bearing of the specialists in the Einsatzgruppen were that they wanted to be counted as full officers; they were put in charge of human beings for the first time, which often explains their extraordinary zeal; they accepted the image of the Jew as a diabolical and dangerous enemy; and they saw the executions as a welcome chance to get noticed and further their career. The cases of the specialists thus once more have demonstrated that Goldhagen's mono-causal argument of anti-Semitism is insufficient to explain the far more complex motivations of the perpetrators.

5. THE ACQUITTED

He was by far the most
empathetic, decent, and only
superior in Sonderkommando 1b
who everyone trusted.

A member of Sonderkommando 1b,
on SS First Lieutenant H.

ON JULY 12, 1963, the District Court in Freiburg found three former Order Police officers not guilty on the charges of murder. The judges justified their decision by arguing that the accused would have lost their own lives if they had not followed their orders to kill Jews in the Soviet Union. The opinion requires explanation because it contradicts the evidence previously presented in this study.

Analyzing the behavior of the acquitted Einsatzgruppen men and their comrades reveals that they generally had more redeeming qualities than any other group of officers. They did not agree with their orders to clear the Soviet Union of Jews, and they remained relatively accountable while participating in astonishing evil. They objected when they were forced to this participation and attempted—some more persistently and successfully than others—to avoid involvement at all. If they had no other choice than to take part directly in the massacres, they tried to ameliorate the situation and have the least possible impact on the killings. Finally, these officers used every opportunity to be transferred to other units and consequently served only a relatively short term in the Einsatzgruppen. Once arrested and tried after the war, they were furthermore cooperative and willing to clear up the circumstances.

From this general description one would assume that the officers in this group were the opposite of the confirmed killers. One would also predict that the attitude and the motivation of these men would contradict Daniel Goldhagen's anti-Semitism thesis more strongly than the other categories. As the evidence shows, however, these assumptions are not always correct.

Education and Career before 1941

In keeping with their middle-class background, the majority of the officers in this group of the acquitted had attended the Gymnasium. SS Maj. Oswald Schaefer, SS Captain Ra., SS First Lieutenant H., SS Second Lieutenant R., and SS Private First Class Conrad Stuhr* subsequently studied or planned to study theology, philosophy, or law.[1] The others attended the required eight to ten years of schooling, then went on to apprenticeships, unskilled jobs, or immediately joined the police force.

As had been the case for most specialist officers, the bleak economic conditions at different times during the Weimar Republic and the early years of the Third Reich also forced some of these officers to abandon their initial career plans and find work in professions that offered a steady income. For six of them, this meant becoming policemen, though sometimes they had traveled a rather lengthy journey through several other jobs before they reached that position. SS Staff Sergeant Si., for example, whose "intelligence, education and perceptive faculty were," according to the court in Munich, "inferior to the other defendants," was, ironically, the son of two teachers.[2] He had to quit his Gymnasium because of bad grades and initially worked as a salesman. Si. could not maintain this position during the economic crisis of 1929, however, and thus decided to learn the printing trade, in which he continued to work until 1938. He then briefly became a fireman and finally entered the Order Police in 1940. Si. was the only Einsatzgruppen officer who received his normal police training at the Border Police School in Pretzsch, the later assembly point of the Einsatzgruppen.

First Lieutenant U. similarly did not prosper as a salesman in the wake of the 1929 stock market crash. He joined the police in 1930 and became a county sheriff in 1936, working in the personnel department. However, after successful graduation from the police academy in 1937, he was made an instructor at a school for Reserve policemen, a position that would later help him leave service in the Soviet Union. In January 1941, he was appointed adjutant to the commanding officer of a police training battalion in Vienna. After the June attack on the Soviet Union, his unit was renamed Police Battalion 322 and put under the command of Higher SS and Police Leader-Center, von dem Bach-Zelewski. The unit was also designated to Einsatzgruppe B, and in particular supported Einsatzkommando 8.

In a remarkable parallel to Hitler's early life, another officer, SS Sgt. Kuno

Grasdübel* was born in the Austrian town of Braunau, where he learned the trade of a mechanic. Grasdübel* later moved to Munich to take on a position with the Bavarian State Police in 1932. To improve his career chances, he joined the SS at the same time. From 1936 to 1938, the last two years of his term of enlistment, Grasdübel* served with an SS engineer unit in Dresden. After his discharge, he requested a return to the Order Police. As Grasdübel* stated in his interrogation, his goal was to enforce the law, not to carry out ideological work. Nevertheless, he was placed with a branch of the Security Police, and in the spring of 1941 he was made a weapons instructor at the Border Police school in Pretzsch. Grasdübel* could have stayed in that position had he not openly criticized the scandalous conduct between some senior SS officers and women from the Arbeitsdienst, the local labor service. His outspoken attitude caused him to be assigned to Einsatzkommando 8.

Another future Einsatzgruppen officer, R., decided that the still weak economic situation did not offer him good prospects if he took over his father's sales business. Therefore, R. applied for police service and began work with the Düsseldorf State Police in December 1935. Four years later, he graduated from the Security Police Leadership School, and afterward briefly served in the Gestapo offices in Düsseldorf and Koblenz. R. excelled in mental and physical tasks, and as a result of his outstanding evaluations, he received a special assignment as bodyguard to Reichsmarschall Hermann Göring in 1940. Although R. lacked the required financial means for university studies, his evaluation as an "extraordinarily gifted member of the police forces" earned him the right to study law. However, in 1941, he was directly drafted from the classroom to Einsatzkommando 8.

Another policeman, H., also could not fulfill his career plans because of the bleak economy. Constantly in need of finances for his theology and philosophy studies at the University of Tübingen, he quit and entered the State Police in 1936. With the rank of first lieutenant, he then served in State Police offices in Cologne, Halle, and Erfurt before he was called to Sonderkommando 1b.

Another of the acquitted, SS Staff Sergeant S., on the other hand, lost his job with the government-owned railroad, the Reichsbahn, in 1921 during the politically and economically unstable beginnings of the new fledgling Weimar Republic when the legislature (Reichstag) had passed a bill to reduce personnel in the civil service. Subsequently, S. worked in unskilled positions until April 1, 1925, when he enrolled for twelve years of service in the Order Police. Like SS 2d Lt. Bruno Schulz, S. resigned with an Eingliederungsschein, the document that guaranteed his future employment in local, state, or federal government agencies, and he went on to become a detective. He attended the Security Police

Leadership School in Charlottenburg and was subsequently transferred to the
Gestapo outpost in Allenstein, a branch of the State Police office in Tilsit. Thus,
in June 1941 S. also became an involuntary member of Einsatzkommando Tilsit,
simply because he was a member of the local Security Police organizations in
the city.

Contrary to the officers who chose a police and SS career because it promised a steady income, SS First Lieutenant Ku. and Schaefer became followers of
the Nazi movement out of conviction and career considerations, respectively.
Ku. had joined the Hitler Youth when he was sixteen years old and had worked
for its Reich Youth Leadership before Hitler came to power. In 1939 he transferred to the Criminal Police and became an SS member. Like R., Ku. was considered especially gifted and was offered the opportunity to study law, which he
began in 1940. His studies were cut short, however, when he received notice to
report to Sonderkommando 1b in May 1941.

Schaefer's career was equally dedicated and straightforward. He graduated
from law school in 1931, joined the Storm Troopers and the Nazi Party in 1933,
and began service with the Berlin Gestapo in 1935. In 1936 he switched from the
emasculated Storm Troopers to the expanding SS. Quickly moving up the career
ladder, Schaefer was soon made leader of the State Police outpost in Weser-
münde. In 1940 he took over the new State Police office in Reichenberg (Reich-
sprotectorate Bohemia/Moravia). After the attack on the Soviet Union, he had to
serve a term in the Einsatzgruppen, as did many other Gestapo officers stationed
in the Reich and previously occupied countries.

One can surmise from their low ranks that SS Private First Class Stuhr* and
SS Pvt. Olaf Förster* never intended to make a career in the SS. Nevertheless, both had joined the Nazi Party in 1933. In addition, Stuhr* became an SS
member in 1934, as he claimed in court, "Only to protect his reputation as a businessman."[3] It appears more likely, however, that his SS connection helped him
to circumvent being drafted into the Wehrmacht. Stuhr*'s membership in the SS
enabled him to stay at home and care for his business. Despite his Nazi Party
background, he remained pragmatic and continued to work with Jewish clients.

Like Stuhr*, Olaf Förster* was protected from the military draft because he
was the director of a lightbulb factory and was considered essential for the economy. After the beginning of the war, however, both received basic military training with the Waffen SS and were assigned to Einsatzkommando 5 in May 1941.

The career paths of the officers in this category of the acquitted eventually
led to the Einsatzgruppen, despite their great difference in age. The oldest, S.,
was almost twice the age of He. when they were drafted to the Einsatzgruppen.
In fact, He., who was born in 1920, is the youngest within the sample group of

Einsatzgruppen officers indicted in West Germany. Full of idealism and youthful enthusiasm, it is furthermore no coincidence that the three youngest, He., Ra., and R., all volunteered for a year in the labor service immediately after they graduated from the Gymnasium. Ra. and R. then enlisted for another voluntary year in the Wehrmacht. Apparently Nazi propaganda had influenced these young men so much that they were eager to make their contribution for the rebuilding of their country.

The steady stream of propaganda did have a particularly strong impact on Ra., who joined the Nazi Party and the SS when he was still in school and only seventeen years old. During his labor and military service he abandoned his plans to study theology and embarked on a full-time police and SS career. He first visited an elite SS Officer Candidate School (Junkerschule), then the police academy. His training was briefly interrupted by his detachment to the predecessors of the Einsatzgruppen in Czechoslovakia, where he was exposed to the treatment of so-called political enemies for the first time. Apparently undisturbed by this initiation, he continued his career until he was assigned to the police training battalion in Vienna. As commanding officer of the 3rd Company in the renamed Police Battalion 322, Ra. spent eleven months in the Soviet Union.

Ra.'s career before 1941 graphically demonstrates how deeply Nazi influence had already penetrated into the German police apparatus by 1937. His superiors found it more important for Ra. to receive his ideological indoctrination at a Nazi Officer Candidate School before his police-specific training at a state institution, the police academy. Ra.'s police schooling therefore also exemplifies the merging of party and state offices in all branches and levels of government. Of course, this observation confirms an important functionalist argument.

Although only four officers in this group were full-fledged SS members, the others, with the exceptions of U. and S., at least also joined different Nazi Party organizations. Ra. and He. were definitely Nazi enthusiasts. The others, however, had more practical reasons to become Nazi converts. R., for example, correctly expected better chances for acceptance in the police if he simultaneously applied for SS and party membership. Again others, such as H. and Si., had been party members since 1933, but advanced in or joined the SS only after the 1940 German victory over France, when the homeland's general wave of adoration and belief in the Führer of the Greater German Reich reached new and unprecedented heights. Despite their early affiliation with Nazi institutions, however, the officers in this group—apart from Ra., who had participated in the Sudeten campaign, and Schaefer, who headed a State Police outpost in the former Czechoslovakia—did not have the positions and responsibilities that might have enabled them to recognize the true intentions of the Nazi regime. Moreover, they had entered Soviet territory still believing that they were to police the newly acquired lands; they knew nothing yet about the fate of the Jews.[4]

Activities and Behavior in the Einsatzgruppen

Being acquitted in a trial, especially when it was held long after the events, does not necessarily signify innocence. The judges in the pertinent courts clearly exonerated only H. and U. from the accusation of having conducted or supported an execution. For all others, the judges deemed the evidence inconclusive and reverted to the principle of "when in doubt, then in favor of the accused." Despite the remaining uncertainties, and contrary to most other defendants in the Einsatzgruppen Trials, however, most officers in this category of the acquitted did preserve a basic level of human decency and took the measures they deemed necessary—albeit often erroneously—to avoid fulfilling the order to kill Jews.

H. stands out from this already exceptional group of officers, and his case deserves special consideration. As a member of Sonderkommando 1b, the court in Karlsruhe indicted H. for his participation in the massacres in the Lithuanian town of Dünaburg.[5] Yet in the end, several reliable witnesses testified that H. was not involved in these activities, including the policeman Zi., who had known H. as a caring superior since their time together at the State Police office in Erfurt. When the execution operations against the Jews began, H. had been in charge of the unit's advance command, which had already departed. However, H. would not be as fortunate for the next operation. His commanding officer, SS Lieutenant Colonel Ehrlinger, insisted that all officers had to participate in the executions. Ehrlinger personally ordered H. to join the next massacre, in Rositten, but H. faked an acute sickness, which Ehrlinger grudgingly accepted. Nevertheless, H. knew that in the long run he could not continue to avoid the despicable and criminal activities of his unit. Therefore, in November of 1941, following a leave in Germany, he did not return to his Sonderkommando, but went to his former unit in Erfurt, where he served during the remainder of the war. After the war, H. did not wait until he was arrested, but rather, when he heard of the trial against his former commanding officer, he volunteered his knowledge to the Central Office, to clear up the crimes of Sonderkommando 1b, even though he thereby incriminated himself.

H., the former theology and philosophy student, apparently did not compromise his integrity before, during, or after his time in the Einsatzgruppen, and thus it is not surprising that the witnesses in unison praised him, one naming him as the only decent superior in Sonderkommando 1b. And it is remarkable that he was allowed to extricate himself from the executions and later the killing fields without consequences, especially under the watchful eyes of the zealous Dr. Erich Ehrlinger. Ehrlinger, indeed, had initiated an investigation into H.'s sudden illness during the Rositten massacre, but the proceedings did not conclude before the war was over. Nor did the SS seem to care much about H.'s desertion, inasmuch as he was promoted to captain shortly after his return to Germany on April 1, 1942.[6] H's case thus again confirms that no one was ever severely punished for refusing to kill Jews.

Unlike H., however, the remaining officers in this group of the acquitted all attended at least one execution, though this usually happened under direct orders and often considerable duress. Ku. was perhaps lucky enough to be hit in the knee by an errant bullet when he observed his first massacre. Thereby unfit for front duty, he served the rest of the war in the Reich Security Main Office and the Hitler Youth leadership.[7] The others were less fortunate, as for example Filbert's successor in charge of Einsatzkommando 9, SS Major Schaefer. As a commanding officer, it was hardly possible to remain uninvolved in the task of the unit. Yet Schaefer claimed that he busied himself with the inspection of POW camps and administrative tasks whenever an execution was scheduled. Ultimately, the court in Berlin could not collect enough evidence to disprove him. Yet in their decision to acquit, the judges also considered that Schaefer's continuing efforts to be relieved of his post succeeded. On December 12, 1941, he received orders to report to the State Police in Munich. A month later, when his replacement Wiebens arrived, Schaefer left the killing fields for good.[8] Obviously that does not necessarily mean that Schaefer disagreed with the extermination program, but he did use his influence to avoid direct participation.

S., on the other hand, did not have the connections Schaefer had. S.'s behavior, however, illustrates how many other subaltern Einsatzgruppen members reacted to their tasks. In court, S. claimed that he never realized that his actions contributed to the destruction of "potential enemies." In S.'s case, the commanding officer of the Tilsit State Police, Böhme, had assigned him and three other officers to secure a former Russian convalescent home for the SS. When the detachment under the leadership of SS Capt. Wolfgang Ilges arrived at the home, a Waffen SS unit had already occupied it.[9] The Waffen SS had arrested the home's staff and guests, altogether about seventy persons of whom fifteen to thirty were Jews. Ilges had his troops interrogate the non-Jews. S. questioned approximately twenty persons and reported to Ilges, concluding that these individuals had belonged to the staff of the convalescent home for many years. To his surprise, the Waffen SS began shooting all Jews and fifteen others, though none of the individuals he had interrogated.

The practice of killing Jews without interrogation or examination was indicative of their lowest position within the Nazi racial hierarchy. As in the Nazi Euthanasia Program, simply being Jewish was sufficient for condemnation to death without further consideration. S. went to the execution only because Ilges had ordered it; he had no special function and was, as the court in Bielefeld found, "Nothing but an innocent bystander." In addition, at the time, S. did not know of the general order to exterminate the Jews.[10] Yet, reason tells us that as a trained law enforcement officer, he should have considered it unusual and questionable that the Jews were singled out and summarily shot.

Although S.'s orders permitted him to remain a bystander, R., Si., and Kuno Grasdübel* of Einsatzkommando 8 were not as fortunate. Against their resistance, and despite some efforts to evade murdering innocent human beings, they became personally involved in the massacres. As the court in Munich established, shortly before the first execution of Einsatzkommando 8, the commanding officer, Dr. Otto Bradfisch, gathered his officers and disclosed that they had orders to liquidate all Jews, racially inferior elements, and Communist functionaries. He had added that this was an explicit Hitler order and that he would initiate special SS and police judiciary proceedings if someone did not comply. According to the Einsatzgruppen Operational Situation Report, Ereignismeldung No. 21, the Einsatzkommando then conducted several executions in Bialystok.[11]

At first R. managed to stay away from the action, but like all confirmed killers, Bradfisch did not tolerate any form of non-compliance. When he noticed that R. had tried to avoid participation, he instructed his deputy to keep track of R. during the next scheduled execution. In the morning of that day, the deputy therefore accompanied R. from his quarters to the execution site and forced him to remain until it was over. A week later, R. again tried to stay away from an execution in Baranowicze.[12] Bradfisch, however, remained adamant and appointed R. as leader of the execution squad. R. served in that function until Bradfisch finally left the scene.[13]

From Baranowicze, Einsatzkommando 8 pushed farther east and reached Minsk in late July 1941. Operational Situation Report No. 36 states, "Liquidations on a daily basis," yet this time R. did not participate.[14] He was present, however, following one of these actions when Himmler spoke to the assembled members of the unit and the men of Police Battalion 322, who had assisted in the killing. It was there, at Minsk, where Bradfisch had questioned Himmler regarding who ultimately would bear the responsibility for the extermination of the Jews. And it was there that Himmler had emphasized that Hitler had taken on this historical task, once and forever, and thus it followed that the Führer automatically assumed responsibility.[15] With similar speeches to other Einsatzgruppen, Himmler hoped to strengthen the sense of purpose and morale of the killing units, but the desired results remained questionable at best.

These motivational efforts definitely left only a small impression on R., who subsequently was put in charge of an independent platoon. With this appointment, he appeared to have escaped Bradfisch's watchful eye for the moment, and from then on he alone decided whether or not to fulfill his orders. According to a member of the platoon, the choice was not easy, and R. repeatedly discussed the options with his subordinates. One possibility for R.'s platoon seemed to be an increased participation in military operations, such as the fight against partisans and scattered Red Army soldiers, and a sympathetic Wehrmacht officer increasingly requested R.'s help in such actions.

Initially the strategy seemed to work, but during the advance on Bobruisk, Bradfisch inspected R.'s platoon and demanded more "Judenaktionen"—actions toward eliminating the Jews. He further declared, "I finally want to see numbers!" R. used the opportunity to reason with his superior, demanding that Bradfisch relieve his platoon of its duties because they could no longer cope with killing. But Bradfisch remained unmoved and replied harshly, "A SS leader cannot dodge a Führer order."[16] Bradfisch also declined to transmit R.'s transfer request to the Wehrmacht. Later, during the regular inspections of the platoon by Bradfisch's superior officer, Arthur Nebe, R. had the chance to directly express his scruples. Predictably, Nebe backed Bradfisch and reminded R. not to break the chain of command. Nebe then told R., "One has to overcome inner scruples (den inneren Schweinehund überkommen)." Nevertheless, Nebe also encouraged R.: "I don't mind that you burn a partisan village every now and then, as long as you don't forget to do your main job [to hunt and kill Jews].[17] This remark exemplifies the SS leadership's contempt for human life. While intended to hearten the spirit of the reluctant R., it underscored only that it did not matter too much whether the victims were Jews or other sub-human beings.

R.'s efforts to be relieved of his command proved to be rather counterproductive. His superiors rejected his pleas and pushed him into finally killing more Jews. As a consequence, R. concluded that in order to avoid being accused of openly defying superior orders, he had no choice but to engage in several small-scale executions. He successfully demonstrated to the court that defiance of orders might have had fatal results, as he had learned during his rigid training. Therefore, he was under considerable duress when he finally committed two massacres in Bobruisk and Sluzk. However, he did not shoot the entire Jewish population of these towns, as his orders had specified. To bolster his low body count of Jews, R. added to his victims the partisans his platoon had killed during a confrontation and the Red Army soldiers they had brought to a POW camp. His superiors never questioned his numbers.

Furthermore, R. made another remarkable effort to leave his terrible job. Against all training, indoctrination, and discipline, he did break the chain of command and contacted his old superior in Göring's bodyguard unit. This attempt was again futile, but in October 1941 R.'s tour of duty in the Soviet Union was finally over. Although in the end he had conducted two executions, he had remained appalled by the assignment, had continued his attempts to be relieved of his duties, and had made an effort to kill as few Jews as possible without raising suspicion. He returned to Germany and resumed his law studies.[18]

Even more restricted than R.'s options to dissent in Einsatzkommando 8 were those of Si., who already had been a shooter during the execution at Baranowicze. Si. had also listened to Himmler's speech in Minsk, but contrary to R., the speech might have had a different influence on the less intelligent Si. To Si., Himmler's presence at the execution site might have had the desired effect: to demonstrate that the highest German authorities approved of the slaughter and to signal that the measures against the Jews indeed had a legal basis.

In September and October of 1941, Si. was detached to an independent platoon, under SS Capt. Werner Schönemann,[19] which committed several massacres in Borissow. Like Bradfisch and most other senior officers, Schönemann was a Nazi zealot who pushed his men to kill Jews. Schönemann additionally would threaten hesitant subordinates with severe punishments and SS courts. On one occasion, Schönemann ordered Si. to shoot an elderly Jewish couple who could not march to the execution site. As always, Si. complied without resistance because he feared for his life and saw no other choice; it appeared to him that within his small detachment of fifteen policemen it was impossible to avoid the killing without raising suspicion. Si. therefore concluded that volunteering for guard or transport duty during future executions was the only way to evade having to pull the trigger. Si.'s dilemma was furthermore compounded by the fact that he did not possess R.'s mental flexibility, persistence, and connections. Therefore, he did not consider transferring from the Einsatzkommando, but stayed with it for more than two years. Despite his deficiencies, he did recognize that killing other human beings was wrong and took the only step he thought possible to avoid being an executioner.[20]

After the outspoken Kuno Grasdübel* had been sent to Einsatzkommando 8 for again criticizing the misconduct of senior officers in Pretzsch, and despite his reputation as a troublemaker and his low rank of sergeant, Bradfisch made him his commanding chief, reasoning that he was the only available noncommissioned officer with military training. As chief, Grasdübel* did not have to be present during the executions, but at least once Bradfisch had required him to participate. After returning from this shocking experience, Grasdübel* told his comrades, "I am so glad that it's over; can't they find somebody else for this?"[21]

Witnesses confirmed Grasdübel*'s basic human qualities; he usually had looked the other way when the local population smuggled food into the jail for their relatives, an action that was strictly prohibited and punishable by death. Moreover, upon his arrival at Einsatzkommando 8, Grasdübel* had immediately requested a transfer to the front or back home, but expectedly Bradfisch had said that was not possible. Grasdübel* remained with Einsatzkommando 8 until April 1943.

In the Einsatzkommando 8 cases of R. and Si., the court in Munich concluded that the defendants could not reasonably be expected to have acted in any other manner. According to the judges' interpretation of "necessity," as it is written in Paragraphs 34 and 35 of the German penal code, heroic disregard of imminent or apparent danger for life and limb could not be expected of the defendants.

§ 34. Necessity as justification: Whoever commits an act in order to avert an imminent and otherwise unavoidable danger to the life, limb, liberty, honor, property or other legal interest of himself or another does not act unlawfully if, taking into consideration all the conflicting interests, in particular the legal ones, and the degree of danger involved, the interest protected by him significantly outweighs the interests which he harms. This rule applies only if the act is an appropriate means to avert the danger.

§ 35. Necessity as excuse: (1) Whoever commits an unlawful act in order to avert an imminent and otherwise unavoidable danger to his life, limb, or liberty, or to that of a relative or person close to him, acts without guilt. . . .(2) If, in committing the act, the perpetrator assumes the existence of circumstances which under subparagraph (1) would excuse his conduct, he shall be punished only if he could have avoided the error. . . .[22]

Yet, both R. and Si. did not choose the easiest way out. R. did everything short of disobeying the actual orders; but Si.'s case looks more ambiguous. However, given that the court noted Si.'s low level of intelligence, his behavioral pattern shows that he *had* assumed the "existence of circumstances" that would have excused his conduct, as stipulated by Paragraph 35. In addition, the court recognized that both defendants clearly lacked the will to participate in the crimes. Therefore, they had to be acquitted.

Again, of course, in actuality no imminent danger for life and limb of the defendants existed, despite the ominous threats of Bradfisch, Schönemann, and other Einsatzgruppen leaders. As noted, historians and the district attorneys at the German Superior Courts and at the Central Office of the State Justice Administrations could not document a single instance when a member of the SS, police, Wehrmacht, or any other German organization was harshly punished for disobeying an order to kill Jews or other innocent civilians. But, again, the judges in Munich based their decision on the *assumed* existence of circumstances that would excuse their conduct, and that on its own was sufficient reason to acquit. The Munich judges' decision is consistent with the verdict of the court in Kiel. With an emphasis on *assumed,* the Kiel jury found the gas van driver, Thomas Gevatter, not guilty on the same grounds as were Si. and R.

Although these judgments appear to be a reasonable application of Paragraph 35 to the historical situation in the killing fields, the judges in Freiburg excused the participation of U., Ra., and He. in the massacres of Police Battalion 322 because an *objective* danger to their lives existed if they had disobeyed their orders, according to Paragraph 34. The judges in Düsseldorf also came to that conclusion, regarding the conduct of the defendants Stuhr* and Förster*. The Düsseldorf and Freiburg courts, however, not only stood alone among the judges in the Einsatzgruppen Trials, they also disregarded the available historical evidence. Because the arguments in both cases are similar, the following analysis of the Freiburg judgment will suffice to refute its erroneous claims.

Police Battalion 322

U., Ra., and He. belonged to Police Battalion 322, the renamed former Police Training Battalion Vienna-Kagran. U. was the adjutant to the battalion commander, Major N. from the Order Police.[23] Ra. was in charge of the Battalion 322 3rd Company; and He. was a platoon leader in its 1st Company. The battalion consisted of three companies, with 150 policemen each, a transport company with 40 policemen, and staff headquarters with approximately 30 people. Police Battalion 322 belonged to the Police Regiment Center, which was subordinated to the Higher SS and Police Leader-Center, SS Lieutenant General von dem Bach-Zelewski. The Higher SS and Police Leader outranked SS Brig. Gen. Arthur Nebe, the leader of Einsatzgruppe B, but both received their orders directly from the Reich Security Main Office and Heydrich. Von dem Bach additionally had to answer to the Main Office Order Police under Gen. Kurt Daluege. The directives concerning participation of Order Police units in the activities of the Einsatzgruppe, however, usually circumvented the latter chain of command and came down directly from the Reich Security Main Office.[24]

When Battalion 322 set out for the Soviet Union, its commander briefed the policemen on the upcoming tasks. They were to enforce law and order in the rear army area, which included safeguarding important military assets such as bridges, roads, and railroads; and they were to be involved with traffic controls and other police-specific duties. Police Battalion 322 additionally had to fight partisans and eliminate political commissars, according to the Kommissar-befehl—Hitler's Commissar Order of June 6, 1941, to kill these functionaries among the Soviet POWs.[25] It was not yet evident, however, from this order, that the killing of Jews should become the primary function of the unit.

The court in Freiburg charged U., Ra., and He. with participation in several massacres committed by their unit and Einsatzkommando 8 from July to October 1941, and after evaluating the evidence, reached the following conclusions. During the first Aktion in Bialystok on July 18, 1941, U. accompanied his commanding officer, Major N., on an inspection tour of the troops. After the two officers had visited the contingent that was rounding up the Jews of the city, the two men returned to staff headquarters. At this point, U. still believed that Battalion 322 was registering the male Jews for work assignments. However, in the evening, N. and the commander of the transport company, Captain Frömsdorf, informed U. that the Jews were not registered, but were being shot. Taken completely by surprise and visibly shaken, U. and the other officers drove to the execution site where they witnessed their policemen kill the group of Jews. As U. testified, he was "paralyzed by terror,"[26] and it took him several minutes before he left the scene and returned to the car. When N. came back to the car, he informed U. that parts of 1st Company were also participating in the shooting. N. promised U. to immediately phone the regimental commander, Lt. Col. Max Montua, and complain about this scandalous misuse of the men. U. strongly supported his commander in this thought. Nevertheless, once N. talked to their direct superior, he was not as adamant.

In general, N. was known as a decent man, but his halfhearted efforts to extricate his battalion from the massacres were bound to be futile. According to other battalion members, N. was known to be a caring and fatherly superior. In fact, his men would fondly call him Papa N. On the other hand, N. lacked the resolve to stand up to senior officers, in particular Montua. N. regularly gave in to Montua's demands and always made sure that his men had executed Montua's directives unconditionally. Moreover, the otherwise open-minded, friendly, and approachable N. did not tolerate input from his officers in that matter. This applied especially to U., his adjutant, to whom N. primarily left everyday routine and especially the implementation of unpleasant battalion orders.

In early September 1941, Battalion 322 again received the order to assist in an action against the Jews of Minsk. On the first day of that operation, parts of 1st and 3rd Companies were to surround a quarter of the city and help with the transport of the Jews to the jail. As in Bialystok, U. had to escort N. on an inspection tour. Later, U. learned that on the next day, parts of the battalion were designated as execution squads. Again U. urged his commander to protest such a terrible order, but N. told him that he had already tried and that they had to obey until their superiors decided otherwise.

On the next morning, N. asked U. and another officer from staff headquarters, the witness W., to accompany him to the execution site and supervise the men. U. replied, "Do we really always have to be present?"[27] N. disregarded the comment and forced them to go with him. The three officers looked at one of the prepared mass graves, but when the execution began, U. immediately turned away from the sight and urged N. to leave the scene as soon as possible. The officers left after only thirty minutes had passed.

In both instances, U. certainly did not have an impact on the decision-making process. Despite his continued efforts, he could not convince his superior to take a stronger stance against the orders. Obviously U.'s rank of lieutenant was insufficient to have a bearing on the events as well. And U. did not support the actions by his presence, because he had no other function than to escort a superior officer. Appalled by the criminal activities that he had been associated with against his will, U. took the first opportunity to leave the battalion in March 1942, when he accepted a position at the police academy. Considering his continuing protests and ameliorating influence on the executions, the court cleared him of all charges.[28]

The judges did not have such a clear-cut decision, however, with the other two officers. Ra. had personally taken over command when his 3rd Company had rounded up the Jews during the first action in Bialystok. The company then returned to its former post, guarding a nearby POW camp, before the execution began. Like the other officers of the battalion, at this time Ra. still believed that the Jews were only registered for work conscription.

The Minsk massacre, however, should have enlightened him. His company was then once again rounding up Jews when several other Security Service members under the leadership of his deputy, First Lieutenant Rasche, and possibly another officer, began to savagely beat the Jews. Rasche, who was known for his anti-Semitism, then volunteered to escort the Jews to the execution site. It could not be established beyond a reasonable doubt, but if Ra. actually had noticed Rasche's behavior, it would have been his duty to restrain his subordinates and prevent their participation in tasks beyond the given orders, which were to seal off the designated parts of the ghetto and round up its Jewish residents, not to torture or herd them to an execution site. Thus, if Ra. abhorred the treatment of

the Jews as much as he claimed in his interrogation, he should have tried everything in his power to keep his men as far away from the execution as possible.

On October 19, 1941, Ra.'s company finally had to serve as shooters during
an execution in Mogilev, the result of an escalating scale of involvement, as was
common for most perpetrators in the Einsatzgruppen. And as before, on the first
day of the action, the policemen helped with the arrest of the Jewish population.
The following day, Ra. transmitted the necessary orders. The execution squad
under the leadership of Rasche was to take position on the left side of the mass
grave; the other policemen either had to guard the Jews, transport them, escort
them to the grave, or later cover their bodies with dirt. Ra.'s company then conducted the execution in a disciplined and efficient fashion, and Ra. tried to
avoid—under the circumstances—unnecessary suffering. He made certain that
the victims were dead and that each group was completely covered with earth
before the next victims were brought forth. Ra. also ordered the drivers of the
trucks that delivered the new victims not to pull too close to the grave, so that
they would be spared seeing the killing of their brethren. Ra. himself later fired
two shots in order to kill still-living victims in the grave.

Nonetheless, the operation did not proceed smoothly in the area immediately to the right of Ra.'s company, where particularly gruesome scenes evolved.
According to the testimony of Ra. and others, there the drunken members of a
Hiwi unit pulled children from the trucks, tossed them high into the air, and shot
them with their submachine guns. Although the overall leadership of the execution was in the hands of Einsatzkommando 8 and Ra. was not immediately in
charge of the Hiwis, Ra. was a captain and should have stopped the inconceivably brutal behavior.

He. had also participated in the Mogilev massacre. He was in charge of the
execution squad from 1st Company, which was positioned on the far right wing
of the mass grave. Like Ra., he made certain that the victims were dead and properly covered and that the action commenced without unnecessary suffering.[29]

Ra. and He. both recognized that these executions of helpless human beings
had nothing to do with the conduct of the war. They also knew that these people
were killed solely because they were Jews, and that the Nazis had decided to to-
tally annihilate them. Given their above-average intelligence—both had graduated from the Gymnasium—they should have realized that there are boundaries
even to orders from the highest state authority. Nevertheless, relying on the testimony of a number of former battalion members, the court in Freiburg established that the officers confronted the danger of being killed themselves if they
had not obeyed their directives.

The judges reached their verdict because they believed that from the moment Ra. and He. had joined the SS, and especially since the battalion's transfer to the Soviet Union in July 1941, they had been taught unconditional obedience and the possible consequences of insubordination, including a penalty of death. These officers had internalized these principles and likewise had instructed the men in their charge. In addition, the SS and police courts responsible for Police Battalion 322 had gained the reputation for being particularly strict, always meting out the harshest penalties. Senior SS leaders consciously intimidated the men, and rumors further amplified the already existing environment of fear. Moreover, the Freiburg judges reasoned that the members of Police Battalion 322 on a daily basis had witnessed the brutal behavior and contempt for human life in Einsatzkommando 8. These policemen furthermore assumed that the Security Service was secretly controlling and constantly monitoring their behavior, as indeed had been the original *raison d'être* of the Security Service. Thus, to fake illness, as other perpetrators had done to avoid participation in the executions, did not seem a wise choice either, because the battalion's hard-line Nazi physician definitely would have exposed such behavior. He had always attended the executions, and once personally had shot a Jew. In the end, the Freiburg judges declared that Ra. and He. participated in the executions only to prevent danger to their own lives.

The court also took into consideration that both officers despised the senseless slaughter and urged their superiors to protest. Ra. had told the judge, "After this action [Mogilev], I lost my belief in everything good"; and his co-defendant, He., had declared that he had regarded the situation as repugnant.[30] It was noted that Ra. also often had reminded his battalion commander to avoid the killings by seeking more front assignments for the unit. Before Mogilev, Ra. had contemplated whether to ask N. to withdraw his company from the action, but given N.'s subservience to Montua, Ra. thought that such an attempt would be of no avail. And Ra., indeed, had voiced his concerns to General Daluege, who was inspecting the battalion, but the Order Police chief did not want to hear complaints either. The court accepted that the response had finally convinced Ra. that his seniors could not be moved from their mission, and his only choice was to achieve a transfer to a military command.

He. also had complained to his commanding officer, Captain Jörke, as did the other platoon leaders of his company. Yet, like N., Jörke was an officer who demanded the exact fulfillment of all orders and tolerated no criticism from the junior ranks. Jörke was also the officer responsible for legal matters of the battalion (Gerichtsoffizier) who rigorously enforced the duty to obey orders but failed to teach the limits of obedience. Thus, the Freiburg judges believed that He. and Ra. were never, or not sufficiently, instructed about the limits of obedience throughout their career.[31] These limitations are set forth in Paragraph 47 of the military penal code (Militärstrafgesetz), which at the time was applicable to the policemen.

> 1. If an order in matters of military duty violates the penal code, the superior who gave the order alone assumes responsibility. However, the obeying subordinate is punished as an accomplice: 1. if his activities go beyond the order, or 2. if he knows that the order demanded an action violating the civil or military penal code.
> 2. If the guilt of a subordinate who helped with a crime is minor, it is possible to refrain from punishment.[32]

Both conditions described in (1) and (2), however, do not apply to Ra. and He. It is reasonable to assume that a young lieutenant, such as He., who had just completed strict SS training, would not dare to question his orders. Ra.'s training also had made him believe that, as he stated to the judge, "An order was something holy and therefore must be obeyed at all cost."[33]

The court here noted—and one can only concur—that both officers should have realized that their duty to follow orders ended where innocent civilians were butchered by the hundreds and thousands. One wonders, then, how the court could ultimately arrive at the conclusion that there was no other option than obedience. The panel of judges argued that because the destruction of the Jews was the first priority of the Reich Security Main Office, and the Einsatzkommandos alone were not of sufficient size and strength to achieve that goal, the Reich Security Main Office had put great emphasis on the prompt fulfillment of all such orders by other police forces as well. And, therefore, if the defendants had refused their participation, Major N. or Colonel Montua would have reported the insubordination along their chain of command. Because of the increased SS control over the German police, it would have been inevitable, then, that the SS would have learned about the case. Himmler eventually would have received the report and most likely would have taken action.

According to the Freiburg court, Himmler then could have reacted in several ways. He could have left the officer unpunished; he could have taken a rather mild disciplinary measure such as degradation; or he could have transferred the officer to another unit. Transfer, however, did not seem to be a viable option because such an example would certainly have set a precedent for others, especially among the less Nazified personnel in the Order Police or Police Reserve, and thus might have jeopardized the success of the entire elimination campaign.

Himmler also could have put the disobedient officer on trial in an SS and police court, though that was not a viable option either, because of the—in Himmler's eyes—onerous Paragraph 47. Had a defendant invoked Paragraph 47 of the military penal code, the SS judges would have had a problematic choice. If they acquitted the defendant, which was not very likely, they would have thereby acknowledged that the order to kill the Jews was criminal. If, on the other hand, the SS court convicted the defendant, it might draw attention to an important section of the military penal code that the SS leaders would have liked to forget.

To solve such a potentially self-incriminating problem, if the occasion arose, Himmler was obligated to revert to an entirely different option: recall the officer in question from his killing unit and secretly assassinate him in Russia, or otherwise have him "disappear" in one of the many concentration camps. And, thus, argued the Freiburg court, disobedience would have led to the death of the pertinent officer, and Ra.'s and He.'s participation in the massacres had been secured only under duress and imminent danger to their lives. Moreover, the judges concluded that both defendants did everything that could reasonably be expected of them to justify their acts according to Paragraph 34 of the penal code. Therefore, it was the judges' opinion that they could only find the defendants not guilty.[34]

Obviously in retrospect, and from the safe distance of the historian, it is extremely difficult to imagine how any human being would have acted in the situation of the perpetrators in Police Battalion 322. Certainly one would have been more inclined to concur with the verdict if the judges had acquitted the defendants on a "subjective danger to life and limb" according to Paragraph 35 (2), as had been the case in Munich and Kiel. Arguing, however, that an "objective threat" existed, according to Paragraph 34, seems to be a misinterpretation of the evidence.

Of course, from a legal point of view, every court is entitled to an independent opinion; yet the Freiburg judgment is contrary to several established legal and historical considerations. First, although several defense witnesses indeed had claimed that officers who refused to shoot Jews were shot clandestinely, none of these cases could be documented or corroborated. Obviously, if such events had occurred, they would have had a decisive impact on all trials involving Nazi criminals. The German justice system under the leadership of the Central Office thus took each of these alleged cases very seriously. After years of investigation, however, none could be substantiated. Furthermore, as the concluding report observes regarding one such incident filed by the Central Office after a decade of careful inquiry:

> Even if the case [of an officer being shot for refusing to kill Jews] should have occurred, it would not be suitable to prove that a general condition of "duress"

existed. In comparison to a substantially larger number of cases in which disobedience did not have any consequences, such a case could only indicate that
such consequences could have happened (but not "certain" or at least "with all
likelihood"), and that only on occasions when the responsible commanding
officer overstepped his disciplinary authority.[35]

Knowing this argument, the Freiburg court should have dismissed all testimony
to the contrary.

In addition, all but two other German courts rejected the commonly used defense argument of "putative duress" and justification according to Paragraphs 34
and 35. Some specifically deny the existence of a subjective or objective threat to
life and limb of the defendants.[36] The court in Cologne concludes, for example,
citing a German Supreme Court decision, "If an individual acts out of blind
obedience or misguided sense of duty, his actions do not fulfill the conditions of
§§ 34 and 35 of the penal code."[37] This interpretation seems applicable to the officers of Police Battalion 322 because they acted primarily out of obedience and
loyalty.

Another panel of judges from Koblenz does not rely on legal precedent alone;
it rather considered the historical evidence:

> Historical research did not reveal a single case when resistance against orders of
> this kind was punished particularly harsh. On the contrary, the historical record
> does not lack instances of courageous resistance.[38]

The judges then cite such cases at length. For example, G., the district governor
of Schaulen (Siaulai), saved the Jews of the town's ghetto from Einsatzkommando 3. When approached by Colonel Jäger's advance command, G. threatened to use his Lithuanian police against the Einsatzkommando if they tried to
shoot ghetto inmates. Although G. clearly had refused to carry out the general
execution order in his district, nothing happened to him.

Another witness in Koblenz, the former Order Police officer P., refused a
Security Service request for policemen under his command to serve as an execution squad. P. reported the incident to the Main Office Order Police, which
backed his decision. P. also told of other similar cases. His overall situation was
comparable to Police Battalion 322. The only difference was that P. challenged
the Einsatzgruppen, reported within his chain of command, and suffered no
consequences. It, therefore, appears as if both Ra. and He. could have refused
to participate in the massacres if they had mustered the necessary courage. They
had multiple channels through which to voice their concerns, one through the

Higher SS and Police Leader to the Reich Security Main Office, and one through the Order Police to the Main Office Order Police. And, again, although both channels ended with Himmler as Chief of the German Police, P.'s case proves that the Order Police channel could have a positive influence on avoiding involvement in the massacres.

Another court relies on the testimony of the witness Bruno Streckenbach, the former SS colonel in charge of personnel in the Reich Security Main Office, who must have known disciplinary procedure and the way the Reich Security Main Office dealth with insubordination. Streckenbach confirmed that even former Einsatzgruppen and Einsatzkommando leaders, among them SS Brig. Gen. Heinz Jost (Einsatzgruppe A), SS Col. Franz Six (Vorkommando—Advance Command Moscow), SS Lt. Col. Dr. Walter Blume (Sonderkommando 7a), and SS Maj. Oswald Schaefer, whose case was discussed earlier, later objected the executions and were relieved of their commands without repercussions.

Before the invasion of the Soviet Union, Blume had requested command over a Sonderkommando rather than an Einsatzkommando because he expected that he could avoid the most horrible massacres if his unit remained closer to the front line. But because in practice there was no difference in the tasks of these differently named killing units, Blume's efforts seem rather hollow. Nonetheless, he was quickly relieved of his duties in the Soviet Union and recalled into the Reich Security Main Office. In his farewell speech, Blume pointedly reminded his men, "When you come to Berlin and have a special wish, come visit me in the RSHA and I will try to help you."[39] Even Bruno Streckenbach later voiced criticism to the Final Solution, requesting a transfer from the Reich Security Main Office to the Waffen SS. Himmler was furious at first and reduced him to the rank of first lieutenant. But ultimately Himmler let Streckenbach go to the Waffen SS, where he quickly rose to lieutenant general and division commander.

The court in Koblenz also mentions other plausible indications why refusing to kill Jews had no worse ramifications than loss of rank and transfer to the front. During the preparations for the attack on the Soviet Union, for example, Heydrich had affirmed that anyone who did not feel up to the task should report this, and he would be used otherwise. The witness H. then named six officers from his department in the Reich Security Main Office who had made use of this opportunity without suffering consequences. Because the Security Service leadership's concern for the mental condition of the Einsatzgruppen members was known, the absence of severe punishment seems to be a reasonable and sound conclusion.

A Heydrich decree had stipulated that Einsatzgruppen members could volunteer for front assignments, but that they had to maintain, or proceed through, the formal chain of command. In actuality, however, the request most often would then be filed in the personnel papers and, in general, was not to be granted. Heydrich's primary intention had been to show that his Security Service men did not dodge from front duty. Yet, many officers in this study were denied such a transfer. Nevertheless, Heydrich's decree also indicates that official channels for leaving the Einsatzgruppen did exist. Former Advance Command Moscow commander Colonel Six summarizes this notion in his postwar testimony: "One could at least try to be transferred out of an Einsatzgruppe. In any case, no one was shot because of that."[40]

The judges in Koblenz also used a passage from Himmler's Poznan speech to prove that he accepted that some officers could not follow the elimination order:

> If one believes that he cannot obey such an order, he has to report it honestly: "I cannot bear the responsibility, I request to be relieved of the task." Then in most cases the order will follow: "You have to do it nonetheless." Or one thinks that he does not have the nerve, he is too weak. Then one can say: "That's okay then, go into early retirement."[41]

Although Himmler had delivered the speech in 1943, it is reasonable to assume that the Security Service leadership shared Himmler's opinion long before he publicly announced it.

If these arguments still do not prove that the decision of the Freiburg judges was wrong, however, the other cases discussed in this study do. For example, Captain K. had attended only three of the many executions conducted by Sonderkommando 1b. When he asked for a transfer because he could not deal with the massacres, it was granted and he was promoted soon thereafter.[42] Another officer, O., a weapons specialist, went on inspection tours or simply stayed in his quarters every time an execution was scheduled. He was never punished for his evasion either.[43] Moreover, two members of Einsatzkommando 8 openly defied direct orders to kill Jews without any negative consequences. In one case, gas van driver Thomas Gevatter* first sabotaged his vehicle and then refused to begin the gassing of the Jews in his van. He was simply transferred back to his old unit.[44] And in another case, which will be discussed in more detail in the following chapter, SS Capt. Herbert Weistermann* disobeyed Ehrlinger's order to execute the remaining Jews of Smolensk. He, too, went without punishment.[45] Finally, SS First Lieutenant H. had faked an illness in order to avoid participation in a massacre and later simply did not return from his leave. Although his commander had begun an investigation into his illness, his quasi-desertion remained unpunished and he was even promoted, serving the balance of the war with his former unit.

Nonetheless, one has to admit that contradictory regulations such as the SS honor code and the duty to disobey criminal orders, combined with threats and rumors, might have fostered a degree of insecurity, in particular among the lesser educated Einsatzgruppen officers. In general, however, historical experts, such as Dr. Günther Seraphim from the University of Göttingen, who were consulted during most Einsatzgruppen Trials, have demonstrated that the SS and police judiciary followed clearly defined and non-arbitrary principles. Himmler's purpose was to create a set of rules that reflected the elite status of the SS. Himmler abided by these rules, and he expected the same from his subordinates. Certainly these regulations were not based on the notion of due process; nevertheless, they did not leave room for arbitrary terror against SS members, as the Freiburg court erroneously believed. In short, the terror the SS perpetrated against outsiders did not apply to its members. Therefore, an atmosphere of fear, as it is portrayed in the Freiburg judgment, clearly could not have existed in the killing units.

Conclusions

In addition to its legal implications, the case of Police Battalion 322 does, of course, invite comparison with the situation in another police unit, Christopher Browning's notorious Reserve Police Battalion 101. In his conclusion, Browning uses Primo Levi's metaphor of the "gray zone" to evaluate the disturbing actions of the Reserve policemen in Poland. Levi had coined the term gray zone for the morally ambiguous behavior among Holocaust victims that cannot be explained sufficiently along the Manichean notions of innocence and guilt. Levi argued that in order to survive in a concentration camp, the inmates were forced to adopt, to varying degrees, the inhuman rules of their Nazi masters. Thus, like those who became the infamous Kapos—the inmates appointed by the SS men in charge to head prisoner work gangs (Kommandos)—they often evolved into perpetrators themselves. Obviously, becoming a Kapo was a Faustian bargain, and for some an extremely difficult moral choice.

Keeping in mind that the Nazi perpetrators obviously faced completely different choices than did their victims, Browning suggests that the paradoxical behavior of many policemen can be described effectively along the lines of Levi's gray zone. One platoon leader in Reserve Police Battalion 101, Lieutenant Gnade, who initially attempted to evade but soon began to enjoy the killings, must be seen at one end of the scale, whereas another platoon leader, Lieutenant Buchmann, who refused to participate in the massacres as long as his commanding officer covered for him, is at the other end. Browning places somewhere in the middle the battalion commander, Major "Papa" Trapp, whose devotion to following orders was stronger than the voice of his conscience.[46]

From the study of Police Battalion 322 it is obvious that the concept of a "perpetrator's gray zone" is applicable to the officers of Police Battalion 322 and to the perpetrators in the Einsatzgruppen in general. For Police Battalion 322 it means that the behavior of its commanding officer, coincidentally also lovingly called "Papa," as well as that of Ra. and He., resembles Major Trapp's dilemma. Their conscience told them that murdering the Jews was wrong, but their superiors, training, and career concerns convinced them that it was acceptable. Ultimately these officers from Police Battalion 322 proved to be too weak to listen to the voice of reason and settled for an uneasy compromise. Their overall comparatively humane behavior was sufficient to lead to an acquittal in a court of law, but it certainly must be despised from a moral point of view.

One noteworthy difference existed between Reserve Police Battalion 101 and Battalion 322. Although the reserves of Battalion 101 were entirely unprepared for their tasks, the men of Battalion 322 were at least informed about the Kommissarbefehl and the Directives for the Behavior of the Troops in Russia, and therefore knew that their assignment might entail the execution of civilians. Some other obvious parallels exist between the two Order Police units, however. Both were chosen to implement the Final Solution not because they were the best-suited institutions for the task, but because they simply were the only available sources of manpower when the initially designated forces proved to be insufficient.

As to their motivations, compartmentalization and bureaucratization played an important role. Although the policemen in both battalions did not enjoy the distance of the desk perpetrators or even the specialists, there was a division of labor, which certainly helped in the habituation process of the perpetrators. Both units started with guarding and driving the Jews from their homes before they graduated to transporting and finally shooting duties. Apparently, once they had crossed the initial threshold, however, taking the next steps became increasingly easier.

General wartime brutalization was another principal motive among the policemen. Browning finds that for the police Reserves, the increasingly brutal conduct of the war and existing racial stereotypes reinforced each other and helped the perpetrators gain the necessary distance from the victims. The experience of Police Battalion 322 clearly supports Browning's conclusion. In addition, historian Omer Bartov established that a combination of several factors—the social and educational background of the junior officers, political indoctrination, the crimes already committed under the cluster of "illegal orders" such as the Kommissarbefehl, and the actual situation at the front—caused the extraordinary ruthless character of the war.[47] And if human life did not count much for "ordinary" German soldiers, it certainly also did not for the members of Police Battalion 322.

Anti-Semitism, apart from the brief reference to Lieutenant Rasche, is not mentioned in the evidence on the Police Battalion. Nevertheless, considering the overall situation of the war, the ideological training of all police forces, and the general propaganda, some form of anti-Semitic sentiments must have affected the actions of the officers and men of Police Battalion 322. Anti-Semitism was at least also an underlying factor for the Einsatzgruppen officers who were acquitted because of reasonable doubt. Si., for example, was the least intelligent in this group and was therefore even more susceptible to Nazi slogans. In addition, after losing his apparently safe job at the railroad because of a government measure in 1921, it is likely that he and the older policemen might have used their service in the Einsatzgruppen to get even with the Jews—the people who were, according to the Nazis, at the root of all evils during the Weimar years.

However, no evidence in the legal records shows that these officers indeed blamed their misfortunes on the Judenrepublik, the name given the Weimar Republic by its right-wing opponents who believed that it was run by Jews, such as then Secretary of State Walther Rathenau. And there is no direct indication of anti-Semitism among the younger officers such as Ra., R., and He., although they grew up in an environment where Nazi values were the only moral guidelines they ever knew, and most likely they had absorbed some. Yet the idealism and enthusiasm with which these officers volunteered for the labor service, the Wehrmacht, and the SS indicates that the Nazi movement and its promises certainly had affected them. On the other hand, the impact of propaganda, political indoctrination, and police training were still not strong enough to eliminate all forms of independent thought. Even careerists and Nazi idealists such as Oswald Schaefer and R. engaged their superiors in discussions about the purpose of the executions, and rather simple-minded individuals such as Si. recognized that they were committing crimes.

In the end, all officers in this group of the acquitted at least took the measures they thought necessary to refrain from personal implication. From a purely ethical perspective, such behavior is objectionable; yet, these men were definitely not "willing executioners."

What primarily forced these officers to act then was not anti-Semitism, but circumstances that were often beyond their control. And obviously the choices for some were more limited than for others. U. had no direct executive function within his unit because he was the adjutant to the battalion commander. In contrast, Schaefer and R. were in charge of independent killing squads and short of

openly defying orders, they had no other choice than to finally "produce numbers." That they at least explored other options, such as an increased engagement against partisans, and that they broke the chain of command with their attempts to be relieved of their positions are remarkable statements of courage for
officers brought up under the strict SS code of honor.

Si., too, had the misfortune of being a policeman in a small detachment
under the leadership of a relentless SS officer. Within his small group of only
fifteen men, evasion of the shootings was much more difficult than in a larger
unit. And for the remaining officers, obedience to authority often appeared to be
the only reasonable option. Obviously the decision to comply was made easier if
the orders did not directly involve them or their units in the killing operations.
While their actions were morally wrong, these officers at least considered what
they believed to be alternatives. Unfortunately, that much cannot be said about
the following group of policemen—those who obeyed.

6. THE OFFICERS WHO OBEYED

On direct orders he would
have killed his best friend, even if
he did not see a reason.

SS Second Lieutenant Gustav Herrscht*

ORMER SS 1st Lt. Georg Heuser was found guilty of participation in the mass murder of the Jews. In his closing statement he argued that he had followed his orders to kill, although he recognized that his actions constituted a monumental injustice. Heuser then explained his apparently irrational behavior with what he called "the political schizophrenia of the time."[1]

Heuser's reaction is typical for the men in this group of obedient officers. Despite being educated in fields that emphasize critical thinking and respect for the process of law, they ultimately followed their orders blindly. Kadavergehorsam, literally "obedience to the corpse," is a descriptive German word for such a behavior, and in court many of the Einsatzgruppen used it as a defense.

The social-psychological research of Stanley Milgram and others has certainly confirmed the all too human propensity to submit to authority and conformity. Obedience alone, however, does not explain why intellectuals and men of at least above-average intelligence were willing to cast aside their conscience and break the simplest of all universally accepted moral principles, the right to live. Influences such as nationalist and conservative traditions, previous service in hierarchical organizations, conformity to the group and, of course, pre-existing notions about the Jews helped to facilitate the absolute acceptance of orders.

Upbringing, Education, and Career before 1941

The background of the officers who obeyed their orders, before they came to the Einsatzgruppen, is rather uniform. They were the sons of soldiers, businessmen, farmers, priests, teachers, or civil servants. All but two were between twenty-seven and forty years of age when they committed their crimes in the Soviet Union. Yet contrary to what one might expect of the children from largely conservative backgrounds, only three defendants mention their parents' nationalist conviction as an influence on the decision to cast their lot with the Nazis.

Like most children from middle-class origins, the majority of the Einsatzgruppen officers in this group had graduated from a Gymnasium and then went on to study at a university. Clearly the law was their discipline of choice—twenty-two out of seventy-eight took up studies in the legal field; economics, history, geography, and engineering were other popular areas of study. A few went into rather unexpected disciplines such as theology, archaeology, ancient languages, or medicine. Yet it is noteworthy that sixteen officers did not finish their studies, usually due to financial and family problems or because they had embarked on a full-time police and SS career. In addition, the draft call to the Einsatzgruppen interrupted the law studies of some officers in this group.[2]

Most future Einsatzgruppen officers absorbed nationalist and racial concepts during their schooling, if not directly in their home. Because many had firsthand experience with the negative impact of the economic depression, it is no surprise that the Nazi program of fiscal revival attracted a number of them years before Hitler came to power. And because these early converts were highly ambitious, they characteristically left the emasculated Storm Troopers after 1934 and joined the more promising SS, Gestapo, or Security Service forces. The remainder of this group came to these organizations through the coordination of the German police under Himmler and Heydrich.

Once in the Security Police, most officers received leadership training and subsequently served in a variety of SS and Security Service functions. Six policemen participated in the "pacification" of Czechoslovakia and Poland. In the time between graduation from leadership school and the dispatch to the Soviet Union, most officers reached at least junior ranks of second lieutenant to captain. As had been the case for the other categories of officers, these men also often met influential Reich Security Main Office and Security Service commanders and forged personal ties that lasted through their time in the Einsatzgruppen. In December 1939, SS 1st Lt. Hans Graalfs became the adjutant to the commanding officer of the Security Service office in Berlin, SS Oberführer Naumann.[3] Another officer, SS Maj. Robert Mohr, met his superior, Bruno Streckenbach, as well as Adolf Eichmann and Dr. Werner Best, during his time at the Office of the Commander of the Security Police and the Security Service (BdS) in Cracow. Mohr returned to the Reich Security Main Office in the spring of 1941, when he selected the personnel for the Einsatzgruppen in the Soviet Union in close cooperation with Streckenbach.[4] Mohr thus had a personal and direct influence

on the destruction of the Soviet Jews, and it is very likely that most other officers at least also knew about the radical policies, methods, and goals of the Nazi
regime by 1941.

Only five cases diverge from the general pattern of obedience to command:
Kluge*, Weistermann*, Schumacher, St., and Freund. These few exceptions did
not agree with the SS rules and regulations at one point or another. SS Maj. Hermann Kluge*, a detective, initially had refused to join the Gestapo, even after
Heydrich tried to convince him in a personal meeting. However, he eventually
became part of the organization through the restructuring of the German police
branches in 1936. The imminent Gestapo takeover, however, might have been
the real reason for Heydrich's restraint from exerting more pressure on Kluge*
a few months earlier.

Kluge*'s first position in the Gestapo brought him to Berlin, where he was
responsible for the monthly Situation Reports. In his drafts, he would harshly
criticize even the slightest digression from the regulations. His immediate superior, the witness Klaus Ahlerich*, showed him "how to tone down the offensive tone to the customary level,"[5] yet Kluge* displayed an unusually critical
behavior and sarcasm toward higher-ranking officials, consistent throughout his
entire career.

In his next function as leader of the Gestapo office in Allenstein and political
adviser to Hermann Koch, the then regional Nazi Party official of eastern Prussia, Kluge* did not hold back with his criticism of his superior and other Nazi
leaders.[6] Friends regularly warned him to be more careful, but he brushed away
the advice replying, "I don't fear these 'bigwigs,' rather they should fear me."
During his term in eastern Prussia, Kluge* additionally began to inform Jewish
friends and acquaintances about the ever more radical racial measures of the
regime. He also managed to help several Jews to emigrate, especially during his
subsequent duties in Vienna and Moravia. Among these emigres was his former
companion, a Jewish woman, whom Kluge* helped to obtain a Romanian pass-
port—at least that is what he claimed in his defense. The court, however, clearly
established that Kluge* was no philo-Semite, and at the time he did not know
that the woman was Jewish. Moreover, Kluge's* apparent acts of kindness were
actually very much in line with "forced emigration," the official Nazi policy toward the Jews during 1938 and 1939.[7]

During the trial, Kluge's* co-defendant, SS Capt. Herbert Weistermann*,
also depicted himself as a benefactor of the Jews. Contrary to Kluge*, however,
Weistermann*'s claims appeared to be more sincere, and several reliable witnesses corroborated them. Weistermann* had been a member of the Operational
Task Headquarters in Czechoslovakia and subsequently stayed with the newly
created State Police office in Reichenberg. Soon after the German takeover, he

began a friendship with a witness named Egon Preker*, who was married to a Jewish woman. Weistermann* not only prevented problems with the German authorities for Ms. Preker* while she lived in Reichenberg, he later helped her leave the country. In addition, Weistermann* advised another witness, the half-Jewish Karl Wendtlinger* to dissolve his engagement to an Aryan woman because once Weistermann* would be relieved of his job, no one would protect Wendtlinger* any longer. Wendtlinger* refused and was indeed arrested after Weistermann* left his post.

One might interject here that Weistermann* had only encouraged Jews to leave, as Kluge* had done, yet Weistermann* stood up for "his Jews" when it became necessary. That was the case when a journalist from the anti-Semitic magazine *Der Stürmer* interviewed the local Jewish Sonderkommando; the journalist was also the deputy regional Nazi Party official of Franconia. The Jews had been arrested by local ethnic Germans before the German occupation and were being put to work for Weistermann*'s office in the Sonderkommando unit. When the journalist beat one of the Jews, Weistermann* stepped in immediately, ended the interview, and sent the journalist home.

Weistermann* certainly displayed courage, as a lowly Criminal Police Captain, in defending his Jews against a much higher-ranking Nazi Party official. One might assume that Weistermann* acted bravely only to assert his position and protect his "property," as was common practice in the Nazi system. However, another noteworthy incident occurred that attested to Weistermann*'s courage. Toward the end of his stay in Reichenberg, the Reich Security Main Office ordered Weistermann* to register his "work Jews." Weistermann* responded by releasing the Jews to the part of Czechoslovakia not yet occupied by the Germans. He then proudly reported to the Reich Security Main Office that Reichenberg was now "judenrein"—literally purged of Jews.[8]

Others in this group of obedient officers were not as brave as Weistermann*. However, like Kluge*, SS Capt. Dr. Hans Karl Schumacher also had declined the offer to join the Gestapo. And he did so, as he told his interrogators, because he did not want to partake in its criminal machinations. Schumacher also later openly criticized his superior officer's attitude during Kristallnacht and was subsequently reprimanded for insubordination.[9]

Another officer, St., had become a policeman because in 1932 a Criminal Police career looked more promising than his law studies. After three years of training, St. was accepted as a temporary first lieutenant. He was given a tenured position only after he joined the Nazi Party. St. was not politically active, however, and he continued his relations with a Jewish friend, although he had received a letter of reprimand from Himmler. He was able to avoid joining the SS, however, and in his position at the Criminal Police office in Düsseldorf, he did not have to wear a uniform. But when he became a teacher of criminal law at the Border Police School in Pretzsch in 1940, an SS uniform was mandatory, and St. accepted the SS equivalent rank of captain. It is interesting that although St. was sentenced to four years in prison, the Berlin court did not disclose his full name.[10]

A final divergent case among those who obeyed was SS Capt. Carsten Freund*, who had been a practicing Catholic throughout his time at the University of Cologne, where he intended to earn a Ph.D. in social and labor law. After the Nazis came to power, Freund* believed he had a better chance to advance in his studies if he joined a nationalist student organization. He thus became a member of the Langemarckring, a student group promoting military training, rather than the "unChristian" Storm Troopers. The Langemarckring was named after the city of Langemarck, where at the beginning of the First World War German volunteers had attempted to storm an Allied stronghold. In right-wing circles, Langemarck became a symbol for the German military spirit; the student volunteers had allegedly attacked and died singing the German national anthem, evidence that the Fatherland was more important than their individual lives.

Freund* eventually did become part of the Storm Troopers when the Langemarckring was forced to merge with them in the summer of 1933. Yet Freund* remained a passive member, and rather engaged himself in another Catholic student organization affiliated with the YMCA. He also spoke out for his Christian belief. This became evident in 1935, when the Nazi student organization (Studentenbund) raided Freund*'s Catholic fraternity house. Freund* and the president of his group, the witness Dr. Bodo Augustin*, reported the incident to the police. Unfortunately, the officials simply refused to register the complaint and brusquely advised them to keep silent.

Soon afterward the Nazis dissolved Freund*'s Christian organization, though Freund* nevertheless kept in touch with Dr. Augustin* and a circle of Catholic friends. At around the same time, he broke off his studies and volunteered for the Wehrmacht. After his discharge a year later, he found a job with the Criminal Police detectives. On advice of his commanding officer, Freund* suddenly renounced his membership in the Catholic Church and joined the Nazi Party and the SS. In November of 1938, the infamous events of Kristallnacht, the night of the nationwide pogrom to destroy Jewish homes, businesses, schools, and synagogues, found him back in Cologne, this time as a member of the Gestapo and in charge of Department II b (Churches, Sects, Jews, Masons). On the day after the pogrom, he interrogated the arrested Jews of the city. Following instructions, he released individuals over the age of sixty-five, but cleared the majority for transport to the concentration camp in Dachau. Thereafter, Freund* served in the Einsatzgruppen in Poland, where he met the subsequent

commander of Sonderkommando 7a, Albert Rapp. Despite psychological problems with the Gestapo methods and the as yet relatively minor horrors of Nazi
racial "reorganization" in Poland (compared to what would happen in the Soviet
Union), Freund* then followed the draft to the Einsatzgruppen.[11] It thus seems
that, like Freund*, all of the "exceptional" obedient officers, except Weistermann*, had fallen back in line with the Nazis by the time they were sent to the
Einsatzgruppen

Two other officers had careers that did not fit into the previous general pattern, but for different and diametrically opposed reasons. Apart from being the
two oldest men in this group, SS Brig. Gen. Carl Zenner and SS 1st Lt. Harm
Willms Harms had nothing in common. Zenner was born in 1899 and joined the
NSDAP in 1925. Because he was a veteran of the First World War and a gifted
orator, he became an official propaganda speaker for the party. In 1926, he also
joined the Storm Troopers and the SS. His assigned membership numbers in the
Nazi Party and the SS were 13,539 and 176, respectively, indicating that Zenner
was one of the earliest party members and an even earlier member of the then
fledgling SS.[12]

The ambitious Zenner quickly advanced to colonel, and Storm Trooper
leader in the demilitarized Rhineland. After Himmler took over the SS in 1929,
Zenner organized the buildup of the SS in that area, specifically in the districts
of Cologne-Aachen, Koblenz, and Trier. In 1934 he was promoted to SS Oberführer and took charge of the Munich SS district. Subsequently he briefly served
in the Security Service Main Office and became police president of Aachen in
1937. In the meantime, he had also been elected as a Nazi delegate to the Reichstag in 1932.

The day the Germans launched the attack on the Soviet Union in June of
1941, Zenner was promoted to SS Brigadier General. This might be a mere coincidence, but it also symbolizes how intricately intertwined were Zenner's career and the turn of Nazi anti-Jewish policies. His elevation to a general's rank
coincided with the implementation of the first systematic Nazi murder program. At another crucial moment for the unfolding of the Holocaust, in the late
summer of 1941, the initial Einsatzgruppen were reinforced with fresh SS shock
troops to accelerate the extermination campaign.[13] Zenner was once again promoted and appointed the SS and Police Leader of White Ruthenia. He was selected for this job because of his unique organizational talents and the ability to
keep in line the governor, Kube, who was known to be weak regarding the Jewish Question. Before he left for his new assignment, the chief of the Order Police, Daluege, told him, as Zenner himself proudly remembered, "You are the
only one who can deal with Kube."[14]

The oldest of all Einsatzgruppen officers indicted in a West German court was Harm Willms Harms, born in 1892. He had volunteered for the army in 1912 and had served in World War I. In 1919, he joined a Freikorps and helped defeat the radical Communist-leaning Spartacus uprising.[15] In October of the same year he joined the Billeted Field Police (Kasernierte Feldpolizei) and subsequently served in different branches of the Hamburg police until the outbreak of the war. Harms also became a member of the Storm Troopers in 1933 and the Nazi Party in 1937. In 1937 his department in the State Police merged with the Gestapo. In January of 1939, Harms was finally transferred to the Tilsit State Police, where he took over the Department II b (Opposition from the Right and Jewish Affairs). Then, in June 1941, Stahlecker recruited him, as he had the other members of Einsatzkommando Tilsit.[16] In short, Harms became a member of the Einsatzgruppen through the reorganization of the German police and his position with the Tilsit State Police, whereas Zenner was, as he expressed it in his closing court statement, "A practicing and convinced old Nazi," who had dedicated his life to Nazism from early on.[17] Nevertheless, it is important to note that these apparently very different officers had made their living in organizations with long-standing radical and authoritarian traditions.

Crimes and Attitudes

Obeying commands without much questioning thought was the defining characteristic for the officers in this category of the obedient. It is, therefore, not surprising that all defendants fulfilled the essence of the order to eliminate the Jews, even if they realized that, as First Lieutenant Krumbach succinctly declared, "State-sanctioned murder still remains murder."[18] These officers' personal involvement in the massacres ranged over the spectrum of functions. Some participated by guarding the victims or the outer limits of the execution site, others rounded up the victims or brought them to the graves, and yet others fired the shots, even if it was "only" to finish off still-living victims in the grave. Some officers supervised the executions, or stood next to the responsible officer, always ready to take charge if necessary. And even if they did not have a special function during the execution, the presence of officers supported and legitimized the actions in the eyes of the enlisted men who did most of the "dirty work." However, in certain cases, officers deviated from the general pattern: some went beyond the orders; some were torn between obedience and the voice of reason; and some decidedly disapproved of the killing of innocent human beings.

Men such as 1st Lts. Georg Heuser and Gerhard Schneider, and Capt. Karl Harder, must certainly be seen as the most extreme and fanatical in this group of the obedient, and their actions and attitudes resemble that of the confirmed killers. In fact, because the courts in Koblenz and Berlin did not convict them as perpetrators is the only reason they have not been discussed with the former category.

Like the confirmed killers, Heuser contributed to several massacres in different functions. Initially a member of Sonderkommando 1b, he came to Minsk in November 1941 and stayed there with the Office of the Commander of the Security Police and the Security Service until the German retreat in June 1944. Heuser served as a shooter during several massacres, including the great March Action of 1942. According to another member of his unit, Heuser shot at least eighty times on one of these days. In addition, he directed away from the scene a member of the civilian administration who had tried to intervene.

On another occasion, the killing of 900 passengers of the train DA 201 from Vienna, Heuser admitted that he shot "like a machine."[19] As the deputy to the commander of the Security Police and the Security Service, Heuser also helped with the organization of seventeen railroad transports from the west. On July 28, 1942, the first day of another major action, Heuser had made certain that the personnel officer, Kaul, went to the execution site.

The terrible routine of the shootings, however, had its effects even on the callous Heuser. When the witness Rum., who had previously guarded the outer perimeter of the execution site, relieved Heuser as a shooter in the afternoon of July 29, he noticed that Heuser's face was pale. Heuser quietly explained, "I am finished [Ich bin fertig]."[20] During another execution, Heuser told a comrade, "It [the killing] makes me sick to my stomach [Es kotzt mich an]."[21]

Yet, despite these reservations, Heuser continued to participate in executions until the end, never showing leniency to his victims. This became particularly evident in the fall of 1943, when his men drove the Jews from their houses during the final dissolution of the Minsk ghetto. The witness Rum. again testified and asserted that a young Jew had pleaded with Heuser to let him go because he had previously worked well for him. Yet Heuser coldly pushed the Jew aside and told him to get onto the truck.[22] Later, the same day, Heuser was part of the execution squad.

If this is yet not enough to prove Heuser's extraordinary dedication and zeal, during the last year of the Minsk ghetto he personally shot two women and a priest who were suspected of espionage. Even when the German retreat was imminent and Heuser was left behind with only ten men, he continued to execute Jews. Only at the last moment, when there was nothing left to do, Heuser told a railroad official, "Now that we are finished with shooting the Jews, it is time to leave."[23]

Gerhard Schneider's actions in Einsatzkommando 9 under the notorious Dr. Filbert parallel Heuser's behavior. Although Schneider and the other officers of the unit did not get along with Filbert, Schneider was always eager to please his superior. In fact, his willingness to fulfill every detail of Filbert's commands, and his devotion to the elimination of the Jews, stood out so much that the members of an affiliated Order Police platoon thought that Schneider and not the higher ranking Greiffenberger was Filbert's executive officer. Whenever Filbert was not present, the same Order policemen also observed that Schneider acted as if he was in charge; thus "he filled Filbert's footsteps perfectly."[24]

Schneider proved how well he could perform his duties without supervision when Filbert put him in charge of an independent contingent of troops. On August 12, 1941, his platoon was to search for a partisan camp near the village of Surash. From early morning on, the men combed the surrounding forests, but their efforts remained futile; not a single partisan could be found. The frustrated Schneider marched back to Surash, then executed the Jews of the village. It was already getting dark when the action was over and the platoon finally retreated to headquarters.

Apart from the obvious moral considerations, there was no need to kill the Jews of the village for several valid reasons—even to a Nazi mind. First, Schneider's orders were to search for partisans, not Jews. Moreover, his platoon was already exhausted after a long day and did not need further strain. And from a military perspective, it was rather foolish to withdraw from partisan-infested areas after darkness. Nonetheless, Schneider decided to commit the massacre because he was concerned about his image as an exemplary, tough SS leader, and he certainly did not want to return emptyhanded.

To underscore his reputation, Schneider had repeatedly boasted that, contrary to other officers, he had no psychological problems with the killing of the Jews.[25] Yet, despite such a bold statement, Schneider attempted to get away from the Einsatzkommando immediately after the Surash massacre. He contacted a friend at Einsatzgruppen headquarters without Filbert's knowledge, and he was indeed transferred away from the killing fields. He did so, however, not because he disapproved of and resented his tasks, as he claimed in his interrogation, but rather, as the jury in Berlin found, because the failure of the Surash expedition made him fear losing his good standing with Filbert. To save face, Schneider had thus secretly asked his friend for help. He then could still hope for a positive evaluation from Filbert and pursue a successful career in the SS.[26] Considering the evidence and given his overall character, the court's explanation of Schneider's behavior seems more convincing.

The third hard-line SS officer, Karl Harder, took part in different yet equally despicable activities of the Einsatzgruppen. He was Paul Blobel's deputy and the technical expert in Sonderkommando 1005, the unit charged with the exhumation and incineration of the bodies in order to destroy evidence of the massacres. In this function, Harder came to Minsk in the fall of 1943 with orders to obliterate the mass graves surrounding the city. Although his endeavor proved to be more difficult than expected, Harder conceived of a method that worked satisfactorily. He ordered Russian POWs to open the graves and pull out the dead with iron hooks. Because the victims had been killed over a period of more than two years, their bodies were in different stages of decay. An Order police-man who guarded the prisoners described the scene at the reopened grave:

> I believe they were all Jews and civilians, but this could not be established clearly because the bodies were in almost completely decayed condition. The clothing was all gone. Most likely the bodies had been buried for more than a year and not much more than skeletons remained. I never risked more than a cursory glance at the bodies because I got nauseous from the vile stench, and I lost my appetite for months.[27]

After the graves were opened, the Russian POWs had to stack alternating layers of bodies and wood, always careful to leave enough space for proper air circulation. When the piles, measuring approximately 161½ feet in length and some 13 feet in width reached the desired height of 10 to 16½ feet, the Russians poured gasoline over them and set them on fire. The pyres took up to two days before they burned down completely. It is hard to imagine how repulsive this job must have been for the Russian prisoners, in particular because they also had to sleep in holes dug into the ground on the site.

Subsequently, in early November of 1943 the Reich Security Main Office in-structed Harder to prepare a special execution for three Jewish prisoners, two men and a woman. These were the people the Office of the Commander of the Security Police and the Security Service had arrested for placing a bomb into the cafeteria of the unit and killing several policemen. On the day of the execution, Harder again had the Russians build the usual pyre, only this time the bodies were covered with branches, and a thick stake was erected in the middle. At dusk, when the Russian workers had left for their bunkers, ten SS officers arrived, among them Ehrlinger and Heuser, along with the three victims. The SS men tied the prisoners to the stake and lit the pyre. One man burned silently, but the woman let out a blood-curdling scream with her last breath. The other man was able to jump off the pyre and rolled on the ground to extinguish the flames. One of the SS officers shot him immediately. Even almost twenty years after the event the witnesses from the guard in unison testified that they would never forget the woman's cry.[28]

To Harder, on the other hand, who knew about the extent of the mass mur-ders through his activity in the Sonderkommando, the deaths of thousands of people had become a daily routine. And the endless exhumations and incinerations made him even more callous and indifferent to human agony and suffering.

Two other officers displayed behavior emblematic of a number of the perpetrators—Storm Trooper Oberführer Bernhard Fischer-Schweder and SS Brigadier General Zenner. Although both were not directly members of the Einsatzgruppen, they played central parts in the organization and the conduct of several large-scale massacres, primarily motivated by their pompous nature and overblown sense of self-importance.

Fischer-Schweder had been the police director of Memel since January 1941,[29] an Order Police position. But as the highest-ranking local police officer, he had learned from his good friend Dr. Frohwann, of the Tilsit State Police, about the Stahlecker order to liquidate Jews within the 15½-mile wide strip east of the former border. In preparing for the first execution in Garsden, the Einsatzkommando leader, Böhme, had requested from Fischer-Schweder an Order Police detachment for guard duties. Once Böhme had notified Fischer-Schweder about the imminent action, Fischer-Schweder became involved. He did so out of his own initiative; he never received specific orders to help with the tasks of the Security Service, and there was no particular reason to grant a lower-ranking officer's request.

But Fischer-Schweder wanted more than to simply support the action. He insisted that his Order Police forces take care of the guard duties, and that they also serve as the execution squad. Thus, he had his Emergency Platoon under the command of his co-defendant Werner Schmidt-Hammer practice the procedure that was to be followed the next day.[30] To lighten the psychological burden for the shooters, Fischer-Schweder intended to give the operation the aura of military necessity. He had Schmidt-Hammer recite the standard statement of justification: "You are executed on orders of the Führer for crimes against the Wehrmacht."[31]

In the late morning of June 24, 1941, Fischer-Schweder arrived at the execution site wearing the uniform of a Storm Trooper Oberführer; he was accompanied by the county Nazi Party leader, whom he had invited to the spectacle. Böhme welcomed the two officials and briefed them on the conduct of the execution and the future tasks of the Security Service in eastern Prussia. Although Fischer-Schweder knew all this, he pretended to be surprised and exclaimed, "By Jove! The Russian campaign has consequences that one previously would not have thought about."[32] Fischer-Schweder then addressed the designated shooters and told them that they were about to execute civilian prisoners who had resisted the Wehrmacht, thereby indicating that the execution was legal according to the rules of war, and that the victims deserved to die. Yet Fischer-

Schweder could not deceive his subordinates because from the victims' cloth-ing, sidelocks, and beards, they were clearly recognizable as Jews. After the ex-ecution began, Fischer-Schweder turned to his guest, the county party leader, and proudly explained why he had taken over: "It is absurd that the State Police and the Security Service, with their few men, have to execute such a large num-ber of prisoners. I therefore decided to conduct the execution with my Order Po-lice detachment."[33] Fischer-Schweder remained at the site all day, and toward the end of the action he even fired several shots at still-living victims in the grave.

From the whole conduct of the operation—Fischer-Schweder's late arrival, Böhme's report, the justification speech, the explanation to the county party leader, and the shots fired into the grave to set an example for the enlisted men—it appeared as if Fischer-Schweder was in charge. And that is precisely how he wanted to be seen, and how he appeared again during the following action in Krottingen. As before, he provided the execution squad from his forces and pre-tended to be in command. This time he also personally shot two Communist prisoners who tried to escape. At the subsequent celebratory Sakuska, Fischer-Schweder bragged that he had saved Harms's life by shooting the Communist who had attacked him. Clearly, he was a man who backed his words with deeds.[34]

Fischer-Schweder's arrogant behavior did not change after the war. Yet he was no fool either. Although later his new superior, the Higher SS and Police Leader of Russia South, evaluated him as unfit for an officer because of his alcoholism, and he was reduced to corporal status in the Waffen SS as a con-sequence, Fischer-Schweder remained unwilling to expose his own and the crimes of the SS leadership who had expelled him from its ranks. On the con-trary, as he proudly put it in his interrogation, because "only the stupid calves look for their own butcher," he assumed a wrong identity, remained out of sight, and easily avoided de-Nazification. Over the years, however, Fischer-Schweder became increasingly bold. First he sued (unsuccessfully) when he was fired from his job as a refugee camp director in 1955, a legal move that attracted at-tention to his Nazi past; then he applied for reinstatement into the police and was promptly discovered in the application process. Ironically, by facilitating his own demise, he became like the stupid calf he described.[35]

Apart from their high rank, remarkable similarities can be seen between the cases of the two Nazi Old Fighters in this group of obedient officers. As SS and Police Leader of Minsk, Carl Zenner was in charge of the Security Police and, like Fischer-Schweder, all Order Police forces of the city. Zenner similarly also vol-untarily offered his troops and his authority in order to help the Einsatzgrup-pen—in this case Sonderkommando 1b—to kill the Jews.

Zenner's participation was particularly evident during the action against the

Jews of the Minsk ghetto, from November 7–11, 1941, during which, according to Operational Situation Report No. 140, 6,624 Jews were shot.[36] The officer nominally in charge of the Sonderkommando and the operation, Zenner's co-defendant SS Maj. Hans-Hermann Remmers, had received orders from the Reich Security Main Office to coordinate the planning—especially the transport, shooting, and guard duties—with the SS and Police Leader. Because Remmers additionally did not want to burden his men with such an apparently unbearable task, he asked Zenner for help, and Zenner was more than willing to oblige. Not only did he promise the Ukrainian Hiwis under his command as the execution squad, he effectively took charge of the entire operation, from the clearing of the ghetto to the closing of the mass graves.

Zenner supplied the manpower and vehicles for the action, including the Order Police units that rounded up the Jews, the forces that guarded the execution site, and, of course, the shooters. During the execution he only briefly inspected the ghetto clearing and the graves, but Remmers's testimony leaves no doubt that Zenner was the mastermind of the action. Of course, the ruling of the court in Koblenz appears to be biased in this case because Remmers might have implicated Zenner in order to clear himself. However, contrary to Zenner, who categorically denied even the slightest knowledge of the execution and thereby tried the judges' patience (how could an SS and Police Leader not know about a large-scale massacre committed in his city?), Remmers was sincerely remorseful and cooperated with the court. Furthermore, additional witnesses, who had no reason to favor one SS officer over the other, corroborated Remmers's version of the events.[37]

To outside observers, Zenner did not seem quite as pompous as Fischer-Schweder, and he had refrained from personally taking over the conduct of the execution. Yet to a witness he disclosed that he felt like a hero whose toughness indeed had been forged, as Heydrich had wished, by the "rough wind" and the tough customs of the east. He also bragged about the "thousands of Jews who had been put to the sword in these days."[38] Certainly this statement, and his earlier comment about being the only one who could keep the governor in check, reveal that Zenner actually was no less arrogant than Fischer-Schweder, and thought he was equally important.

The following observations shed an even more revealing light on Zenner's personality. Although he held a general's rank, his behavior and manners were not as refined as one would expect from a man of his standing. On the contrary, Zenner usually socialized with other brutal persons who preferred activities of the baser human instincts. Not coincidentally, two of his favorite drinking associates (Saufkumpane), as the witness He. put it so well, were the notorious SS

Lt. Col. and "Jew butcher" Eduard Strauch and another SS officer who was known for killing children by smashing their heads against walls and other hard objects.[39]

In addition, a letter that Order Police General Herf wrote to a friend on December 18, 1941, is even more telling. Herf complained that General Zenner was much too jovial with the lower ranks. Even Himmler had heard of Zenner's often intolerable behavior. In 1942 he initiated a trial against Zenner and "strongly reprimanded" him for neglect of duty and lack of soldierly bearing, for tolerating sexual relations between local Russian women and county sheriffs under his command, and for evacuating a village without permission.[40]

In the letter, Herf furthermore criticized that Zenner had demoted a captain in front of the enlisted men, which was (and still is) considered inappropriate and unworthy of an officer. Finally, Herf noticed how Zenner brutally punched a civil administration official in the face during a formal dinner.[41] It is evident that the behavior of both Zenner and Fischer-Schweder was motivated by their sense of self-importance, career concerns, and a great deal of innate brutality that very likely was exacerbated by decades of service in Nazi organizations.

The career of SS Maj. Robert Mohr also is characteristic of many Einsatzgruppen officers. These men had recognized that they were participating in mass murder and even had some positive personal qualities, but in the end their sense of duty and career considerations compelled them to follow their orders. Mohr is a striking example because he spent part of his student time studying Human Rights in Geneva, the seat of the League of Nations and the birthplace of the regulations for the humanitarian conduct of warfare. As a student, Mohr had supported the pacifist goals of the League. Nevertheless, upon his return to Germany in 1933, he joined the Nazi Party and the SS. After the Röhm Putsch, he was shocked that the German conservatives condoned Hitler's illegal behavior. As a trained attorney, he particularly disliked the scandalous way Hitler bent the existing laws to justify the murder of the Storm Trooper leaders. Like most other Germans at the time, however, Mohr believed that the violence of the Nazis was a necessary and short-lived by-product of a great national rebirth and that, as the German proverb notes, "Where there is planing, there must be shavings (Wo gehobelt wird fallen Späne)."

Four years later, Mohr worked in the Interior Ministry and knew that the violent nature of the Nazi regime would not change. He did not like the prospect much, but he found a rather easy solution to placate his conscience. He accepted the brutality and, of course, the promotions that came with serving his masters, but attempted not to get directly involved. Thus, during Kristallnacht he locked himself into his house and pretended not to notice what was happening around him. That general reaction did not change much in his subsequent positions in the Reich Security Main Office, in Poland, and later in the Einsatzgruppen.[42]

In September 1941 Mohr received his transfer from the Reich Security Main Office to Einsatzgruppe C, where he initially became a personnel officer. Mohr had agreed to serve in the Einsatzgruppen as part of an arrangement that afterward would allow him to get his preferred job as the leader of the State Police office in Darmstadt. When he learned about the executions, he expressed his reservations to his commanding officer, who allowed him to draft a report to Gestapo Müller. In the memorandum, Mohr correctly assessed that the mass executions of helpless civilians prevented the Russian population from cooperating and therefore led to a significant increase in the partisan movement. He hoped to persuade Müller to stop with the killings, but Müller was unimpressed. Mohr then traveled to Berlin and met with Müller, who finally reminded him that the Führer orders had to be fulfilled regardless of the consequences. Mohr immediately gave up his resistance and returned to the Soviet Union, where he took over Einsatzkommando 6. Still pretending to look the other way, he usually had his executive officer command the executions. Additionally, in order to slow down the progress of the killings, Mohr instructed his men to prepare interrogation protocols. He thought that such bureaucratic measures, for which his superiors criticized him, would keep the policemen busy and morally fit for normal police work at home. From March 1942 on, however, Mohr also personally supervised the use of gas vans. He did not even stop the gassings on Easter, when indigenous Hiwis took over the procedures while his Einsatzkommando members celebrated the holiday in the traditional manner with colored eggs.[43]

In the final evaluation of Mohr's behavior, it is evident that despite his earlier pacifist convictions and "inner rejection" of the massacres, as he claimed, Mohr became a loyal Nazi follower who never forcefully professed his disapproval with their crimes. He spoke up for what was right only when he could be certain that he was supported by the Nazi rules, as when he once saved a Pole because the man had a German mother; Mohr knew that the Nazis would not condemn valuable German blood. Likewise, Mohr complained to Müller only if he believed that he could convince him with reasonable arguments. But Müller's words "Führer order" signaled that Mohr's concerns were against the Nazi goals, which might jeopardize his career. Mohr, therefore, immediately complied with his duties, even if he still tried to avoid direct personal involvement. In short, Mohr appears to have been another policeman who quickly abandoned all humanitarian considerations when professional success and career advancement were at stake.

SS Major Kluge*, Otto Bradfisch's successor as commanding officer of Einsatzkommando 8, is similarly a case of interest. He was not as much concerned about his career as was Robert Mohr, but he did not agree with his orders either, and followed them only reluctantly. Upon his arrival in the Soviet Union, Kluge* found that the unit was already well trained and did not need further instructions or supervision. Although Kluge* did no more than necessary to keep operations running smoothly, he never openly protested against his assignment and certainly never refused to obey direct orders, as he stated in court. To his defense, Kluge* maintained that his superior, SS Oberführer Naumann, once drafted a motion to bring him before an SS tribunal for insubordination. Although the court established that a draft of a motion accusing Kluge* did indeed exist, the document did not cite insubordination but rather Kluge*'s known sarcasm and disrespect. Regardless, Naumann had not followed through with the SS tribunal.[44]

From his defensive attitude, it is obvious that Kluge* wanted to present himself to the judges in the most positive light. Although he generally lied about his degree of participation and resistance during his term in the Einsatzgruppen, he nonetheless had an impeccable history of criticizing and revealing corruption among the Nazi establishment. This goes back to his first Gestapo position in eastern Prussia and manifested itself even more after his transfer from Einsatzkommando 8 to the Office of the Commander of the Security Police and the Security Service in Paris in September 1942. According to Dr. Franz Hauser*, the investigating attorney for operations in France, in the Reich Security Main Office, Kluge* soon initiated disciplinary proceedings against several high-ranking police and Security Service officials for the surprisingly common corruption in the SS. His most noted case was an investigation of SS Lt. Gen. Karl Oberg who allegedly had appropriated diamonds from the valuables collected from the French Jews.

Kluge* definitely enjoyed his job as an investigator, and he was promoted to lieutenant colonel in November 1943. Yet in his overly inquisitive zeal to root out corruption, he often went too far for his superiors and was removed from Paris in 1944.

Kluge* became leader of the State Police in Frankfurt/Oder. As such, the Reich Security Main Office instructed him to arrest 250 former Socialists and Center Party members who had been implicated in the aftermath of the failed attempt on Hitler's life. Kluge* and his deputy filed a written objection to the list in which they argued that "these men had done nothing wrong." The Reich Security Main Office thereupon shortened the list to only thirty persons, and Kluge* had them arrested.[45] From this evidence it seems that Kluge* definitely had a great deal of courage and a remarkable sense for justice; however, it is even more noteworthy that despite these positive attributes, Kluge* never once spoke up against a far greater crime, the mass murder of the Jews.

Two more cases exemplify the position of the officers in this middle group-
ing of men with some positive qualities, who were neither as brutal in their
killings as Zenner, nor as critical as Schumacher and Weistermann*. First Lieutenant Krumbach, who in court often found the appropriate words for his and his
comrades' behavior, claimed that he, too, had been opposed to the order to kill
the Jews. Yet, he never even thought about disobedience or at least a form of non-
compliance. Only in cases when the existing laws backed his decision had he
been lenient. Krumbach thus let two Jewish women go free because they could
prove that they were baptized. But when his career or reputation were on the
line, as during the first execution in Garsden, Krumbach had no problems with
his conscience. Although he questioned whether he was capable of shooting
innocent people, he specifically set out to show that he would carry out his responsibilities.[46] In fact, he soon became so cynical and indifferent that he used
the massacres to go on sightseeing tours, dine out lavishly, or appropriate special
foods and other valuables.[47]

Like Kluge* and Krumbach, the defendant Harm Willms Harms obeyed
some orders and objected to others. His case is important because it shows that
his refusal to kill Jews had no negative repercussions. Harms was not an SS member, but he had already participated in the early massacres of Einsatzkommando
Tilsit without hesitation. When Böhme had ordered him to supervise an execution of women and children, however, Harms replied, "Sir, I cannot do that."
Böhme then threatened, "What, Kommissar? I have put you in an SS uniform
and have given you a direct order." Harms remained adamant and Böhme finally
excused him, saying, "That's all right then. You can go. You do not have to do
that. You have a wife and children."[48] This case confirms that Böhme, like many
other senior SS officers, tolerated the inability of his subordinates to follow the
killing orders, at least if they had other willing shooters to do the job.

But the description of the officers who followed orders is not complete without looking at two policemen whose efforts to have a direct influence on the executions were decidedly different: SS Capt. Dr. Hans Karl Schumacher, who had
refused to join the Gestapo earlier and in general displayed a critical attitude toward Nazi policies even before the outbreak of the war; and SS Capt. Herbert
Weistermann*. In both cases, their renegade behavior had no apparent consequences for their careers. Schumacher continued to serve as a detective, and his
superiors apparently did not much mind his criticism as long as he provided his
expertise to the task at hand. They recognized that he was an excellent policeman, even appointing him as instructor of criminal law in Pretzsch. Because of
problems with his vocal cords, however, Schumacher was released from that position in May 1941 and became deputy director of the Criminal Police office in
Duisburg. Although Schumacher left Pretzsch before the Einsatzgruppen were

training there, he could not escape his duty; only five months later he was transferred to Einsatzkommando 5.[49]

Schumacher's career and detachment to the Einsatzkommando thus corroborates Christopher Browning's observations about the problems with the
Einsatzgruppen. Initially the Einsatzgruppen were rather small and consisted
only of physically fit personnel. Yet a few months later, shootings by small execution squads had proved to be an insufficient method to eliminate the large population of Soviet Jews. Even officers with handicaps, such as Schumacher with
his vocal cord problem, were consigned to build up the manpower in the killing
fields. And at about the same time, their vile work would be assisted by the gas
vans, which had just appeared on the scene.[50]

Schumacher arrived in Kiev in October 1941 when the mobile Kommandos
of Einsatzgruppe C were transformed into stationary offices. Therefore, he simultaneously belonged to Einsatzkommando 5 and the stationary Office of the
Commander of the Security Police and the Security Service Kiev (KdS Kiev) for
awhile. His first task was to organize a Ukrainian detective force. In January 1942,
however, partisan activities in the Kiev area increased significantly, and the Office
of the Commander of the Security Police and the Security Service ordered
Schumacher to primarily engage in Security Police work. Schumacher knew that
the euphemism meant participation in the elimination of the Jews, which he
wanted to avoid. At first he tried to convince his superior with logical arguments.
As a trained detective, he argued, he was not qualified for such duty. When that
approach had no effect, Schumacher became more explicit and disclosed his
general reservations about the treatment of the Jews. The commander replied
that the elimination was a Führer order and that he would report Schumacher to
Himmler if he did not comply. The commander, however, also promised that
Schumacher would only have to stay in Kiev until a replacement arrived. Hoping
that would be soon, Schumacher gave in. As he emphasized in court, he never
once felt that the SS would punish him for disobedience, but loyalty as a civil servant and the oath he had sworn to Hitler demanded that he obey.

From the beginning of 1942, Schumacher dedicated most of his time to the
Security Police assignment. He was in charge of the former Communist Secret Police (NKVD) prison where the Einsatzkommando kept its prisoners. Of
course, except for the control of partisans, saboteurs, and enemies of the state,
Security Police work was the accepted code word for the arrest and liquidation of the Jews. When Schumacher came to Kiev, the combined efforts of Sonderkommando 4a and Einsatzkommando 5 had already significantly decimated
the Jewish population of the city. In addition, because Schumacher had only ten
members of Einsatzkommando 5 and a few ethnic German interpreters under his
command, it was impossible to conduct expeditions into the surrounding coun-

tryside or large-scale searches of the city. Yet that was not necessary. Denuncia-
tions by the local population and arrests by other German occupation forces
helped to keep the cells of the prison filled, and Schumacher's men had to interrogate all prisoners and then file detailed reports. A suggestion as to whether
the prisoner should be released or executed was the most important part of each
report. As usual, when a prisoner was identified as a Jew, he was automatically
designated for execution. Schumacher had to countersign each report before
the Einsatzkommando leader, SS Lt. Col. August Meier, made the final decision. And Schumacher and his men also had to gas the condemned.[51]

Although it appeared that Schumacher had overcome his reservations, he
continued to show his disapproval and at least to exert some influence on how
the victims were treated. According to witnesses and his own testimony, he once
had asked a German agricultural expert who had just brought a Jew to the jail
whether he did not have anything better to do with his time. The agricultural expert replied that he was only doing his duty as every "good German" should,
and warned that he could denounce Schumacher for his subversive comment.
Moreover, when Schumacher took command of Einsatzkommando 5 in Meier's
absence, he had refused to countersign the reports on the prisoners, as he was
required. That way, as his court records show, he thought he could distance
himself from the elimination of innocent people.[52] Obviously, that measure was
a mere token activity and did not change the fate of the Jewish prisoners.

Another solution, however, proved to be more successful. On Schumacher's
initiative, the newly appointed commander of the Office of the Security Police
and the Security Service, Erich Ehrlinger, had established the work-education
camp. Despite the ominous and euphemistic name and the terror Ehrlinger perpetrated there during every inspection, the camp actually saved Jewish lives because it allowed the investigating officers to propose "work education" as a third
option to release and death. The new assignment system even applied to Jews,
although the ultimate decision still rested with Ehrlinger.

Eventually, however, because Schumacher and his crew were subjected to
the most horrible scenes when they unloaded the gas vans, Schumacher suggested reverting to the less psychologically burdensome shooting method. Ehrlinger agreed, but the Reich Security Main Office insisted on gassing because it
was a more sophisticated technique and prevented the direct involvement of the
perpetrators. Consequently, both killing methods remained in use in Kiev until
the German retreat.[53]

In the end, Schumacher participated in at least eight to ten massacres. He
even shot the victims because he believed that an officer never asks of his men
what he is not willing to do himself. Yet Schumacher continued to voice disapproval and disgust, and he was certainly not a willing follower of Nazi racial

policy. The primary reason he did not object more emphatically is that he believed in the honor code of the German civil servants and officers: to obey one's superiors and to set an example for one's men. He did not realize, however, that the Nazis had systematically perverted such time-honored values, and that proper behavior would have been exactly the opposite of his obedience. Schumacher recognized his errors only when it was too late, after the war. When the newly founded West German Secret Service (Bundesnachrichtendienst) and other government institutions offered him a position, Schumacher declined, stating, "I am not worthy to serve again. . . ."[54]

Although disobedience was out of the question for the arch-conservative Schumacher, Herbert Weistermann* defied superior orders on at least two occasions. Both happened shortly before the German retreat from Smolensk in the fall of 1943. In the first case, an army general ordered Weistermann* and his squad to execute twenty Russian and Jewish prisoners. Weistermann* refused to obey on the grounds that an army general had no authority to issue directives to the Security Service.

In the second case, SS Lt. Col. Erich Ehrlinger, who had become the new leader of Einsatzgruppe B, instructed Weistermann* to shoot the last Jewish prisoners before they would fall into Soviet hands. Ehrlinger then emphasized that if Weistermann* did not follow that order, he would refer the matter to an SS court. Nevertheless, disregarding his orders, Weistermann* put the Jews on a train to Minsk, where they were used to built tank ditches and other defenses. Unexpectedly, for a confirmed killer such as Ehrlinger, he accepted Weistermann*'s justification for his action and overlooked the insubordination.[55] The fact that Ehrlinger found it necessary to threaten with punishment immediately after he issued a direct order also indicates that Weistermann* already must have had a reputation of following such orders only reluctantly. On the other hand, Weistermann* did what he was asked to do during the other executions of Einsatzkommando 8.

The Obedience Paradigm

The officers who obeyed comprise the largest and perhaps most homogeneous group within the Einsatzgruppen. Although these men had above-average intelligence and sometimes a clearly developed sense of justice, they all carried out their orders when it mattered most, in the killing fields of the Soviet Union. Thus we must revisit and apply Stanley Milgram's research, and the body of criticism it has spawned, to the behavior of these men.

Psychologists and other scholars have criticized Milgram's work from four main directions: the substance of obedience, the ethics of the experiments, the methodology of the experiments, and, most important, the work's relevance to the destruction of the European Jews. The critics' main contention is whether the laboratory setting is, as Milgram claims, "Something not apart from life that carries to an extreme and very logical conclusion certain trends in the ordinary functioning of the social world," and that, therefore, it is possible for people who are not unusual, deviant, sick, mentally ill, or otherwise pathological to be capable of committing acts of horrible violence and evil.[56]

In his review of the existing literature, Arthur G. Miller suggests that despite some minor reservations, the majority of the psychological research confirms that Milgram's work is applicable to the conditions of the Holocaust and other genocidal activities. Miller particularly emphasizes the existence of a hierarchic system, as it existed under the Nazis, and the willingness of individuals to relinquish personal responsibility to larger and distant authorities.[57] Subordination to higher agencies and obedience to superior orders is, of course, exactly what the Einsatzgruppen officers claimed at their trials. Therefore, we must determine if the situation of these officers in the Soviet Union does indeed compare to Milgram's university laboratory.

Milgram conducted his initial experiments at Yale University with subjects, who were to enforce the "learning" behavior of trained actors through the delivery of electric shocks. The subjects were randomly chosen through newspaper advertisements; the person in charge of the experiment—the authority figure—wore a standard laboratory coat and instructed the subjects in a matter-of-fact, businesslike tone. The entire atmosphere surrounding the tests projected a legitimate position of authority and scientific justification. Milgram additionally ran a series of control experiments, changing variables such as location, distance between experimenter and subject, distance between subject and victim, and two experimenters giving contradictory instructions to the subject. The outcome of the variations validated Milgram's basic assumptions. Moreover, three of his control experiments have special relevance to the behavior of the Einsatzgruppen officers.

First, the level of obedience increased when the victim was further removed from the person who administered the punishment. Second, the degree of noncompliance rose when the person of authority was further removed from the person who administered the punishment. And, finally, it was much easier for victims to stand up against legitimate authority as a group than as isolated individuals.

The situation Milgram created in his laboratory setting contained nearly all the basic ingredients of the Russian killing fields. What Milgram could not simulate, however, was the situation of the increasingly brutal war that was fought far away from Germany and other civilized countries. No one was watching the

Einsatzgruppen members; therefore they had even more license to act brutally and with no regard for human suffering than did the subjects in Milgram's experiment. Like the subjects who followed the directives of the instructor in the laboratory coat, the Einsatzgruppen officers obeyed the general elimination order because it originated from an apparently legitimate authority. In addition, the apparently legitimate leader of the nation, Hitler, had declared the Jewish victims subhuman and deserving of death, just as the experimenter had made clear that the laboratory victims deserved to be punished if they refused to learn correctly.

Although the Einsatzgruppen officers were not selected randomly as were Milgram's subjects, they clearly displayed behavior similar to that of these "teachers." When Milgram increased the distance to the victim, the subjects' willingness to inflict punishment increased, and compliance was especially high when the process of punishment was broken down into several smaller steps, and the subjects were thus gradually introduced to their tasks. Milgram writes, ". . .The subject is implicated into the destructive behavior in piecemeal fashion."[58] The Einsatzgruppen officers also were exposed to the task of killing the Jews "piecemeal," through a series of prior, lesser, and more removed assignments such as guarding and transporting the victims, and delivering the weapons and ammunition of death among others.

Another of Milgram's conclusions is also evident in the Einsatzgruppen cases, that a larger distance between the figure of authority and the subject results in an increased degree of non-compliance, in particular, in acts of undermining rather than in overt defiance of orders. Officers such as Schumacher and Mohr came up with bureaucratic measures such as reports, interrogation protocols, and work-education camps to slow down the scope and speed of the massacres, rather than refusing to carry out their duties. Other officers, who were discussed in previous chapters, also often tried to evade fulfilling their orders by engaging in military actions or pretending to be busy with other tasks. Perhaps some of these men simply wanted to assert their humanity by having a somewhat ameliorating influence on the massacres, a behavior similar to some of Milgram's subjects who tried to administer the shortest possible electric shocks to their learners. In the end, however, all measures to soften the brutal reality of the Einsatzgruppen killings had little or no effect on the overall elimination of the Jews, just as the efforts to sabotage Milgram's experiments had little impact on the punishment of his learners. Contrary to Milgram's randomly chosen subjects, most Einsatzgruppen officers had the additional disadvantage of believing in traditional military responsibilities, and others had been exposed to a long process of indoctrination and propaganda. Clearly, to these men, a direct supervisor did not need to be present when they decided to carry out what they had been ordered to do.

Milgram also found that it was much easier for his subjects to voice disagreement and objections as a group than as individuals. Heydrich and his followers must have been aware of this, as well, when they selected the personnel for the Einsatzgruppen. They had made certain that potential "troublemakers" would remain isolated yet kept in line by the groups of closely knit officers who had served together in previous functions. Thus, the Einsatzgruppen officers who objected in one form or another to the massacres looked for opportunities to extract only themselves, and they usually did not confide in other members of the unit. The atmosphere of anxiety and uncertainty created by a series of conflicting orders, decrees, threats, and speeches; the repeated instruction in the following of orders; and the perceived consequences of disobedience also explain why many officers complied so uncritically.

For these reasons, Milgram's conclusions are applicable to the situation of the Einsatzgruppen members. However, other important factors contribute to their behavior. To this group of officers in particular, devotion to a traditional and conservative sense of loyalty, duty, and obedience played a significant role, albeit mistaking the Nazi violence as a necessary but ephemeral stage in the restoration of German society. The officers from traditionally conservative backgrounds were certainly accustomed to service in hierarchical organizations and submission to authority. They never—or only after a long time—realized the true character of the Nazi system, that it was anything but a traditional conservative, right-wing organization. When this realization came, it was usually too late, for the officers did not want to jeopardize their blossoming careers. Two cases that prove this point involved Schumacher and Mohr, who both made private and uneasy arrangements with the Nazi regime and the Einsatzgruppen murders. Schumacher acted out of resignation and to set an example for his subordinates; Mohr acted out of conviction. In a similar way, the SS leadership was able to harness and exploit the expertise, energy, and ideals of so many police officers for its criminal goals.

Nevertheless, an overblown sense of national pride and devotion to duty clearly was not the impetus for other officers in this group. One wonders whether anti-Semitism, thus, *is* a better explanation. Officers whose affiliation with the Nazis went back to the early fighting years, such as Zenner and Fischer-Schweder, certainly had absorbed the negative stereotypes about the Jews. This is evident from Fischer-Schweder's actions before and during the executions in Lithuania, and especially from his disingenuous comment about the elimination of the Jews being an unforeseeable "consequence" of the war with the Soviet

Union. In reality, he knew all too well that this war was designed to annihilate Jewish-Bolshevism for good. Furthermore, his colleague, Zenner, was specifically selected to become SS and Police Leader in White Ruthenia in order to counterbalance the influence of the Jew-friendly governor. Obviously, only an officer who had distinguished himself in terms of his toughness toward the Jews would have been chosen for such an important position.

The other officers in this group had also joined the Nazi Party and the Storm Troopers or SS before Hitler came to power and, therefore, had time to become familiar with the regime's anti-Semitism. It was an inherent part of their training. Some had learned to hate the Jews even earlier. SS Maj. Werner Hersmann grew up in Frankfurt, a city with a prominent Jewish minority, and he therefore claimed to know the destructive influence of the Jews. It is no surprise that he encouraged his superior officer to immediately include the entire Jewish population in the executions.[59] In Hersmann one might thus indeed detect a deeply rooted form of eliminationist anti-Semitism, but it was not as evident in most other cases. Some, like Remmers, admitted that they hated the Jews and that restrictions should be imposed upon them, yet they had never envisioned the killing and eradication of an entire people to be among such measures.[60]

Even notorious fanatics among the Einsatzgruppen officers had spared individual Jews, in particular if they could be beneficial to the Germans. Ehrlinger had allowed Weistermann* to put the remaining Jews of Smolensk to work rather than shoot them on the spot. SS Capt. Werner Schönemann, another usually zealous officer, had allowed a Jewish businessman to go free because he supplied the Einsatzkommando with mineral water.[61] And other officers believably demonstrated to the courts that they never harbored hostilities toward the Jews. Like Weistermann*, St., and Graalfs, they maintained their relations with Jewish friends even though they were criticized and reprimanded. Weistermann* often had intervened on behalf of the Jews in Reichenberg. And St. had risked his life to save a friend's Jewish wife by contacting a colleague in the Gestapo and asking him to allow the woman's file to disappear. Yet, in general, the court documents are silent on the issue of anti-Semitism. It is, therefore, difficult to draw valid conclusions. However, it would appear that anti-Semitism on its own was neither a sufficient nor total explanation for the behavior of the Einsatzgruppen.

The actions of the officers in this chapter—those who obeyed—confirm both Browning's and Goldhagen's observations about the indifference and brutality of the perpetrators, particularly when considering Karl Harder's activities in Sonderkommando 1005. Harder had regarded himself as a legitimate scientist and innovator and discharged his task with the same dedication other people bring to a civilian position. Although he was not as removed from the killings as the so-called desk perpetrators, his behavior must also be seen as a form of compartmentalization. Like the bureaucrats and pseudo-researchers who organized the deportations, ordered, shipped, and stockpiled the poison gas, or tested the proper use of the gas vans, Harder easily forgot the impact of his work on actual human beings—or in his case, their remains. This one-dimensional focus on the task at hand, no matter what it entailed, perhaps also explains how he and the other officers in this category could return to normal professions after the war, such as civil servant, attorney, teacher, banker, salesman, or police officer, as if nothing had happened in the interim. The only exceptions were Schumacher, who refused every government position, and the former SS 2d Lt. Max Brünnert, who believed that he could redeem himself through hard physical labor in a Ruhr area coal mine.[62]

Other officers, in addition to Harder, "distinguished" themselves by their indifference and lack of human emotions. Alfred Krumbach, for example, had enjoyed a good meal in a farmer's house before he joined his unit and shot the Jews, and had used the opportunity of the execution to sightsee or to acquire merchandise of prewar quality. And his talents in finding first-class products did not go unnoticed by his superiors. They promptly put him in charge of organizing the customary celebrations after the massacres. Krumbach also often paid for the Sakuskas with the valuables he had collected from executed Jews.

The otherwise relatively sensitive Mohr, in addition, did not seem to mind that the auxiliaries operated the gas vans while he and his men celebrated the Easter holidays. And finally, even a man who had evidenced some integrity such as Schumacher could seriously discuss the advantages of one method of killing— shooting—over another—gassing.

Whereas most officers usually avoided being directly involved in the massacres, Heuser had fired his weapon "like a machine" and perhaps single-handedly killed more victims than any other Einsatzgruppen officer tried in German courts. Another officer, Zenner, simply had a crude and brutish character. Did the Reich Security Main Office then, as Browning asks in his conclusion, select for brutal personality traits among the Einsatzgruppen leaders?[63] Looking at Zenner, Harder, and Heuser among the officers in this group, the answer is definitely yes. Yet on the other hand, Schumacher and Mohr were usually not brutal and somehow managed to maintain the delusion that they could reconcile their dislike of violence with successful careers in the SS and the Einsatzgruppen.

Of course, it is abundantly clear that for the officers in this group of those who obeyed, career considerations superseded all notions of human decency. Before the war started, only Weistermann* unsuccessfully had attempted to take the most logical step, namely to quit his position in the Gestapo. All others never considered resignation from their well-paying, respected jobs. Even

Schumacher, who had persistently refused to join the Gestapo, left the Protestant Church in 1938 in order to have better chances to advance his career.

The perfect example for this behavior, however, is SS First Lieutenant Schneider. His career was more important than his honor as an officer, the well-being of his men, and sound military decision-making. Thus, in order to further his chances for early promotions, Schneider broke the chain of command and jeopardized the lives of his subordinates for questionable results. Schneider's search for partisans remained futile, and an action against the Jews in the next village gave him the opportunity to relieve his frustration and to redeem himself in the eyes of his superior. It is therefore possible to argue that Schneider did not commit the massacre because he did not like the Jews, but simply because he believed that he needed to return with some results. To him, it did not much matter that the victims were Jewish, but that they were easily available targets. In a similar vein, Schneider repeatedly emphasized that he could kill Jews without experiencing psychological problems because he wanted to project a tough image, which would help him advance in his career—not because of anti-Semitism.

Although fulfilling the demands of their superiors was a strong motivation for the officers in this category, leaving a favorable impression with their peers was even more important. Conformity to the group influenced all officers, but some more than others. During his police training, Krumbach, for example, had already fainted twice at the sight of the bodies. Before the Garsden massacre, he had been extremely worried that he might faint again, and he firmly believed that another such failure would have finished him in front of his comrades. His fear was compounded because in the meantime he had also received the SS uniform and rank, which in his view brought even more expectations. Thus, Krumbach forced himself to deal with the execution. Remarkably, after he had crossed that threshold, he showed less scruple in the subsequent actions. His behavior, therefore, represents another case of habituation to the tasks.

Another officer, SS 1st Lt. Walter Helfsgott, already had the reputation of being weak before he came to the Kiev Office of the Commander of the Security Police and Security Service. When he was briefed on his new assignment, Helfsgott voiced his objections. His superior then derogatorily called him a "home-front warrior." Helfsgott thus set out to prove that he was indeed a real warrior.[64] Another officer, Werner Schmidt-Hammer, who had recited the standard execution statement in Garsden and other Lithuanian towns, also believed in the traditional honor of the officer corps. Although he recognized the criminal nature of his activities, he believed officers had to follow their orders at all cost.[65] Similarly, most policemen had participated in the massacres because they thought that their reputation as officers and soldiers was at stake, a notion that is best expressed in the court's evaluation of SS 1st Lt. Adam Schild*.

The defendant's zeal to participate in partisan actions was primarily based on his distinct military attitude. During an inspection by Oberführer Naumann in the summer of 1942, he told him that he did not come to Russia to shoot human beings but to defend his fatherland. Moreover, the defendant was always extremely concerned to act in a militarily correct and exemplary fashion. Even during the executions he was very active in order to set a good example and project an ideal image to his subordinates.[66]

Finally, we can examine the two old Nazis who felt circumvented in the decision-making process. Zenner took over the organization of the massacre in Minsk because he wanted to demonstrate that he was in charge of the city and that nothing could happen without his consent. Fischer-Schweder also had an inferiority complex. He was only a member of the by then rather insignificant Storm Troopers, and as Order Police chief he was cut off from the important Security Service operations. His seemingly naive, surprised realization of the consequences of the Russian war certainly indicates that he knew he was not part of the so-called usual information loop. And, thus, in order to compensate for his weak position, Fischer-Schweder thought it essential to present himself at the forefront of events. This might be his main reason for inviting the county Nazi Party leader to the execution. Fischer-Schweder needed a witness to and validation of his importance.

And, yet, the behavior of the men who had followed their orders was to a large degree circumscribed by the situation of the moment. Even apparent acts of bravery such as Weistermann*'s insubordination happened only after it was evident that Germany would lose the war. Weistermann* most likely refrained from using similar reasoning to save the Jews during the German advances, because he knew then that Ehrlinger would not have been as forgiving.

Weistermann*'s one-time commanding officer, Kluge*, also was courageous only before and after his service in the Einsatzgruppen. In fact, Kluge*'s zeal in persecuting corruption can be explained logically from an entirely different angle: Kluge* relished the power invested in his office with the Gestapo and in particular as an investigator in Paris. These positions put the lowly Major Kluge* into a position to be respected and feared even by generals and governors. To consolidate that power, Kluge* secretly organized a private circle of informers to observe his fellow Security Police officers, thereby turning the surveillance officers of the Security Service into victims. Certainly if Kluge*'s own comrades were not beyond suspicion, why should he care that his unit in the Soviet Union had its way with such lowly and insignificant beings as the Jews?

In conclusion, then, this group of obedient officers followed their orders unconditionally. Only a select few, however, did so because they believed in the

Nazi cause or anti-Semitism. The majority were motivated by a combination of factors, including a misguided sense of duty, loyalty, and discipline, by career-ism, by peer pressure, and by the desire to show their power and importance. Most important, as Stanley Milgram established in his laboratory experiments, unquestioning obedience is often the easiest, most convenient, and perhaps most natural reaction to a situation such as the killing fields in the western Soviet Union.

7. ATYPICAL MEN—
EXTRAORDINARY SITUATIONS

Each assumed the right to decide the
fate of men, and death was the intended
result of his power and contempt.

Benjamin Ferencz, U.S. Chief Prosecutor for the
Nuremberg Einsatzgruppen Trial, 1947

IN THE introduction to his report on the first major West German trial of ten former Einsatzgruppen members, Ralph Giordano describes the Einsatzgruppen as "unique formations, beings seemingly from another planet that no author of horror stories could have conceived in his fantasies."[1] At a time when the German public still refused to believe that more than a few hundred or thousand Nazi fanatics had committed such monumental crimes, Giordano lacked a comparison within this world and could only describe the mobile killing units as extraterrestrial entities. Considering that the Einsatzgruppen members indeed displayed an utter disregard for all human values, one must concur. Certainly no normal human being could be capable of mercilessly machine-gunning or gassing row after row of innocent men, women, and children.

Eight years later, in 1966, Heinz Höhne wrote, "Even Himmler must have known that only a small minority of these men were born sadists and killers."[2] The previous chapters have shown that the Einsatzgruppen officers, with few exceptions, were not psychopaths. In fact, most possessed very human sensibilities. These apparently normal human beings then became some of the worst possible Holocaust perpetrators. The effort to understand why they participated in such an unprecedented mass murder campaign reveals important insights into the depth of human behavior. Obviously each case presented in this study has unique elements, and consequently care must be exercised in drawing general conclusions.

Christopher Browning titled his pioneering book *Ordinary Men,* thereby indicating that he wrote about average, normal people one might encounter. The subjects of his study, 210 out of 500 original members of Reserve Police Battalion 101, were unexceptional men, with no outstanding qualities or abilities, no Nazi background, and they had joined the Police Reserve only when it became apparent that they might be drafted to the front. They had formulated their political opinions before the Nazis took charge. They were, indeed, "ordinary men," not an expected source of mass murderers. In the Police Reserve they received introductory weapons training, and after only three weeks of duty in occupied Poland, they were ordered to shoot Jews. Although their commanding officer gave them the option to perform other tasks rather than the killings, without fear of retribution, a majority of the policemen chose their roles as killers, roles that involved the murder of thousands of Jews over weeks, months, and sometimes years.

The Einsatzgruppen officers certainly came from a more promising pool from which to draw potential Jew killers. As Raul Hilberg pointed out regarding the senior Einsatzgruppen officers tried at Nuremberg, many were bureaucrats, intellectuals, and convinced Nazis, and once they were drafted to the Einsatzgruppen, they committed both their ideological convictions and their technical expertise to the elimination of the Jews in the Soviet Union. It was precisely the fusion of ideology and professional skills that made them so effective.[3]

A look at the background of the 136 Einsatzgruppen officers brought before the German courts confirms Hilberg's evaluation. A majority of the defendants were highly trained professionals with a long career in Nazi organizations, and sixty-eight of them had studied at a university.[4] The Einsatzgruppen officers were thus definitely not ordinary men, although one category, the specialists—the drivers, administrators, interpreters, and technical experts—comes close to Browning's definition. Like the Police Reserves, the specialists were older and in general not as educated as their comrades. Most however, were very ambitious and driven to have successful careers, even if this included participation in mass murder. Yet this ambition does not mean that it is more appropriate to view the specialists and the other Einsatzgruppen officers as Daniel Goldhagen did—Hitler's willing executioners.

Goldhagen's book purports to be a sweeping refutation of every previous interpretation of the Holocaust. He uses the evidence from Reserve Police Battalion 101 and two other institutions involved in the annihilation of the European Jews to prove that more German citizens than previously assumed were, like the Police Reserves, actual or potential Jew killers. Contrary to Browning, Goldhagen finds that the men of the police battalion constituted a rather representative sample of the German population. Therefore, he states, they were not "ordinary" in Browning's sense, but ordinary only because they came from a culture that had harbored radical anti-Semitic sentiments for generations and only waited for the opportunity to act upon their deeply ingrained racial hatred.

Analysis of the different types of Einsatzgruppen perpetrators, however, demonstrates that Goldhagen's simplistic thesis does not sufficiently account for their behavior.[5] Most Einsatzgruppen officers were obviously neither willing executioners nor ordinary men. Rather, they were atypical men confronted with exceptional situations. The evidence confirms that the choices they made reflect individual responses to the circumstances in the killing fields that were determined by many variables. Nevertheless, some general observations about their behavior can be made.

Anti-Semitism in various forms was definitely an important, but not the only, explanation for the motivation of the Einsatzgruppen officers. Understandably, the German court judgments are usually silent about the role of anti-Semitism, because one cannot expect that defendants accused of such horrible crimes and facing lifelong prison terms if convicted would freely admit that they were virulent anti-Semites. Only two or three former Einsatzgruppen members were honest or proud enough to confess that they had killed Jews because they hated them. A few others used character witnesses to attest to their good relations with Jews before and after their term in the Einsatzgruppen, rather than focus on their negative deeds during their time in the Soviet Union. In general, however, anti-Semitism was not openly mentioned in a majority of the cases. Nevertheless, it is possible to draw conclusions about the influence of Jew hatred by examining the background, career, and activity of the defendants as they were established in court.

The anti-Semitic training and indoctrination in the SS and other Nazi organizations must have left an impression on most officers, inasmuch as they had been members since the early 1930s. The judges in Frankfurt wrote regarding one officer: "The defendant was raised and educated along the principles of National Socialist ideology as a result of his early membership in the NSDAP and the SS."[6] Similarly, most other Einsatzgruppen members had been exposed to constant propaganda and systematic degradation of the Jews for at least eight years before they came to the Einsatzgruppen. The context of the increasingly brutal war of annihilation with the Soviet Union then amplified previously existing and propaganda-nurtured images of the enemy and the Jews. "The Jew" in Nazi ideology thus not only controlled both Soviet Communism and the Western capitalist powers, but he had forced the war upon Germany and had made its population suffer. Once the Einsatzgruppen officers internalized this equation, it began to make sense to wage a war against the Jewish people, even defenseless men, women, and children. In this respect, then, service in the Einsatzgruppen indeed could be considered equivalent to duty at the front, as Himmler, Heydrich, and other SS leaders had so often emphasized.

A long-standing tradition of dehumanization of the victims also helps to explain the moral indifference, mockery, and victory parties of the Einsatzgruppen officers. Yet, the executioners should have had problems with killing Jews they knew and had acknowledged as human beings. Browning's work describes cases where the Reserve policemen had recognized their victims as former neighbors and therefore had much greater difficulty overcoming their inhibition to kill.

The Einsatzgruppen officers, especially the members of Einsatzkommando Tilsit, also often had to face people they knew. Yet contrary to the men of Reserve Police Battalion 101, who left the shooting of their native Hamburg Jews to the auxiliaries, Einsatzkommando Tilsit reverted to even more cruelty when faced with the task of killing familiar members of the community. During the execution in Polangen on June 30, 1941, Security Service men had picked a skinny young man to push into the grave the body of a particularly large victim known to the Security Service, a baker named Gurewicz. They had also forced the well-known gynecologist to stack bodies in the grave.[7] It seems that in cases of familiarity with the victims, additional brutality helped the executioners to overcome remaining scruples. Moreover, looking back at what they had done, again the killers could blame the Jews to justify their actions.

The extended period of service in the SS and other Nazi organizations exposed the Einsatzgruppen members to anti-Semitic propaganda, and certainly also taught them about submission to authority and blind faith in the Führer and his leadership cult. The motto of the time, as coined by Goebbels, was "The Führer commands, we follow." Nevertheless, it is evident from the court records that in spite of all Nazi indoctrination, training, and dehumanization of the Jews, the majority of Einsatzgruppen officers still realized the full dimensions of their crimes. We cannot forget First Lieutenant Krumbach's assertion in court, "State-sanctioned murder still remains murder."[8]

Among the officers who had followed their orders, men such as Captain Schumacher and First Lieutenant Schild* acted out of a traditional German civil servant's sense of duty and loyalty that demanded setting examples for subordinates, even in difficult situations. Such action was, of course, a time-honored tradition. But following the Prussian ideals of doing what was best for one's country would actually have demanded quite the opposite behavior of challenging their orders and preventing their subordinates from committing such horrible crimes. Clearly, the handful of officers who obeyed for this reason did not properly evaluate the circumstances. Most others, however, referred to superior orders to justify their actions, and the German courts too often accepted that argument.

Although it is hard to conceive that men of such high education and professional qualification did not recognize the legal implications of their behavior, the activities of the Einsatzgruppen officers in the Soviet Union definitely confirm that all human beings have a propensity for violence and destruction. As D. G. Myers writes, "It is even harder to attribute the Holocaust to *unique* character traits in the German people."[9] For most, these dormant traits will never be awakened, but for the Einsatzgruppen, the conjunction of the right circumstances, and the fusion of ideology and intellect, activated the worst. That was definitely the case with T. Sgt. Martin Weiss, who had appeared to be a model citizen before his service in the Einsatzgruppen.

Most Germans chose a career for life. However, most Einsatzgruppen officers were flexible in times of crisis, and in general when it was to their advantage. Thus, it was not simply due to tradition and investment of time and experience that many later Einsatzgruppen officers stayed with the Security Police, but rather that a career in the police organizations guaranteed a good salary, a respected profession, and, most importantly, opportunities for advancement. Men such as the Maj. Robert Mohr had deliberately volunteered for a term in the Einsatzgruppen as part of an arrangement that allowed him to pick a preferred position in Germany afterward. Others such as Naumann and Filbert thought of their tenure in the Einsatzgruppen as a chance to gain or regain the favor of their superiors.

Yet, once the policemen had been transferred to service in the Einsatzgruppen, they usually occupied a rather precarious position, as the majority held junior ranks between second lieutenant and captain. And most of these young and idealistic men certainly sympathized with Hitler's policies, as did their counterparts in the Wehrmacht. Omer Bartov states:

> They had grown up under the impact of the Great Depression and the social and political crisis which destroyed the Weimar Republic and brought the Nazis to power. They had come of age under Hitler's rule and absorbed the ceaseless propaganda and indoctrination of his regime in school, at the university, from the media and in the various youth and labour organisations. These young officers spent the most formative period of their lives under National Socialism, and those years must have left a lasting impression on their mentality.[10]

Moreover, the junior officers in the Einsatzgruppen not only had to obey the commands from the higher-ranking officers, they had to transmit them to the enlisted men. They thus became the central link in the chain of command in the

Einsatzgruppen. Service in the Einsatzgruppen was also the first operational assignment for many of these junior officers, and they had the chance to prove to
their superiors, their men, and themselves that they could apply what they had
learned at the leadership school and establish themselves as exemplary police
officers. And if they were executive officers, they had to analyze and perhaps correct their commanding officers' decisions when necessary in order to secure the
overall efficiency of the unit. This task often became a difficult balancing act, especially if the officers aspired to their own commands—they had to obey their superior, yet at the same time serve as a control to his decision-making. The easiest
way out of this predicament, thus, was precise execution of the general elimination order—no questions, no conflict.

In the killing fields, the Einsatzgruppen officers indeed were exposed to the
additional pressure of conformity to the group. Even among the confirmed
killers, who definitely did not need further incentives, the competition for the
highest numbers must be seen as peer pressure. The closely knit groups—the
Seilschaften—created a bond and motivation that none dared to break. Moreover, few wanted to risk their reputation in front of superiors, comrades, and subordinates. Christopher Browning carefully examines the impact of all these elements on the decisions of the killers in Reserve Police Battalion 101.

The court evidence of the Einsatzgruppen officers also has demonstrated
that the influence of alcohol and what Daniel Goldhagen called habituation—
the gradual exposure and acceptance of the tasks of massacre—were even
greater than scholars thought. For the Police Reserves in Poland and the executioners in the Soviet Union, alcohol significantly helped to lower the threshold
to commit murder and made the gruesome task of killing at close range more
bearable. Captain Werner Schönemann stated, "This was our sad destiny. We
could only stand it drunk. We believed that we had to shoot our way through
to the Ural Mountains."[11]

An understanding of the motives of the Einsatzgruppen officers is possible if
the influencing factors in combination are considered: alcohol, habituation, careerism, peer pressure, deference to authority, political indoctrination, and anti-
Semitism. It is also obvious that the crimes of the Einsatzgruppen would have
been unthinkable without the provided context of the largest and most brutal
military and racial elimination campaign in history. Without the war in the Soviet Union, the Einsatzgruppen officers might have remained policemen doing
their duties at home, much as Robert Jay Lifton suggests regarding the infamous
Josef Mengele: "Had there been no Auschwitz, he might have led an unremark-
able life as a professor or physician."[12]

Certainly most Einsatzgruppen members had already become instruments

of terror as Gestapo or Security Service officers, and they had already committed numerous crimes before the war. However, the situation in the Soviet Union
allowed them to freely unleash unrestricted power over a group of people who
had long been given less than human status. The Einsatzgruppen officers and
their crimes thus will always stand as shocking, horrifying examples of human
capabilities.

AFTERWORD

German Justice and the Einsatzgruppen Crimes

*Justice cries out for punishment because we
are humans and we deny our own humanity
if we let these crimes go free, if we let them be
amnestied, if we let them be subject to time
limits, or if we simply don't bother to
prosecute them for one reason or another.*

Geoffrey Robertson, British Barrister,
Lecture, September 15, 2000,
United States Holocaust Museum

T HE TREATMENT of former Nazi
criminals in the courts is a significant indicator of the success of how Germany
has come to terms with its Nazi past—Vergangenheitsbewältigung. The long
shadow of the country's recent history has been discussed in many historiographical works,[1] and it appears that although the debate is far from over, the re-
united Germany is definitely on the right course. Nonetheless, the sources used
for this study and the process of acquiring them prove that the German justice
system and its efforts to bring an important group of Holocaust perpetrators to
justice fell short in two important aspects: the leniency of the sentences, and the
bureaucratic measures taken to protect the perpetrators.

In Eric Johnson's work *Nazi Terror: The Gestapo, Jews, and Orginary Germans,* the last chapter is appropriately titled "Christmas Presents for the Gestapo." Johnson states that many former Gestapo officers were allowed to return
to their lives after the war, even if they had participated in numerous crimes
against humanity. They were hardly ever punished, received overwhelming support from many dignitaries, and were usually able to regain their positions and
pensions. In other words, they were completely reintegrated into German society.[2] In his memoirs, Robert Kempner, a prosecutor at the Nuremberg Trials,
similarly regrets that a "fever of mercy" (Gnadenfieber) regarding former Nazi
criminals befell the new German republic after 1949.[3] Unfortunately, these au-
thors' observations definitely apply to the Einsatzgruppen officers as well. Of the

136 indicted Einsatzgruppen members, 44 re-entered the German corps of civil servants after 1945. Many others also quickly reached respectable positions.[4]

The prosecutors' decisions to charge the majority of the Einsatzgruppen officers as accomplices, which carried a lesser penalty, greatly facilitated the reintegration of these criminals. Legal observers of the trials, however, noted that the leniency of the sentences had helped to document the activities of the Einsatzgruppen, because the prospect of short prison sentences had ensured the cooperation of the defendants. Furthermore, as so many courts believed, it was perhaps impossible to find earthly justice for the Einsatzgruppen officers.

Considering the magnitude of the crimes, however, it seems woefully inadequate to point to the technicalities of the German penal code when prosecuting mass murderers such as the Einsatzgruppen members. One certainly has to question why these individuals were punished with no more than a few years in prison when they literally had not only the blood of hundreds of victims on their hands but the substance of their shattered brains as well.

Based on the evidence presented by the expert witnesses from the intentionalist school of thought, the judges in the German courts declared that the National Socialist rulers, in particular Hitler, Himmler, and Heydrich, were primarily responsible for the mass murders because they had planned and ordered these crimes against humanity. And whereas Hitler, Himmler, and Heydrich had usurped and used the power of the state illegitimately and had the will to commit the crimes, the majority of the Einsatzgruppen officers did not. The Einsatzgruppen members, their argument notes, did not organize the mass murder; they only received and implemented instructions. Because the Einsatzgruppen officers had found an already existing machinery of mass murder that worked efficiently without their participation when they had joined their respective killing squadrons, they were little more than proverbial cogs in the machine.

In reality, however, only a select few Einsatazgruppen officers "did not much more than absolutely necessary," as SS Lt. Col. Dr. Bradfisch noted in evaluating one of his subordinates; most others had contributed significantly to the elimination campaign.[5] And, yet, despite their at times difficult to follow reasoning, the German judges clearly recognized the unfathomable depth of the crime. The court in Kiel states:

> The objective injustice of the defendants' deeds was enormous. The killing operations of the Einsatzgruppen and the number of human beings killed make the most infamous murders in criminal history for which the perpetrators were punished with the highest penalty look insignificant in comparison. The crimes of the Einsatzgruppen were at least as evil as other capital crimes.[6]

The Jews were shot or asphyxiated in gas vans out of racial hatred, a motive that definitely fulfills the requirements of "depraved indifference." The innocent victims regardless of age or gender suffered unbearably as they were cruelly shot or gassed. Moreover, most defendants did little to alleviate the suffering. Yet, the Kiel judgment concludes: "In the end, the dimension of the crimes weigh so much that the maximum penalty for accessory to murder would be appropriate, were it not for a series of mitigating circumstances."[7]

Like the court in Kiel, the other courts granted extenuating circumstances that in most cases led to far lesser sentences than the maximum of fifteen years in prison for accessory to murder.[8] Some courts even went as far as to completely refrain from penalties because of duress, or the defendants' "minor" contributions to the massacres.[9] But what did the courts accept as mitigating conditions? First, most held in favor of the defendants that they came from a solid, bourgeois background, that they did not openly condone violence, and that they had never committed a crime before they were transferred to the Soviet Union. The courts noted that the Einsatzgruppen members had willingly joined the Nazi Party and the SS early, which should have been held against them, but the judges concluded quite the opposite. They argued that extended membership in organizations that denied the free will of the individual had conditioned the Einsatzgruppen officers to follow a strict code of honor and blind obedience and made it extremely difficult for them to understand the criminal intent of an apparently legitimate regime.

Second, the judges saw as a mitigating circumstance the general character of the Nazi regime. They thought that the defendants were links in the chain of command within a brutal political system that disregarded all notions of justice and was not adverse to the most heinous crimes. However, due to the intensity of anti-Semitic propaganda and the systematically aroused anti-Semitic sentiments of the German population at large, avoiding participation in the massacres would have required a high degree of ethical independence, courage, and sacrifice that the courts felt could not be expected. For these reasons, most courts believed that the defendants were not "Jew haters" and had participated in the massacres only because of personal weakness and the overall situation.

Third, the judges argued that the delay in bringing the defendants to justice—more than twenty or twenty-five years since they had committed the crimes—could not be held against them. As the court in Essen writes, "It must be measured that the effect of the sentence is much harsher on them in their old age than it would have been immediately after the war."[10] If they had been arrested and sentenced immediately after the war, they would have had an opportunity to atone for their guilt, be rehabilitated into society, and lead a meaningful life after their release. At the time the court wrote its opinion, however, in December 1966, the defendants were already too old and would have been beyond proper rehabilitation by the time of their release if the judges had given longer sentences.

A final, crucial explanation remains that, at least in the eyes of the German judges, warranted the lenient penalties. The Einsatzgruppen officers had committed only one singular crime because in a legal sense every Jewish action in which they had participated was just part of one larger, "natural action." The justification was not, as one might expect from the previous reasoning, the existence of Hitler's general elimination order, but rather, from the judges' finding, that a "machinery of destruction" was present within the Einsatzgruppen that would have worked as effectively independent of the contribution of individual members. It was concluded that most Einsatzgruppen officers had knowingly and willingly become part of this already established killing machine, and thus their subsequent activities within the larger framework of the Einsatzgruppen campaign justified evaluating their behavior as a singular act of accessory. The judges in Essen write:

> Their actions in the Einsatzkommando from the moment they reported for duty in the Soviet Union to the end of their term represents one singular, natural action, regardless of their physical or psychological contributions to the murderous activities of the Einsatzkommando.[11]

Therefore, according to the judges, when the gas van replaced the submachine gun and carbon monoxide took the place of the bullet to the head as the frequency of large-scale executions diminished and jail clearings increased in the summer of 1942, the Einsatzgruppen officers still committed only one continuous crime. The judges believed that variations in the technology of killing did not substantially alter the overall organization of the murder plan. The defendants did not have to make a new resolution to participate because they already had made that choice when they joined their units. Even if they had made new decisions regarding the minute details of the gassings, the entire operation remained nevertheless only one action because of the close organizational connection.

The courts based their decision on a ruling of the Supreme Court of the German Federal Republic. The Supreme Court, in BGHSt 2219, had determined that a perpetrator who committed multiple crimes within a close spatial connection can be charged for only one action, even if he had made multiple decisions to commit each individual deed.[12] The German lower courts then applied this verdict and concluded that the close organizational connection of the Einsatzgruppen crimes also warranted their treatment as a singular act.

Obviously, one could, with good reason, object to the judges' reasoning.

Why did the courts not hold the Einsatzgruppen officers accountable as perpetrators? It was these officers who had mercilessly killed their victims. And even if, until the late 1960s, the prevailing historical interpretation tended to see the Nazi leadership as the responsible party for the crimes, why did later judges not follow the functionalist reasoning and finally put the blame where it belonged, with the men who actually pulled the trigger?

It is even more difficult to understand that many courts granted extenuating circumstances to men who had committed some of the most heinous crimes in history. Why did the judges count the bourgeois upbringing and good education favorably for the defendants? If almost half (sixty-eight) of the indicted Einsatzgruppen officers had studied at a university and forty-four were trained as lawyers (one, SS Major Mohr even studying Human Rights!), should not their education have provided them with the high degree of ethical independence and critical thinking required to recognize the criminal intent of the Nazi regime? And if many chose, despite better knowledge as they admitted in court, not to stand up and act against their criminal orders, should not their punishment have been enhanced? Furthermore, if the German courts cooperated so closely with the Central Office and therefore knew that the Nazis never punished anyone harshly for refusal to carry out orders and kill Jews, then the judges should not have counted the defendants' claimed fear of punishment as an extenuating circumstance and should have extended their penalties.

Also questionable is why the courts opted for a shorter sentence in order to make rehabilitation possible. One can argue whether or not the Einsatzgruppen officers deserved consideration of leniency, but we must recognize the reasons why these men were not brought to justice earlier. First, the Einsatzgruppen members, with the exceptions of SS Capt. Hans Karl Schumacher and a few others, had deliberately covered their tracks. Some, such as Erhard Kroeger and Anton von Krell*, even fled the country when they were in jeopardy of being discovered, and led law enforcement agencies on chases around the world. Thus it appears that the German courts rewarded the Einsatzgruppen officers for hiding their crimes as long as possible or for escaping from the arms of justice. Second, in some cases, the defendants profited from the authorities' inability to investigated these crimes in a timely manner.

And then there remains the questionable "unity of action" issue. Why did the German courts extend the Supreme Court ruling concerning close spatial connection to the organizational connection of the Einsatzgruppen officers? How could they interpret the multiple murders committed by most Einsatzgruppen officers as a singular act? Did it not require an independent and new decision each time a bullet was fired or a gas valve was opened?

For all the warranted criticism, one has to bear in mind, however, that the German courts are bound to the existing regulations. The penal code applies universally to all citizens and cannot be altered for the prosecution of special groups of defendants. Arbitrary dispersion of justice had been a defining characteristic of the Nazi regime, and the German judges certainly were aware of the fact that they could not fight against a past evil by employing its very methods. In addition, one also has to acknowledge that human error is possible.

On the other hand, if proper prosecution of the Einsatzgruppen officers was prevented by both legal and ethical considerations, at least the offices and archives responsible for keeping the trial records should have done everything to make their material accessible to researchers and the public. Unfortunately, that was not always the case with this project. Beginning in the summer of 1998, I contacted by letter twelve district attorneys' offices with the request to access the pertinent judgments. After an often considerable amount of time had passed, I received responses. Six district attorneys' offices referred me to the responsible state archives. The archives then wrote that according to the laws of the states, by which they were bound, the final judgments could not be released within thirty years after the judgment was entered. Therefore, I had to request special permission from the Department of Justice. In general, that permission was granted, but under certain conditions, ranging from a simple statement such as, "It is to be understood that all personal data will be used with a pseudonym,"[13] to an entire list of requests, as in the following particularly stringent example:

> According to § 33 Section 1 of the Hessian Data Protection Code, I hereby give Mr. Helmut Langerbein permission to evaluate the pertinent files for his dissertation project under the following conditions: As far as the purpose of the project allows, the pertinent personal data is to be erased or at least to be used with a pseudonym; the personal data is to be kept secret and stored safely; it can only be used for the project; publication must be with a pseudonym and in a manner that makes it impossible to identify the actual person. Moreover, I oblige the petitioner to emphasize that the defendants in this case were *acquitted*.[14]

Three other district attorneys' offices immediately granted permission and supplied me with copies of the material under similar conditions. Another three offices completely ignored my letters. Ultimately, I was able to collect the necessary records at the Central Office.

Of course, one wonders whether these privacy regulations should be applied to the people who put themselves beyond the pale of human law when they mur-

dered hundreds of thousands of Soviet Jews. Yet, reflecting upon German political, social, and educational developments since the 1960s and early 1970s, when
the majority of the trials were held, it is obvious that the country has made great
strides in dealing with its history. However, the uncooperative behavior of some
offices may indicate that a few government officials unfortunately still apply the
exact letter of the law rather than its intent, in order to prevent proper access to a
part of German history they would rather see covered by a mantle of silence.

NOTES

Introduction: The German Einsatzgruppen Trials

1. Landgericht (hereafter, LG) Berlin, 3 PKs 1/62, June 22, 1962, 29.

2. Ibid.

3. C. F. Rüter and D. W. de Mildt, *Die westdeutschen Strafverfahren wegen national-sozialistischer Tötungsverbrechen 1945–1997,* Amsterdam and Maarsen, Holland University Press, xii.

4. Christopher R. Browning, *Ordinary Men. Reserve Police Battalion 101 and the Final Solution in Poland*; and Daniel Jonah Goldhagen, *Hitler's Willing Executioners. Ordinary Germans and the Holocaust.*

5. For a summary of the Goldhagen debate and some of the most balanced criticisms, see Ian Kershaw, *The Nazi Dictatorship. Problems and Perspectives of Interpretation,* ch. 10; Omer Bartov, "Ordinary Monsters," *New Republic* (April 29, 1996): 32–38; and essays in Robert R. Shandley, ed., *Unwilling Germans? The Goldhagen Debate.*

6. Stanley Milgram, *Obedience to Authority. An Experimental View.*

7. Stanley Milgram, "Behavioral Study of Obedience," *Journal of Abnormal and Social Psychology* 67, 4 (1963): 371.

8. For a good discussion of Milgram's work, see Arthur G. Miller, *The Obedience Experiments. A Case Study of Controversy in Social Science.*

9. Herbert Jäger, *Verbrechen unter totalitärer Herrschaft. Studien zur nationalsozialistischen Gewaltkriminalität,* 168, 343.

10. An interview with Staatsanwalt Tönnies at the Central Office of the State Justice Administrations for the Investigation of National Socialist Homicide Crimes (Zentrale Stelle der Landesjustizverwaltungen zur Verfolgung nationalsozialistische Gewaltverbrechen) in Ludwigsburg confirmed this conclusion.

11. Fritz Bauer et al., *Justiz und NS-Verbrechen. Sammlung Deutscher Strafurteile wegen nationalsozialistischer Tötungsverbrechen 1945–1966.* References to page numbers of published verdicts are to the page used within the Bauer volumes. References to page numbers in unpublished judgments are to the page number in the original court record.

12. Rüter, *Die westdeutschen Strafverfahren,* xi. The Central Office became part of the German National Archives in January 2000.

13. Quoted in Michael Burleigh, *The Third Reich. A New History,* 340–41. See also Ian Kershaw, *Hitler: 1936–1945 Nemesis,* 489; Michael R. Marrus, *The Holocaust in History,* 37, among others.

14. Ernst Nolte, *The Three Faces of Fascism,* 291.

15. Edward M. Wise, ed. *The Penal Code of the Federal Republic of Germany.*

16. See the work of Hans Mommsen.

17. Karl A. Schleunes, *The Twisted Road to Auschwitz. Nazi Policy Toward German Jews, 1933–1939.* For a brief summary of the intentionalist/functionalist debate, see Marrus, The *Holocaust in History,* 31–54, and Donald L. Niewyk, ed., *The Holocaust. Problems and Perspectives of Interpretation,* 9–50.

18. Heinz Höhne, *Der Orden unter dem Totenkopf. Die Geschichte der SS,* 77.

19. See Martin Broszat, *The Hitler State.*

20. Christopher R. Browning, "The Decision Concerning the Final Solution," in *Fateful Month: Essays on the Emergence the Final Solution,* 8–38; and "Beyond 'Intentionalism' and 'Functionalism': The Decision for the Final Solution Reconsidered," in *The Path to Genocide. Essays on Launching the Final Solution,* 86–121.

21. Ibid.

22. Ian Kershaw, *Hitler: 1936–1945 Nemesis.*

23. Ibid, xlvi.

24. Quoted ibid, 484.

Chapter 1: The History of the Einsatzgruppen

1. The first number (one million) is from International Military Tribunal (hereafter, IMT), *Trials of War Criminals Before the Nuremberg Military Tribunals,* vol. 4, Military Tribunal II, Case No. 9, The United States of America against Otto Ohlendorf et al., iv. The United States Holocaust Memorial Museum's *The Historical Atlas of the Holocaust,* 51, cites more than one million murdered Jews. The 2.35 million number is from Yehuda Bauer, *A History of the Holocaust,* 197. Daniel Goldhagen, in *Hitler's Willing Executioners,* 158, estimates the number of victims at two million. Using newly available data from Soviet archives, Sergei Maksudov arrives at 970,000 Jewish victims within the Soviet borders of 1939 alone, in "The Jewish Population Losses of the USSR from the Holocaust," Lucjan Dobroszycki and Jeffrey S. Gurock, eds., *The Holocaust in the Soviet Union,* 207–14. Raul Hilberg gives an estimate of 1.35 million Jewish victims in *The Destruction of the European Jews,* vol. 1, 390, and 700,000 Jews within the Soviet territories in vol. 3, 1213—14. Thus, 1.5 million victims seems to be an approximate average.

2. Ibid.

3. Heinz Höhne, *Der Orden unter dem Totenkopf (The Order of the Death's Head);* Helmut Krausnick and Hans-Heinrich Wilhelm. *Die Truppe des Weltanschauungskrieges. Die Einsatzgruppen der Sicherheitspolizei und des SD 1938–1942.*

4. Der Reichsführer SS und Chef der deutschen Polizei, EAP 161-c-30–10/6, T 175, roll 161, frame 2693261, National Archives (hereafter, NA); items of unknown provenance, photostats probably of an SS booklet containing the basic orders of the SS, organizational and descriptive material on the SS units in the field and the administrative office, historic dates for the future growth of the SS, letters and testimonials from the Germanische SS, no date.

5. See Karl Dietrich Bracher, *The German Dictatorship,* 350–62.

6. Werner Best, *Die deutsche Polizei,* 78–87.

7. Typengrundrisse für SS- und Polizeiwohnungen, EAP 161-b-12/74, T 175, roll 35, frames 2543938–40, NA.

8. See, for example, the case of SS Sturmführer Louis Evers. According to a letter from the SS Personnel Main Office, Evers had been expelled from the SS because he had, without permission, married a woman from a family with a criminal background. EAP 161-b-12/74, T 175, roll 35, frame 2543950, NA.

9. Microfilm, items of unknown provenance; scenario for *The Path to Obedience (Der Weg zum Gehorsam—Bildfolge)*, probably prepared by members of the Schulungsamt (Education Department), no date, EAP 161-c-30–10/12, T 175, roll 161, frame 2694386; *The Struggle Is Ours,* EAP 161-c-30–10/6, T 175, roll 161, frame 2693261; NA.

10. *The Path to Obedience,* NA.

11. *The Organizational Book of the NSDAP.* Quoted in LG Kiel, 2 Ks 1/69, November 28, 1969, 10.

12. Die 12 Julsprüche der SS, EAP 161-c-30–10/1, T 175, roll 161, frame 2693007, NA.

13. Uns ist der Kampf, EAP 161-c-30–10/6, T 175, roll 161, frames 2693224–2693226, NA.

14. Das Judentum. Seine blutgebundene Wesensart in Vergangenheit und Gegenwart, Zusammenfassung, EAP 161-c-30–10/2, T 175, roll 161, frame 2693797, NA.

15. Hans Heinrich Wilhelm, *Die Einsatzgruppe A der Sicherheitspolizei und des SD 1941–42,* 46–48; Helmut Krausnick and Hans-Heinrich Wilhelm, *Die Truppe des Weltanschauungskrieges. Die Einsatzgruppen der Sicherheitspolizei und des SD 1938–1942,* 13–31; LG Koblenz, 9 Ks 2/62, May 21, 1963, 17–19. See also Hilberg, *The Destruction of the European Jews,* vol. 1, 274–84.

16. IMT, *Trials of War Criminals,* vol. 19, 44.

17. Die Laufbahn des leitenden Dienstes in der Sicherheitspolizei und im Sicherheitsdienst des Reichsführer SS, EAP 161-c-30–10/6, T 175, frame 2693265, NA.

18. LG Darmstadt, Ks 1/67 (GstA), November 29, 1968, 8.

19. See Peter Longerich, *Die braunen Bataillone. Geschichte der SA,* 206–19; Höhne, *Der Orden unter dem Totenkopf,* 90–124.

20. Krausnick and Wilhelm, *Die Truppe des Weltanschauungskrieges,* 35; Höhne, *Der Orden unter dem Totenkopf,* 242–44; and Eric A. Johnson, *Nazi Terror: The Gestapo, Jews and Ordinary Germans,* 55, 303.

21. LG Koblenz, Ks 2/62, May 21, 1963, 17.

22. Krausnick and Wilhelm, *Die Truppe des Weltanschauungskrieges,* 17–21.

23. LG Ulm, Ks 2/57, August 29, 1958, 187–88.

24. Quoted ibid., 19.

25. Helmut Krausnick and Harold C. Deutsch eds., *Helmuth Groscurth: Tagebücher eines Abwehroffiziers 1938–1940.*

26. Krausnick and Wilhelm, *Die Truppe des Weltanschauungskrieges,* 21–29.

27. Kershaw, *Hitler: 1936–1945 Nemesis,* 246.

28. Krausnick and Wilhelm, *Die Truppe des Weltanschauungskrieges,* 30–36.

29. Ibid., 63.

30. Ibid., 34–71. For the letter, see Bauer, *A History of the Holocaust,* 148–51.

31. Quoted in Krausnick and Wilhelm, *Die Truppe des Weltanschauungskrieges,* 51.

32. Ibid., 80–106.

33. For the events in Poland, see also Kershaw, *Hitler: 1936–1945 Nemesis,* 235–52.

34. The overall strength of the Reich Security Main Office on January 1, 1944, was 50,648 officers. Reichssicherheitshauptamt, Reichstärkemeldung, January 1, 1944, EAP 173-b-10–05/32, T 175, roll 240, frame 2720236, NA.

35. Krausnick and Wilhelm, *Die Truppe des Weltanschauungskrieges*, 146.

36. For von Toll see LG Koblenz, 9 Ks 2/62, May 21, 1963, and the discussion in ch. 4. For Gehfluss* see LG Hannover, 2 Ks 3/68, October 14, 1971, 270–72.

37. LG Essen, 29 Ks 1/64, March 29, 1965, 10.

38. LG Karlsruhe, VI Ks 1/60, December 20, 1961, 5; and LG Darmstadt, Ks 1/67 (GStA), November 29, 1968, 46–47.

39. LG Darmstadt, Ks 1/67 (GstA), November 29, 1968. See also LG Wuppertal, 12 Ks 1/62, December 30, 1965, 7.

40. LG Berlin 3 Pks 1/62, June 22, 1962, 6; and LG Karlsruhe, VI Ks 1/60, December 20, 1961.

41. See LG Köln, 24 Ks 1/63, May 12, 1964, 2; LG Kiel, 2 Ks 1/64, April 8, 1964, 3; and LG Würzburg, Ks 15/49, February 3, 1950, p.2.

42. Hilberg, *The Destruction of the European Jews*, vol. 1, 287–89; Höhne, *Der Orden unter dem Totenkopf*; Wilhelm, *Die Einsatzgruppe A*, 53–55; and LG Koblenz, 9 Ks 2/62, May 21, 1963, 9.

43. LG Wuppertal, 12 Ks 1/62, December 30, 1965, 14–15; Krausnick and Wilhelm, *Die Truppe des Weltanschauungskrieges*, 283–85.

44. The routes and positions of the individual commands can be easily traced from the Einsatzgruppen Situation Reports, as it has been done in Hilberg, *The Destruction of the European Jews*, vol. 1, 299–300; in Krausnick and Wilhelm, *Die Truppe des Weltanschauungskrieges*, 173–204; and in the pertinent West German judgments.

45. Copied in Bundesarchiv/Militärarchiv (hereafter, BA/MA), RH 22/155, OKH, GenQu, AZ Abt Kriegsverwaltung, Nr II/2101/41 geh, April 28, 1941.

46. Omer Bartov, *The Eastern Front 1941–45. German Troops and the Barbarization of Warfare*, 106; and Christian Streit, *Keine Kameraden*, 31–50.

47. BA/MA, RH 22/155; LG Essen, 29 Ks 1/64, March 29, 1965, 7.

48. Ulrich von Hassell, *Vom andern Deutschland. Aus den nachgelassenen Tagebüchern 1938–1944*, 153; English language edition, *The Von Hassell Diaries 1938–1944. The Story of the Forces against Hitler inside Germany as Recorded by Ambassador Ulrich von Hassel, a Leader of the Movement*, 129.

49. Quoted in Dmitri Volkogonov, *Stalin*, 409.

50. For the increasing Nazification of the Wehrmacht before the attack on the Soviet Union, see Manfred Messerschmidt, *Die Wehrmacht im NS-Staat. Zeit der Indoktrination*; Andreas Hilgruber, *Hitlers Strategie. Politik und Kriegführung 1940–1941*, 61–66; Streit, *Keine Kameraden*, 14–61; and Jürgen Förster, "Die Vorgeschichte des Angriffskrieges gegen die Sowjetunion," Jürgen Förster et al., *Deutschland und das bolschewistische Russland von Brest-Litovsk bis 1941*.

51. BA/MA, RH 21–2, 656, Der OB der 4, Armee, Ia/III/IIa/Ic Nr 2000/41 geh, September 11, 1941.

52. BA R 58/218, Ereignismeldung aus der UdSSR (hereafter, Ereignismeldung) No. 106, October 7, 1941, 15–16; and LG Darmstadt, Ks 1/67 (GstA), November 29, 1968.

53. BA R 58/215, Ereignismeldung No. 38, July 30, 1941, 9; and BA R 58/216, Ereignismeldung No. 58, August 30, 1941, 12.

54. BA R 58/218, Ereignismeldung No. 119, October 20, 1941, 5.

55. BA R 58/214, Ereignismeldung No. 14, July 6, 1941, 5; and BA R 58/214, Ereignismeldung No. 28, July 20, 1941, 10.

56. LG Köln, 24 Ks 1/57, May 4, 1957, 5.

57. LG Essen, 29 Ks 1/64, March 29, 1965, 36; and LG Berlin 3 Pks 1/62, June 22, 1962, 17.

58. See, for example, LG Hannover, 2 Ks 2/68, April 1, 1970, 16; and LG Düsseldorf, 8 Ks 3/70, January 1, 1970.

59. BA R 58/214, Ereignismeldung No. 14, 6.

60. BA R 58/215, Ereignismeldung No. 58, p.12.

61. Quoted in LG Essen, 29 Ks 1/65, February 10, 1966, 45.

62. Ibid., 48–51. Because author Eric Johnson already published information about Matschke in *Nazi Terror,* the original name is also used here.

63. The narrative follows the widely accepted version of Krausnick and Wilhelm, *Die Truppe des Weltanschauungskrieges.*

64. LG Köln, 14, Ks 1/63, 5–6.

65. For the Operational Order, see BA R 58/214, Ereignismeldung No. 10, July 2, 1941, 2–3, Der Chef der Sicherheitspolizei und des SD an alle Einsatzgruppen, July 1, Einsatzbefehl No. 2, July 1, 1941; and Kershaw, *Hitler: 1936–1945 Nemesis,* 463–92.

66. The Communications Regarding the Situation in the Soviet Union (Mitteilungen zur Lage in der Sowjet-Union) had been a modest forerunner to the Ereignismeldungen even before the war with the Soviet Union. See Der Chef des Sicherheitshauptamtes (Ifa), *Mitteilungen zur Lage in der Sowjet-Union,* No. 1–4, 7–8, Feb–Jun, Oct, and Nov 1939, EAP 173-b-22–10/9–14, T 175, roll 579, frames 681–1410, NA.

67. Ronald Headland, *Messages of Murder. A Study of the Reports of the Einsatzgruppen of the Security Police and the Security Service, 1941–1943,* 92–100; Krausnick and Wilhelm, *Die Truppe des Weltanschauungskrieges,* 333–41.

68. Hilberg, *The Destruction of the European Jews,* vol. 1, 292–96; Bauer, *A History of the Holocaust,* 197; and Maksudov, "The Jewish Population Losses of the USSR from the Holocaust."

69. Theo Richmond, *Konin. A Quest,* 72, 363. In contrast to Christopher Browning, Richmond also presents an account of the massacre in Jozefow, committed by Reserve Police Battalion 101, from a Jewish perspective. See 365–73.

70. BA R 58/218, Einsatzmeldung No. 128, October 29, 1941, 6.

71. BA R 58/214, Ereignismeldung No. 23, July 15, 1941, 11.

72. See LG Frankfurt, 4 Ks 1/65, March 12, 1966, 27; for other cases see LG Essen, 29 Ks 1/65, February 10, 1966, 48, 50, 61.

73. Wilhelm, *Die Einsatzgruppe A,* 64–67; Hilberg, *The Destruction of the European Jews,* vol. 1, 318–20.

74. LG Essen, 29 Ks 1/64, March 29, 1965, 23.

75. LG Dortmund, 10 Ks 1/61, October 12, 1961, 12.

76. LG Essen, 29 Ks 1/64, March 29, 1965, 37.

77. Ibid., 23; and LG Essen, 29 Ks 1/65, February 10, 1966, 69–70. According to these two

references, SS Oberscharführer Hermann Glockmann was killed by a bullet ricocheting from the frozen walls of the grave. His death was officially treated as if he had been killed in action against partisans. For a similar case, see LG Koblenz, 9 Ks 2/62, May 21, 1963, 12.

78. LG Karlsruhe, VI Ks 1/60, December 20, 1961, 32.

79. Reichsicherheitshauptamt I A 6 Nr. 1602/41, EAP 161-b-12/75, T 175, roll 35, frames 2544123–24, NA.

80. LG Essen, 29 Ks 1/65, February 10, 1966, 34.

81. LG Kiel 2 Ks 1/69, November 28, 1969, 5.

82. Goldhagen, *Hitler's Willing Executioners,* 9.

83. See BA/MA, RH 22/156, Der Reichsführer SS Tgo Nr 114/41 g Kdos, May 21, 1941.

84. See, for example, BA/MA, RH 22/6, 377a and 377, Organizational Chart of HSSPF South, August 19, 1941; BA/MA, RH 22/47 Bfh H Geb Süd, Abt Ia/VII/Nr 934/42, July, 21, 1942.

85. Hilberg, *The Destruction of the European Jews,* vol. 1, 297–98.

86. After the occupied territories passed from military to the civilian administration, Alfred Rosenberg and the Reichsministerium für die besetzten Ostgebiete (RmBO) established the Reichskommissariate Ostland and Ukraine. The Higher SS and Police Leaders (HSSPF) cooperated with the commanders of the respective rear army areas and the Reichskommissare. See BA/MA, RH 22/156, Der Reichsführer SS Tgo Nr 114/41 g Kdos, May 21, 1941.

87. LG Ulm Ks 2/57, August 29, 1958, 101.

88. For a discussion of the uneasy relationship between the HSSPFs and the Einsatzkommandos, see also LG Koblenz, 9 Ks 1/61, June 12, 1961, 10.

89. The numbers are according to Hilberg, *The Destruction of the European Jews,* 341.

90. The courts in Koblenz and Hamburg estimate the number of Jews brought to Minsk and Riga in November 1941 at 50,000. LG Koblenz, 9 Ks 1/61, June 12, 1961, 14; LG Koblenz, 9 Ks 2/62, May 21,1963, 28; and LG Hamburg, 147 Ks 1/76, August 2, 1977, 8. Wilhelm states about 60,000 Jews altogether, in *Die Einsatzgruppe A,* 117, 425.

91. An intermediary sweep between the German offensives of 1941 and 1942 included the screening of the POW camps for Jews and other inferior races. A letter signed by Streckenbach ordering that temporarily suspended Gestapo and police officers in Germany (due to pending investigations or punishment) should be utilized to free Einsatzgruppen members for other Security Police tasks again demonstrates the lack of qualified personnel. Der Reichsführer SS, February 16, 1942, EAP 161-b-12/75, T 175, roll 35, frame 2544042 and 2544043, NA.

92. Central Office, Ar-Z 22/60, 330–31.

93. LG Dortmund, 10 Ks 1/61, October 12, 1961, 27.

94. For Einsatzkommando 1005 see Central Office, AR-Z 22/60, 306–398. See also Krausnick and Wilhelm, *Die Truppe des Weltanschauungskrieges,* 437–38; and Hilberg, *The Destruction of the European Jews,* vol. 1, 389.

95. Hilberg, *The Destruction of the European Jews,* vol. 1, 273.

96. Ibid; Bauer, *A History of the Holocaust,* 193–94; Hans Mommsen, "The Realization of the Unthinkable," in Gerhard Hirschfeld, ed., *The Policies of Genocide*; and Goldhagen, *Hitler's Willing Executioners,* 153.

97. See for example, Arno J. Mayer, *Why Did the Heavens Not Darken? The "Final Solution" in History.*

98. BA, NS 19/3874, Ernennung von Reichsleiter Alfred Rosenberg, April 20, 1941.

99. Although many Einsatzgruppen members were indeed decorated with medals, only a few received them for military action against regular Red Army soldiers. SS 1st Lt. Egon Nolte*, for example, received the Iron Cross (Second Class) for saving five wounded soldiers from the advancing Red Army. See LG Essen, 29 Ks 1/65, February 10, 1966.

100. Here the Einsatzgruppen officers' intent or attitude of "working towards the Führer" is not to be confused with the traditional German military "Auftragstaktik," in which a leader sets a clear objective but leaves the details of how to reach it up to the subordinate. Although the two behaviors appear similar, Auftragstaktik requires a system of clearly defined structures, organization, and responsibilities. "Working towards the Führer," on the other hand, only functions in situations devoid of any fixed structures and clear-cut chains of command, characteristic of the internal dynamics of the Nazi regime and Hitler's form of government.

Chapter 2: The Confirmed Killers

1. BA R 58/218, Ereignismeldung No. 101, October 2, 1941, 2.

2. For a detailed description of the massacre, see LG Darmstadt, Ks 1/67 (GStA), November 29, 1968, 437–543.

3. Quoted in Gerald Fleming, "It Is the Führer's Wish," in Donald L. Niewyk, ed., *The Holocaust. Problems and Perspectives of Interpretation,* 22.

4. Best became Plenipotentiary of Denmark in 1940. The Danes tried and sentenced him to death after the war, but his sentence was later commuted to five years in prison. See Hilberg, *The Destruction of the European Jews,* vol. 3, 1091.

5. LG München, IV 9/69, February 2, 1970, 6–9.

6. Quoted ibid., 86–87.

7. Quoted ibid., 88–89.

8. Seilschaften literally means a group of climbers who are tied together along the same rope. When the first climber in a Seilschaft wants to advance to a higher position, the following members of the group must move in unison. Similarly, when one member falls, he pulls the others down with him.

Within German government institutions and private businesses, the metaphor is used to describe how the promotion of one employee also facilitates the promotion of others who have worked under him.

9. LG Essen, 29 Ks 1/64, March 29, 1965, 4.

10. Dienstleistungszeugnisse Erich Ehrlinger, EAP 173-b-10–05/12, T 175, roll 240, frames 2729909–2729914, NA.

11. LG Berlin, 3 Pks 1/62, June 22, 1962, 2.

12. For Wiebens, see LG Berlin, (500) 3 P(K) Ks 1/65, May 6, 1966.

13. LG Berlin, 3 Pks 1/62, June 22, 1962, 22.

14. LG Karlsruhe, VI Ks 1/60, December 20, 1961, 16.

15. LG Berlin, 3 Pks 1/62, June 22, 1962, 14.

16. LG Frankfurt, 4 Ks 1/65, March 19, 1971, 13.

17. LG Berlin, 3 Pks 1/62, June 22, 1962, 19.

18. LG Essen, 29 Ks 1/64, March 29, 1965, 14.

19. LG Berlin, 3 Pks 1/62, June 22, 1962, 28.

20. LG Berlin, (500) 3 P(K) Ks 1/65, May 6, 1966, 36.

21. LG Berlin, 3 Pks 1/62, June 22, 1962, 14.

22. LG München I, IV 9/69, February 2, 1970, 95.

23. LG Berlin, 3 Pks 1/62, June 22, 1962, 29. Walter Blume was indeed punished, but not by an SS court. The tribunal in Nuremberg sentenced him to death, which was later commuted to life in prison. See Hilberg, *The Destruction of the European Jews,* vol. 3, 1092.

24. Quoted in LG Essen, 29 Ks 1/64, March 29, 1965, 22.

25. LG Essen, 29 Ks 1/65, February 10, 1966, 63.

26. Ibid., 64.

27. LG Essen, 29 Ks 1/64, March 29, 1965, 22–23.

28. From de Mildt, *Justiz und NS-Verbrechen (Nazi Crimes on Trial),* quoted on www1.jur.uva.nl/junsv/brd/brdengfiles/brdeng588.htm.

29. LG München I, IV 9/69, February 2, 1970, 55–66, 92.

30. LG Karlsruhe, VI Ks 1/61, December 20, 1961, 52–54.

31. LG Berlin, (500) 3 P(K) Ks 1/65, May 6, 1966, 5–7.

32. LG München I, 22 Ks 1/61, July 21, 1961, 32.

33. The White Ruthenia district was part of the Reichskommissariat Ostland under Gauleiter Hinrich Lohse. Its territory was roughly equivalent with the Byelorussian Soviet Republic. LG Koblenz, 9 Ks 2/62, May 21, 1963, 20–22.

34. For Stark's personal history, see ibid., 11.

35. Parts of the report are cited in LG Koblenz, 9 Ks 2/62, May 21, 1963, 95. Strauch was later sentenced to death in Nuremberg, then extradited to Belgium, where he was sentenced to death again. However, there was a stay in the imposition of the sentence because of Strauch's insanity. Von dem Bach was first sentenced to 3½ years for his participation in the Röhm Putsch of 1934. He was finally sentenced to life in 1962. See Hilberg, *The Destruction of the European Jews,* vol. 3, 1091, 1107.

36. See also Wilhelm, *Die Einsatzgruppe A,* 341–92.

37. LG Koblenz, 9 Ks 2/62, May 21, 1963, 95.

38. Ibid., 94–100.

39. Ibid., 148.

40. LG Würzburg, Ks 15/49, February 3, 1950, 8.

41. Ibid., 5.

42. Ibid., 11.

43. Ibid.

44. Ibid., 10.

45. Ibid., 11.

46. Ibid.

47. Goldhagen, *Hitler's Willing Executioners,* 417.

48. Ibid., 519, n. 74.

49. LG Karlsruhe, VI Ks 1/60, December 20, 1961, 36.

50. Goldhagen, *Hitler's Willing Executioners,* 377–78.

51. See also Eberhard Jäckel, *Hitlers Weltanschauung*, 81, 146; and Jäger, *Verbrechen unter totalitärer Herrschaft*, 81–82, 95–122, 158–60.

52. Further research into the issue of disobedience and punishment would certainly shed new light on the current understanding of Nazi criminals.

53. LG Berlin, 3 PKs 1/62, June 22, 1962, 19.

54. Goldhagen, *Hitler's Willing Executioners*, epigraph to pt. 6.

55. Kershaw, *Hitler: 1936–1945 Nemesis*, xliii.

56. LG Karlsruhe, VI Ks 1/60, December 20, 1961, 44.

57. Goldhagen, *Hitler's Willing Executioners*, 148–58.

58. Ibid., 519, n. 72.

Chapter 3: The Officers from the Eastern Borderlands

1. Wise, *The Penal Code of the Federal Republic of Germany*.

2. Matschke, however, was allowed to wear the insignia of an SS Captain (Hauptsturm-führer).

3. For Kroeger and von Krell*, see LG Tübingen, Ks 1/68, July 31, 1969, 2–9. See also LG Koblenz 9 Ks 2/62, November 10, 1965, regarding BGH (Federal Supreme Court), 1 StR 260/70, February 9, 1971, which commuted the postwar penalty to probation. The case originally began as LG Koblenz, 9 Ks 2/62, November 10, 1965, was then reviewed by the Federal Supreme Court, and subsequently referred back to the same court as LG Koblenz 9 Ks 2/62, November 10, 1965. For Greiffenberger, see LG Berlin, 3 Pks 1/62, June 22, 1962, 6–7. For K., Sakuth, Behrend, and Carsten, see LG Ulm, Ks 2/57, August 29, 1958, 6–15. For von Toll, see LG Koblenz, 9 Ks 2/62, May 21, 1963, 12. Upon intervention of the Federal Supreme Court, BGH, 1 StR 463/64, LG Koblenz, 9 Ks 2/62, November 10, 1965, reconsiders the time spent in British internment camps, but does not add significant information. For Döring, see LG Bonn, 8 Ks 2/62, February 19, 1964, 1–4. For Hering, see LG Würzburg, Ks 15/49, February 3, 1950, 3. For von der Rohde*, see LG München I, IV, 9/69, February 2, 1970, 12–15. For Matschke, see LG Essen, 29 Ks 1/65, February 10, 1966, 11–18; and for Winter, see LG Essen 29 Ks 2/65, December 22, 1966, 21–23.

4. Frohwann escaped prosecution by committing suicide after the war.

5. See LG Ulm, Ks 2/57, August 29, 1958, 16–17; and November 3, 1960, 5–6.

6. LG Würzburg, Ks 15/49, February 3, 1950, 1–2; the other information about Hering is from 3, 12.

7. LG München I, IV 9/69, February 2, 1970, 38–40.

8. Ibid., 76.

9. LG Ulm, Ks 2/57, August 29, 1958, 151, 176–80; and November 3, 1960, 38–40.

10. Ibid, August 29, 1958, 106–109; and November 3, 1960, 15–16, 35–36.

11. Ibid, August 29, 1958, 180; and November 3, 1960, 40.

12. Ibid, August 29, 1958, 176–77; and November 3, 1960, 39–40.

13. Ibid, August 29, 1958, 52, 75, 88.

14. Ibid., 178.

15. Ibid., 190–91.

16. Future pilots in basic military training.

17. LG Ulm, Ks 2/57, August 29, 1958, 141–47.

18. Ibid., 168.

19. Ibid., 156–58.

20. LG Essen, 29 Ks 1/65, February 10, 1966, 50–51.

21. Ibid., 80–81.

22. LG Koblenz, 9 Ks 2/62, May 21, 1963, 12, 104.

23. Lucy S.Dawidowicz, *The War Against the Jews*; Bauer, *A History of the Holocaust*; and Hilberg, *The Destruction of the European Jews*. For a different and universal perspective on the problem of compliance with totalitarian methods of control, see Hannah Arendt, *The Origins of Totalitarianism* and *Eichmann in Jerusalem: A Report on the Banality of Evil*. To Arendt, passivity and cooperation in the face of powerful and all-encompassing bureaucracies were not a particularly Jewish reaction but an expression of fundamental truths about human behavior.

24. Hilberg, *The Destruction of the European Jews*, vol. 1, 318.

25. Ibid., 319.

26. In one exception, BA R 58/220, Ereignismeldung No. 155, January 14, 1942, 16–17, reports that Jews at an execution in Zagare pulled knives and pistols and attacked their guards. As a result, seven policemen were wounded and all Jews killed.

27. See LG München I, IV 9/69, February 2, 1970, 68, 76; LG Würzburg, Ks 15/49, February 3, 1950, 6; and LG Kiel 2 Ks 1/69, November 28, 1969, 22.

28. See LG Berlin, 3 PKs 1/62, June 22, 1962, 17; LG Köln, 24 Ks 1/63, May 12, 1964, 8; and LG Ulm, Ks 2/57, August 29, 1958, 114, 174, 180. The incidents on 114 and 180 involved Communists.

29. LG Ulm, Ks 2/57, August 29, 1958, 157; and LG Tübingen, Ks 2/61, May 10, 1961, 47.

30. LG Essen, 29 Ks 2/65, December 22, 1966, 80–85.

31. LG Karlsruhe, VI Ks 1/60, December 20, 1961, 27.

32. LG Berlin, 3 PKs 1/62, June 22, 1962, 19.

33. Ibid., 29–30.

34. Ibid., pp.6–7.

35. LG Tübingen, Ks 1/68, July 31, 1969, 23–39.

36. LG Bonn, 8 Ks 2/62, February 19, 1964, 5–6.

37. Ibid., 7. The event is also mentioned in BA R 58/219, Ereignismeldung No. 148, December 19, 1941, 10.

38. LG Bonn, 8 Ks 2/62, February 19, 1964, 4.

39. Ibid., 9.

40. Ibid., 4.

41. See Hilberg, *The Destruction of the European Jews*, vol. 2, 405, 437–39.

42. LG Essen, 29 Ks 1/65, February 10, 1966, 17.

43. Ibid. For Matschke's later activities in Cologne, see Johnson, *Nazi Terror*, 3, 5–6, 60, 477.

44. See Hilberg, *The Destruction of the European Jews*, vol. 1, 72; vol. 2, 417–26.

45. LG Berlin, 3 PKs 1/62, June 22, 1962, 7.

46. For K., see LG Karlsruhe, VI Ks 1/60, December 20, 1961, 7; for von Toll, see LG Koblenz, 9 Ks 2/62, May 21, 1963, 12.

47. LG Ulm, Ks 2/57, August 29, 1958, 16–17, 12. Incidentally, the northern German town of Northeim was the subject of William Sheridan Allen's famous study, *The Nazi Seizure of Power: The Experience of a Single German Town, 1930–1935.*

48. LG Ulm, Ks 2/57, August 29, 1958, 15.

49. See Table 1.

50. LG Berlin, 3 PKs 1/62, June 22, 1962, 39.

51. LG Tübingen, Ks 1/68, July 31, 1969, 6, 9, 38.

52. LG Würzburg, Ks 15/49, February 3, 1950, 8; LG Koblenz, 9 Ks 2/62, May 21, 1963, 12; and LG München I, IV 9/69, February 2, 1970, 148–60.

53. LG Ulm, Ks 2/57, August 29, 1958, 126.

54. The court in Ulm called former Lithuanian citizens who were residing in the United States as witnesses against Lukys, and used affidavits deposited at the German Embassy in Chicago.

55. LG Ulm, Ks 2/57, August 29, 1958, 130, 249.

56. LG Koblenz, 9 Ks 2/62, May 21, 1963, 126.

57. LG Ulm, Ks 2/57, August 29, 1958, 51.

58. LG Koblenz, 9 Ks 2/62, May 21, 1963, 124–25.

59. For examples, see LG Ulm, Ks 2/57, August 29, 1958, 134–36.

60. LG Koblenz, 9 Ks 2/62, May 21, 1963, 120.

Chapter 4: The Specialists

1. LG Kiel, 2 Ks 1/69, November 28, 1969, 31–33.

2. The best German translation for these specialists is "Fachoffiziere."

3. LG Tübingen, Ks 2/61, May 10, 1961, 21.

4. A German law gave soldiers and policemen who enlisted for at least twelve years the right to be re-employed as civil servants after their term expired. Like Schulz, they would receive a so-called Eingliederungsschein or Versorgungsschein, and a special Versorgungsamt helped them find a new position. In the meantime, they received a minimal pension. The law was initially passed in order to attract a long-term leadership cadre for the Reichswehr and thus secretly to counterbalance the restriction imposed on the German military by the Versailles Treaty. The men who served under the conditions of this law were commonly known as Zwölfender. Today, a similar clause of the Soldier's Provisioning Law (Soldatenversorgungsgesetz) gives Zwölfenders a choice to either ask for an Eingliederungsschein or to receive educational benefits comparable to the American GI Bill for a limited time. This author served twelve years in the German Air Force and received such benefits under the conditions of the law.

5. LG Tübingen, Ks 2/61, May 10, 1961, 22.

6. See Longerich, *Die braunen Bataillone,* pp.165–75.

7. Anton Hoch, "Das Attentat auf Hitler im Münchner Bürgerbräukeller 1939," 383–413.

8. Hilberg, *The Destruction of the European Jews,* vol. 3, 864; and Martin Broszat, "The Concentration Camps," 405–406.

9. For Oswald, Merbach, and Kaul, see LG Koblenz, May 21, 1963, 7–9, 116, 149. LG Koblenz, 9 Ks 2/62, November 10, 1965, does not give any new information. For Wiechert and

Schulz, see LG Tübingen, Ks 2/61, May 10, 1961, 20–23. For Kl. and P., see LG Karlsruhe, VI Ks 1/60, December 20, 1961, 8–10. For Kretschmer and Fahnemann*, see LG Darmstadt, Ks 1/68 (GstA), April 18, 1969, pp.18–26. LG Darmstadt, Ks 1/68 (GstA), December 23, 1971, changes the sentence for Fahnemann* from no punishment to three years and one month in prison, but does not add new information. For Gevatter*, see LG Kiel, 2 Ks 1/69, November 28, 1969, 2–8; for Reil*, see LG Hamburg, 147 Ks 3/74, March 11, 1975, 2–4, 9, 24; and for Wachholz*, see LG München I, 119 Ks 6ab/70, November 15, 1974, 9–12.

10. LG Tübingen, Ks 2/61, May 10, 1961, 38.

11. Ibid., 40.

12. Ibid., 39.

13. Ibid., 37–42.

14. LG Ulm, Ks 2/57, August 29, 1958, 158.

15. LG Tübingen, Ks 2/61, May 10, 1961, 46–47.

16. Ibid., 53.

17. Ibid., 52–55.

18. On Strauch, see Hilberg, *The Destruction of the European Jews,* vol. 1, 318.

19. LG Koblenz, 9 Ks 2/62, May 5, 1963, 86.

20. Ibid., 85–89.

21. Quoted in LG Kiel, 2 Ks 1/69, November 28, 1969, 25. 22. Ibid., 27–33.

23. LG Darmstadt, Ks 1/68 (GstA), April 18, 1969, 28.

24. Ibid., 30–31.

25. Ibid., 47.

26. LG München I, 119 Ks 6ab/70, November 15, 1974, 24–32.

27. LG Karlsruhe, VI Ks 1/60, December 20, 1961, 50–52.

28. LG Hamburg, 147 Ks 3/74, March 11, 1975, 13–18, 49, 54.

29. LG Koblenz, 9 Ks 2/62, May 21, 1963, 84–85.

30. Ibid., 63, 84, 121–22, 147.

31. LG Tübingen, Ks 2/61, May 10, 1961, 87.

32. Of course, the most determining factor in the calculation of the sentence always remained the seriousness of the crime. For Oswald, Merbach, and Kaul, see LG Koblenz, 9 Ks 2/62, May 21, 1963, 1–9, 116, 148–49. For Wiechert and Schulz, see LG Tübingen, Ks 2/61, May 10, 1961, 1, 20–23, 87. For Kl. and P., see LG Karlsruhe, VI Ks 1/60, December 20, 1961, 1–10, 48–52. For Gevatter*, see LG Kiel, 2 Ks 1/69, November 28, 1969, 1, 61–73; and for Reil*, see LG Hamburg, 147 Ks 3/74, March 11, 1975, 60.

33. LG Darmstadt, Ks 1/68 (GstA), April 18, 1969, 64.

34. Ibid., 70–72.

35. Kretschmer had been extradited to the Soviet occupation zone in 1946. The East German authorities then kept him in jail until 1948. After his release, he went to the western zones where the De-Nazification Board (Spruchkammer) at Nordbaden (a region in southwestern Germany along the upper Rhine River where Karlruhe is the main city) sentenced him to eight years of forced labor for belonging to Sonderkommando 4a. However, he was released for bad health only a year later, his sentence suspended. Ibid., 22.

36. LG Tübingen, Ks 2/61, May 10, 1961, 21. SS First Lieutenant Harms was a member of the Tilsit State Police. He was tried by the court in Ulm. See LG Ulm, Ks 2/57, August 29, 1958.

37. Milgram, *Obedience to Authority,* 87–89.

38. Quoted in Michael R. Marrus, *The Holocaust in History,* 37; Burleigh, *The Third Reich,* 340–41. Hitler's often cited speech to the Reichstag on January 30, 1939, plays a key role in most intentionalist arguments.

39. Quoted in Bartov, *The Eastern Front,* 83.

40. Ibid., 83–105; Streit, *Keine Kameraden,* pp.18–61.

41. Browning, *Ordinary Men.*

42. The letters of SS 1st Lt. Karl Kretschmer are also mentioned in Richard Rhodes's *Masters of Death: the SS-Einsatzgruppen and the Invention of the Holocaust,* 218–21. Although Rhodes deals with a similar topic, he does not use the same sample group of officers. Moreover, Rhodes dismisses both Goldhagen's and Browning's explanations for the behavior of the perpetrators. He then unsuccessfully applies American criminologist Lonnie Athens's "violent socialization" model to the Einsatzgruppen. I have not further drawn from his work.

43. IMT, *The Trials of War Criminals,* vol. 19, 110. Himmler gave the speech in front of SS Major Generals in 1943. In this instance he referred to the extraordinary difficulty required of the men to kill thousands of Jews, for they all knew their "one good Jew."

44. LG Kiel 2 Ks 1/69, November 28, 1969, 45, 57.

45. LG Karlsruhe, VI Ks 1/60, December 20, 1961, 50–52.

46. Milgram, *Obedience to Authority,* 148–50.

Chapter 5: The Acquitted

1. The abbreviations Ra., He., and Si. were chosen to distinguish between the two defendants with the same initials in this chapter.

2. LG München I, 22 Ks 1/61, July 21, 1961.

3. LG Düsseldorf, 8 IKs 1/66, August 5, 1966, 28.

4. For U., Ra., and He., see LG Freiburg, I AK 1/63, July 12, 1963, pp.1–3. For Si. and R., see LG München I, 22 Ks 1/61, July 21, 1961, 4–6. For H. And Ku., see LG Karlsruhe, VI Ks 1/60, December 20, 1961, 6–7. For Stuhr* and Förster*, see LG Düsseldorf, 8 Iks 1/66, August 5, 1966, 28–32, 38–42. The following judgments entered October 30, 1968, and February 8, 1973, do not offer new information on Stuhr* and Förster*. For Schaefer, see LG Berlin, (500) 3 P(K) Ks 1/65, May 6, 1966, 3–5. The judgment from March 18, 1968, does not offer new information. For Grasdübel, see LG Frankfurt, 4 Ks 1/65, March 19, 1971, 2–4.

Acquitted because their actions did not warrant the charges of accessory to murder were S. Sgts. Franz Siepmann* and Karl Seifert* (both LG Düsseldorf, 8 IKs, 1/66, August 5, 1966), First Lieutenant Herbert Stamman* (LG Kassel, 3 Ks 1/63, November 23, 1966), Second Lieutenant Werner Barke* (LG Düsseldorf, 8 IKs 3/70, January 1, 1973), and Markus Scharm* (LG Kassel, 2(4) Ks 132 Js 29806-81, September 26, 1991). Therefore, these men will not be discussed further.

5. See BA R 58/214, Ereignismeldung No. 24, July 16, 1941, 4.

6. LG Karlsruhe, VI Ks, 1/60, December 20, 1961, 15–26.

7. Ibid., 7, 27.

8. LG Berlin, (500) 3P(K) Ks 1/65, May 6, 1966, 26–29, 61.

9. Ilges was a witness in this case. For his trial, see LG Köln, 24 Ks 1/57, May 4, 1957.

10. LG Bielefeld, 5 Ks 2/59, November 4, 1959, 2–4, 9.

11. BA R 58/214, Ereignismeldung No. 21, July 13, 1941, 12.

12. For the Baranowicze massacre, see BA R 58/215, Ereignismeldung No. 32, July 24, 1941, 4.

13. LG München I, 22 Ks 1/61, July 21, 1961, 11–13.

14. BA R 58/215, Ereignismeldung No. 36, July 28, 1941, 2.

15. LG München I, 22 Ks 1/61, July 21, 1961, 13.

16. Ibid., 23–24.

17. Ibid.

18. Ibid., 17–24.

19. On Schönemann, see LG Köln, 24 Ks 1/63, May 12, 1964.

20. LG München I, 22 Ks 1/61, July 21, 1961, 16, 24, 38.

21. LG Frankfurt, 4 Ks 1/65, March 19, 1971, 28.

22. Wise, *The Penal Code of the Federal Republic of Germany.*

23. N. was not tried, because of a severe illness. LG Freiburg, I AK, 1/63, July 12, 1963, 8.

24. See also ch. 2.

25. LG Freiburg, I AK 1/63, July 12, 1963, 8–9.

26. Ibid., 26.

27. Ibid., 29.

28. Ibid., 25–34.

29. Ibid., 25, 26, 30, 35–38.

30. Ibid., 43.

31. Ibid., 38–44.

32. The wording of § 47 is my translation. From Rudolf Absolon, ed., *Das Wehrmachtstrafrecht im 2. Weltkrieg. Sammlung der grundlegenden Gesetze, Verordnungen und Erlasse,* 14.
This paragraph has not changed too much since 1945. The current § 17 (6) of the military penal code excuses crimes against the military order such as disobedience, "If an order demands committing an act punishable by the penal code." Obeying such an order is in itself a crime. See Militärstrafgesetz-MilStG, http://zoom.mediaweb.at/material/milstgb.html.

33. LG Freiburg, I AK 1/63, July 12, 1963, 43.

34. Ibid., 44–56.

35. Central Office, IV 401 AR 593/63, 54. Parentheses in original.

36. See LG Ulm, Ks 2/57, August 29, 1958, 236, 242; LG Tübingen, Ks 2/61, May 10, 1961, 81; LG Köln, 24 Ks 1/63, May 12, 1964, 17; LG Essen, 29 Ks 1/65, February 10, 1966, 136, 168; LG Essen, 29 Ks 2/65, December 22, 1966, 186, 194–97; LG Kiel, 2 Ks 1/68, April 11, 1969, 132–33; LG Hannover, 2 Ks 3/68, October 14, 1971, pp.159–60; LG Darmstadt Ks 1/67 (GstA), November 29, 1968, 222–24, 276–77, 341; LG Darmstadt, Ks 1/68 (GstA), April 18, 1969, 14; and LG Kiel, 2 Ks 1/64, April 8, 1964, 27.

37. LG Köln, 24 Ks 1/68, July 8, 1968, 91.

38. LG Koblenz, 9 Ks 1/61, June 12, 1961, 23.

39. Quoted in LG Essen, 29 Ks 2/65, December 22, 1966, 38.

40. Quoted in Höhne, *Der Orden unter dem Totenkopf,* 328. My translation.

41. Quoted in LG Koblenz, 9 Ks 1/61, June 12, 1961, 25. For the cases of disobedience, see 23–26, 43, 46.

42. LG Karlsruhe, VI Ks 1/60, December 20, 1961.

43. LG Koblenz, 9 Ks 2/62, May 21, 1963, 121, 126.

44. LG Kiel, 2 Ks 1/69, November 28, 1969, 31–33.

45. LG Kiel, 2 Ks 1/68, April 11, 1969, 34, 154.

46. Browning, *Ordinary Men,* 186–88. The concept of the "gray zone" is described in Primo Levi, *The Drowned and the Saved.* See also, Primo Levi, *Survival in Auschwitz,* especially the chapter "This Side of Good and Evil," 77–85.

47. Bartov, *The Eastern Front,* Introduction.

Chapter 6: The Officers Who Obeyed

1. LG Koblenz,9 Ks 2/62, May 21, 1963, 61.

2. See Table 1.

3. LG Kiel, 2 Ks 1/64, April 8, 1964, 3.

4. LG Wuppertal, 12 Ks 1/62, December 30, 1965, 2–3.

5. LG Kiel, 2 Ks 1/68, April 11, 1969, 14.

6. Gauleiter Koch was later appointed governor of the newly conquered northern area of the Soviet Union, the so-called Reichskommissariat Ostland.

7. LG Kiel, 2 Ks 1/68, April 11, 1969, 12–18.

8. Ibid., 30–33.

9. LG Karlsruhe, VI Ks 1/60, December 20, 1961, 4.

10. LG Berlin, 3 PKs 1/62, June 22, 1962, 5–6.

11. LG Essen, 29 Ks 1/65, February 10, 1966, 25–30.

12. For a brief history of the SS, see Hilberg, *The Destruction of the European Jews,* vol. 1, 200–201, and Hajo Holborn, *A History of Modern Germany 1840–1945,* 747–49. The best survey on the development of the SS from the beginning to the end is still Höhne, *Der Orden unter dem Totenkopf.*

13. See Christopher R. Browning, "The Decision Concerning the Final Solution," in *Fateful Month: Essays on the Emergence the Final Solution,* 8–38, and "Beyond 'Intentionalism' and 'Functionalism': The Decision for the Final Solution Reconsidered," in *The Path to Genocide. Essays on Launching the Final Solution,* 86–121. See also Hans Mommsen, "The Thin Patina of Civilization," in Robert R. Shandley, ed. *Unwilling Germans? The Goldhagen Debate,* 183–95.

14. LG Koblenz, 9 Ks 1/61, June 12, 1961, 51. On Kube's problems with the Security Service, see also ch. 2.

15. By January 1919 the Spartacists, under the leadership of Karl Liebknecht and Rosa Luxemburg, had embarked on a radical Communist course in Germany. In early January, their uprising was crushed by the army and Freikorps units; Luxemburg and Liebknecht were

murdered on January 15. For a brief account of the events from a socialist and liberal-democratic approach, respectively, see Wolfgang Ruge, *Weimar—Republik auf Zeit,* 25–27, and Hans Mommsen, *Die verspielte Freiheit. Der Weg der Republik von Weimar in den Untergang 1918-1933,* 46–49.

16. LG Ulm, Ks 2/57, August 29, 1958, 13–14.

17. LG Koblenz, 9 Ks 1/61, June 12, 1961, 52.

18. LG Dortmund, 10 Ks 1/61, October 12, 1961, 37.

19. LG Koblenz, 9 Ks 2/62, May 21, 1963, 45.

20. Ibid., 50.

21. Ibid., 58.

22. Ibid., 57.

23. Ibid., 61. The narrative is based on 41–61, 73–80.

24. LG Berlin 3 PKs 1/62, June 22, 1962, 38.

25. Ibid., 25.

26. Ibid., 17, 25, 33, 37–39.

27. Central Office, AR-Z 22/60, 325.

28. LG Koblenz, 9 Ks 2/62, May 21, 1963, 66–70.

29. LG Ulm, Ks 2/57, August 29, 1958, 6.

30. For Schmidt-Hammer, see LG Ulm, Ks 2/57, August 29, 1958, and March 11, 1960. He was sentenced to three years in prison in both trials.

31. Ibid.

32. LG Ulm, Ks 2/57, August 29, 1958, 48.

33. Ibid., 49.

34. For Fischer-Schweder's activities in Garsden, see ibid., 46–52; for Krottingen, see ibid., 107–22.

35. All information on Fischer-Schweder's postwar career, including the quote, are from LG Ulm, Ks 2/57, August 29, 1958, 7.

36. BA R 58/219, Ereignismeldung No. 140, December 1, 1941, 5.

37. LG Koblenz, 9 Ks 1/61, June 12, 1961, 12–13, 19, 26–38, 49.

38. Ibid., 50.

39. Ibid.

40. Der Reichsführer SS, September 28, 1942, EAP 161-b-12/139, T 175, roll 58, frames 2573846–47, NA.

41. Ibid., 51.

42. LG Wuppertal, 12 Ks 1/62, December 30, 1965, 2–3.

43. Ibid., 3, 9–15.

44. LG Kiel, 2 Ks 1/68, April 11, 1969, 76–77, 86, 90, 115–16.

45. Ibid., 20–22.

46. LG Dortmund, 10 Ks 1/61, October 12, 1961, 34.

47. Ibid., 19–25, 34–35.

48. LG Ulm, Ks 2/57, August 29, 1958, 188.

49. LG Karlsruhe, VI Ks 1/60, December 20, 1961, 4.

50. See Browning, *Fateful Month* and *The Path to Genocide.*

51. Meier died while in custody in 1960. LG Karlsruhe, VI Ks 1/60, December 20, 1961, 31.

52. Ibid., 35.

53. Ibid., 31–37.

54. Ibid., 4.

55. LG Kiel, 2 Ks 1/68, April 11, 1969, 34.

56. Milgram, *Obedience to Authority,* 12.

57. Miller, *The Obedience Experiments,* 227–28.

58. Milgram, *Obedience to Authority,* 167.

59. LG Ulm, Ks 2/57, August 29, 1958, 214.

60. LG Koblenz, 9 Ks 1/61, June 12, 1961, 22.

61. LG Köln, 24 Ks 1/63, May 12, 1964, 8.

62. LG Karlsruhe, VI Ks 1/60, December 20, 1961, 5.

63. Browning, *Ordinary Men,* 165–69.

64. LG Wuppertal, 12 Ks 1/62, December 30, 1965, 17.

65. LG Ulm, Ks 2/57, August 29, 1958, 56.

66. LG Frankfurt, 4 Ks 1/65, March 12, 1966, 31.

Chapter 7: Atypical Men—Extraordinary Situations

1. H. G. van Dam and Ralph Giordano, eds., *KZ-Verbrechen vor deutschen Gerichten,* vol. 2, 5; LG Ulm Ks 2/57, August 29, 1958.

2. Höhne, *Der Orden unter dem Totenkopf,* 334.

3. See Hilberg, *The Destruction of the European Jews,* vol. 1, xxx.

4. See Table 1.

5. For one of the most sensitively written reviews of Goldhagen's book, see Bartov, "Ordinary Monsters," 32–38. For a summary of the Goldhagen debate, see Shandley, *Unwilling Germans? The Goldhagen Debate.*

6. LG Frankfurt, 4 Ks 1/65, March 11, 1966, 31.

7. LG Tübingen, Ks 2/61, May 10, 1961, 39–40. See also ch. 5.

8. LG Dortmund, 10 Ks 1/61, October 12, 1961, 37.

9. Quoted in Miller, *The Obedience Experiments,* 201. Emphasis in the original.

10. Bartov, *The Eastern Front,* 66.

11. LG Köln, 24 Ks 1/63, May 12, 1964, 17.

12. Robert Jay Lifton, *The Nazi Doctors. Medical Killing and the Psychology of Genocide,* 16.

Afterword: German Justice and the Einsatzgruppen Crimes

1. See for example Charles S. Maier, *The Unmasterable Past: History, Holocaust, and German National Identity*; Richard J. Evans, *In Hitler's Shadow: West German Historians and the Attempt to Escape from the Nazi Past*; and Ian Kershaw, "'Normality' and Genocide: The Problem of 'Historicization,'" in *The Nazi Dictatorship,* ch. 9, 218–36.

2. Johnson, *Nazi Terror*, 463–87.

3. Robert M. W. Kempner and Jörg Friedrich, *Robert M. W. Kempner, Ankläger einer Epoche. Lebenserinnerungen*, 336–99.

4. See Table 1.

5. LG Kiel, 2 Ks 1/68, April 11, 1969, 152.

6. Ibid, 150–51.

7. Ibid.

8. In 1968 the maximum sentence for accessory to murder was commuted from life to fifteen years. See Rüter and de Mildt, *Die westdeutschen Strafverfahren*, xii.

9. See for example LG Hamburg, 147 Ks 3/74, March 11, 1975, 75. The verdict is based on the court's interpretation of § 47 Section 2 of the military penal code, which stipulates, "If the guilt of a subordinate who helped with a crime is minor, it is possible to refrain from punishment."

10. LG Essen, 29 Ks 2/65, December 22, 1965, 205.

11. Ibid., 129.

12. Cited ibid.

13. Der Leiter der Zentralstelle im Lande Nordrhein-Westfalen für die Bearbeitung von nationalsozialistischen Massenverbrechen bei der Staatsanwaltschaft Dortmund to Professor Peter Kenez, University of California–Santa Cruz, August 3, 1999.

14. Der Leitende Oberstaatsanwalt, Staatsanwaltschaft bei dem Landgericht Kassel to Professor Peter Kenez, University of California–Santa Cruz, September 29, 1999. Emphasis in the original.

GLOSSARY
German Terms and Abbreviations

Abitur   Secondary School diploma (qualifying students for university studies)

Abschussziffern   Body counts

Abwehr   German military intelligence service responsible for counter-espionage

Aktionen   Actions/operations

Aktionsgruppen   Action Groups

alter Kämpfer   Old Fighter of the early NSDAP (Nazi Party)

Angleichungsdienstgrad   An adjusted, equivalent rank between military and police services

Arbeitsdienst   Voluntary labor service instituted to rebuild Germany's economy

Arbeitserziehungslager   Work-education camp

BdS   Office of the Commander of the Security Police and the Security Service (Befehlshaber der Sicherheitspolizei und des SD), the stationary successor agencies to the Einsatzgruppen. On the level of the Einsatzkommandos and Sonderkommandos, called KdS (Kommandeur der Sicherheitspolizei und des SD)

BGH   Bundesgerichtshof. Supreme Court of the Federal Republic of Germany

Blutorden   Blood Medal; created to honor Old Fighters of the NSDAP

Bundesnachrichtendienst   Branch of the West German Secret Service responsible for collecting foreign intelligence

Bundeswehr   Federal Army since 1953

Eingliederungsschein   Document that guarantees employment in the Civil Service after a former soldier or policeman serves for twelve or more years

Einsatzbefehl   Operational Order

Einsatzgruppen   Operational Task Forces; the mobile killing units of the SS

Einsatzkommando   Independent unit within the Einsatzgruppen

Einsatzstäbe   Operational Task Headquarters

Ereignismeldungen   Einsatzgruppen Operational Situation Reports

Freikorps   Free Corps. Paramilitary organizations consisting of former World War I soldiers and other right-wing elements that helped with the suppression of the leftist uprisings during the early phase of the Weimar Republic

Gauleiter   Nazi Party official on the regional level—in Nazi Party matters subordinated only to Hitler

Gebietskommissar   Territorial Commissar or Governor (called Reichsprotektor in Bohemia and Moravia)

Gefängnisräumung   Prison evacuation—SS euphemism for routine execution

Geheime Reichssache   Top Secret

Gehilfen   Accomplices

Gendarm   County sheriff

Generalgouvernement   General Government; German territory governed by Hans Frank; the former Poland minus the territories that had been incorporated into Germany (Wartheland, western Prussia, southeastern Prussia)

Gestapo   Secret State Police

Genickschussspezialisten   Specialsts at shooting in the back of the neck

Gerichtoffizier   Officer responsible for legal matters in military and police units; approximately comparable to Judge Advocate General (JAG) in the U.S. military

Gnadenfieber   Fever of mercy

Grenzschutz   Border Patrol (illegal Reichswehr organization)

Gymnasium   Form of secondary school; to graduate, students have to pass an exam, the Abitur, which qualifies them for studies at the university level

Hauptamt Ordnungspolizei   Main Office Order Police

Hauptamt Sicherheitspolizei   Main Office Security Police; consisting of the Criminal Police and the Gestapo; predecessor of the RSHA

Haupttäter   Main perpetrators

Herrenmensch   Member of the Master Race

Hitlerjugend (HJ)   Hitler Youth organization; for boys between fourteen and eighteen

Hiwi   Indigenous auxiliary volunteer (Hilfswillige); Eastern European volunteer for noncombat service with German forces

HSSPF   Higher SS and Police Leader (Höhere SS and Polizeiführer)

Judenaktionen   Actions/operations to eliminate the Jews

Judenräte   Jewish Councils

Judenrein   Purged of Jews

Judenrepublik   Name given the Weimar Republic by right-wing opponents who believed it was run by the Jews

Jugendsozialwerk   West German Youth Welfare Organization

Junkerschule   Officer Candidate School within the Nazi Party

Kadavergehorsam   Blind obedience (literally, "obedience to the corpse")

Kapo   Prisoner foremen

Kasernierte Feldpolizei   Billeted Field Police

KdS   See BdS

Kinderaktion   Children's action/operation; all children under eighteen were to be executed

Kommissarbefehl   Commissar Order; Hitler's order to kill political functionaries among Soviet prisoners of war

KP   Communist Party

Kriegsgerichtsbarkeitserlass   Hitler's 1941 decree regarding the occupied Soviet population under military jurisdiction

Kreisleiter   Nazi Party leader on the county level

Kristallnacht   "Night of the Broken Glass"; the pogrom against Jewish shops, homes, schools, synagogues, November 9, 1938, across Germany and Austria

Kripo   Criminal Police

Landgericht (LG)   District Court

Landrat   County supervisor

Langemarckring   Right-wing youth organization formed in memory of the World War I battle at Langemarck

Luftwaffe   German air force

Meldungen   Reports; as in Meldungen aus den besetzten Ostgebieten, Reports from the Occupied Eastern Territories

Militärstrafgesetz   Military penal code

Mischlinge   Individuals of mixed Jewish blood

Mitläufer   Legal term: a minor accessory (literally, "a fellow traveler")

NKVD   Communist Secret Police (Narodnyi Komissariat Vnutrenykh Del)

NSDAP   Nazi Party (National Socialist German Workers' Party; Nationalsozialistische Deutsche Arbeiterpartei)

Oberführer   Rank of the SS (no Germany army or U.S. military equivalents)

Obersekretär   Criminal Police Detective

OKH   Army (Land) High Command (Oberkommando des Heeres)

OKW   Armed Forces High Command (Oberkommando der Wehrmacht)

Ordnungspolizei   Order Police

Rasse- und Siedlungshauptamt   SS Race and Resettlement Main Office; responsible for implementation of Nazi "resettlement" schemes in Eastern Europe

Rayon   A small territorial administrative unit in the Soviet Union; a "district" within a city

Rechsstaat   State of Law

Reichsbahn   Government-owned railroad

Reichsführer   Reich Leader of the SS (Himmler)

Reichskommissar   Reich Commissioner (for a particular occupied territory)

Reichskommissariat Ostland   Northern part of the RmBO; the Reichskommissariat Ukraine was the southern part of the RmBO

Reichsmarschall   Highest German military rank; held only by Hermann Göring (no U.S. military equivalent)

Reichsprotektor   Governor (in Bohemia and Moravia)

Reichstag   German Legislature until 1945

Reichswehr   German military during the Weimar Republic, 1919–33

Reiter SS   Organization within the SS dedicated to horsemanship

RmBO   Reich Ministry for the Occupied Eastern Territories (Reichsministerium für die besetzten Ostgebiete)

RSHA   Reich Security Main Office (Reichssicherheitshauptamt)

SA   Storm Troopers (Sturmabteilung); Brown Shirts

Sakuska   Victory party, usually held after an execution; Lithuanian term

Sardinenpackung   Packing victims' bodies like sardines in a can

Saufkumpane   Drinking companions

Schattengewächse   Shadow growths

Schülerbund   National Socialist Pupils League

SD   Security Service (Sicherheitsdienst) within the SS, under Heydrich

Seilschaft   A closely knit group; literally a closely connected group of mountaineers. Within the government and business world, the term could be described as networking, when the promotion or appointment of one employee results in the promotion of co-workers

Sicherheitsdienst   See SD

Sicherheitspolizei   Security Police

Sonderkommando   Independent special commando unit within the Einsatzgruppen; also, special squad of concentration camp prisoners or ghetto inmates

SS   Elite Protection Squads (Schutzstaffel)

SSPF   SS and Police Leader; subordinate to the HSSPF

SS Totenkopfverbände   SS Death Head Squads; the concentration camp guards

SS Verfügungstruppe   SS Common Disposal Troops; one of three main branches of the SS

Staatsanwalt   District Attorney

Standgerichte   On-site Einsatzgruppen courts in Poland

Stapo   State Police Office

Stosstruppen   Shock troops

Studentenbund   Student organization

Täter   Criminal perpetrators

Täterwille   The will and intention to commit a crime

Untermenschen   Subhuman individuals

Urteilsbegründung   Judicial opinions (part of a judgment)

Vergangenheitsbewältigung   Coming to terms with the past

Vernichtungsbefehl   Extermination Order

Volksdeutsche Mittelstelle   Ethnic German Liaison Agency (VoMi); responsible for reintegrating ethnic Germans from the conquered territories into the Reich.

Vorkommando   Advance Command

Waffen SS   Armed SS; military units of the SS

Wandervogel   Nonpolitical youth movement (literally, "migratory birds")

Wehrmacht   German Armed Forces (Army) during Third Reich

zbV   Special purpose (Zur besonderen Verwendung)

Zentrale Stelle   Central Office of the State Justice Administrations for the Investigation of National Socialist Homicide Crimes, Ludwigsburg, Germany

BIBLIOGRAPHY

Documents

Bundesarchiv (BA)(Federal Archive), Berlin, Germany

NS 19/3874. Reichsministerium für die besetzten Ostgebiete

R 58/214–221. Ereignismeldungen aus der UdSSR

R 58/222–224. Meldungen aus den besetzten Ostgebieten.

Bundesarchiv/Militärarchiv (BA/MA)(Federal Archive/Military Archive), Freiburg, Germany.

RH 21–2. Der Oberbefehlshaber der 4. Armee

RH 22/47. Der Befehlshaber Heeresgebiet Süd

RH 22/155. Das Oberkommando des Heeres

RH 22/156. Der Reichsführer SS

National Archives and Records Administration, Washington, D.C.

Microfilm Publication T 175, Rolls 35–36, 58, 161, 240, 574.

Microfilm Publication T 733, Rolls 2, 8.

Zentrale Stelle der Landesjustizverwaltungen zur Verfolgung nationalsozialistischer Gewaltverbrechen (Central Office of the State Justice Administrations for the Investigation of National Socialist Homicide Crimes), Ludwigsburg, Germany.

AR-Z 22/60. Aktion 1005

IV 401 AR 593/63. Helmut Lalla

Landgericht (* indicates documents published in Bauer et al., *Justiz und NS-Verbrechen.*)

Berlin, 1/62*, 1/65 (May 6, 1966; March 18, 1968), 2/65

Bielefeld, 2/59*

Bonn, 2/62*

Darmstadt, 1/67, 1/68 (April 18, 1969; December 23, 1971)

Dortmund, 1/61* (October 12, 1961; February 5, 1963)

Düsseldorf, 1/66 (August 5, 1966; October 30, 1968), 3/70

Essen, 1/64*

Frankfurt, 1/65 (March 11, 1966; March 19, 1971; August 24, 1976)

Freiburg, 1/63*

Hamburg, 3/74, 1/76, 1/83

Hannover, 2/68, 3/68

Karlsruhe, 1/60* (December 20, 1961; December 13, 1963)

Kassel, 1/63, 29806/81

Kiel, 1/64*

Koblenz, 1/61*, 2/62* (May 21, 1963; November 10, 1965)

Köln, 1/57*, 1/63*, 1/68

München I, 1/61*, 9/69, 4a-c/70, 6ab/70, 2a-c/71, 6/71, 1/72, la-d/72
Tübingen, 2/61*, 1/68
Ulm, 2/57* (August 29, 1958; November 3, 1960)
Würzburg, 15/49*
Wuppertal, 1/62*
Staatsanwaltschaft (Office of the District Attorney) Essen, Germany.
Landgericht Essen, 1/65, 2/65
Staatsanwaltschaft Kiel, Germany.
Landgericht Kiel, 1/68, 1/69

Correspondence and Interviews

Kenez, Peter, and Helmut Langerbein. Letters to German District Attorneys' offices and State
Archives, including responses.
Langerbein, Helmut. Interview with Staatsanwalt Tönnies. Ludwigsburg, March 16, 2000.

Books and Articles

Absolon, Rudolf, ed. *Das Wehrmachtstrafrecht im 2. Weltkrieg. Sammlung der grundlegenden
Gesetze, Verordnungen und Erlasse.* Kornelimünster: Bundesarchiv Abteilung Zentralnach-
weisstelle, 1958.
Allen, William Sheridan. *The Nazi Seizure of Power: The Experience of a Single German Town,
1930-1935.* Chicago: Quadrangle Books, 1965.
Arendt, Hannah. *The Origins of Totalitarianism.* New York: Harcourt, Brace & World, 1951.
———. *Eichmann in Jerusalem: A Report on the Banality of Evil.* New York: Viking Press, 1963.
Bartov, Omer. *The Eastern Front 1941–45. German Troops and the Barbarization of Warfare.*
Basingstoke, Hampshire, U.K.: Macmillan, 1985.
———. "Ordinary Monsters." *New Republic* (April 29, 1996): 32–38.
Bastian, Till. *Furchtbare Soldaten. Deutsche Kriegsverbrechen im II. Weltkrieg.* Munich: Verlag
H. Beck, 1997.
Bauer, Fritz, et al. *Justiz und NS-Verbrechen. Sammlung Deutscher Strafurteile wegen national-
sozialistischer Tötungsverbrechen 1945–1966.* 23 vols. Amsterdam: Amsterdam University
Press, 1976.
Bauer, Yehuda. *A History of the Holocaust.* Danbury, Conn.: Franklin Watts, 1982.
Best, Werner. *Die deutsche Polizei.* Darmstadt: L. C. Wittlich Verlag, 1941.
Bracher, Karl Dietrich. *The German Dictatorship.* Chicago: Holt, Rinehart, and Winston, 1970.
Broszat, Martin. *The Hitler State.* London: Longman, 1981.
———. "The Concentration Camps." Institut für Zeitgeschichte. *Anatomy of the SS State.*
New York: Walker and Company, 1968.
Browning, Christopher R. *Fateful Month: Essays on the Emergence of the Final Solution.* Rev. ed.
New York: Holmes & Meier, 1991.
———. *The Path to Genocide. Essays on Launching the Final Solution.* Cambridge: Cambridge
University Press, 1992.

———. *Ordinary Men. Reserve Police Battalion 101 and the Final Solution in Poland.* New York: HarperCollins, 1992, 1998.

Burleigh, Michael. *The Third Reich. A New History.* New York: Hill and Wang, 2000.

Dawidowicz, Lucy S. *The War Against the Jews.* New York: Bantam Books, 1986.

Dobroszycki, Lucjan, and Jeffrey S. Gurock, eds. *The Holocaust in the Soviet Union.* London: M. E. Sharpe, 1993.

Evans, Richard J. *In Hitler's Shadow: West German Historians and the Attempt to Escape from the Nazi Past.* New York: Pantheon Books, 1989.

Fleming, Gerald. "It Is the Führer's Wish." Donald L. Niewyk, ed. *The Holocaust. Problems and Perspectives of Interpretation.* Boston: Houghton Mifflin Company, 1997.

Förster, Jürgen, et al. *Deutschland und das bolschewistische Russland von Brest-Litovsk bis 1941.* Berlin: Duncker und Humblot, 1991.

Gilbert, Martin. *The Dent Atlas of the Holocaust.* 2nd ed. London: J. M. Dent Ltd., 1993.

Goldhagen, Daniel Jonah. *Hitler's Willing Executioners. Ordinary Germans and the Holocaust.* New York: Knopf, 1996.

Headland, Ronald. *Messages of Murder. A Study of the Reports of the Einsatzgruppen of the Security Police and the Security Service, 1941–1943.* London: Associated University Presses, 1992.

Hilberg, Raul. *The Destruction of the European Jews.* Rev. ed. 3 vols. New York: Holmes & Meier, 1985.

Hilgruber, Andreas. *Hitlers Strategie. Politik und Kriegführung 1940–1941.* Frankfurt: Bernhard und Gräfe, 1965.

Hirschfeld, Gerhard, ed. *The Policies of Genocide.* Boston: Allan & Unwin, 1986.

Hoch, Anton. "Das Attentat auf Hitler im Münchner Bürgerbräukeller 1939." *Vierteljahreshefte für Zeitgeschichte* 17 (1969): 383–413.

Höhne, Heinz. *Der Orden unter dem Totenkopf. Die Geschichte der SS.* Hamburg: Verlag Der Spiegel, 1966. Richard Barry, transl. *The Order of the Death's Head: The Story of Hitler's SS.* New York: Coward-McCann, 1970.

Holborn, Hajo. *A History of Modern Germany 1840–1945.* Princeton, N.J.: Princeton University Press, 1982.

Institut für Zeitgeschichte. *Anatomy of the SS State.* New York: Walker and Company, 1968.

International Military Tribunal (IMT). *Trials of War Criminals Before the Nuremberg Military Tribunals.* 23 vols. Washington D.C.: U.S. Government Printing Office, 1949.

Jäckel, Eberhard. *Hitlers Weltanschauung*: Entwurf einer Herrschaft. Stuttgart: Deutsche Verlags-Anstalt, 1981.

Jäger, Herbert. *Verbrechen unter totalitärer Herrschaft. Studien zur national-sozialistischen Gewaltkriminalität.* Frankfurt: Suhrkamp, 1982.

Johnson, Eric A. *Nazi Terror: The Gestapo, Jews and Ordinary Germans.* New York: Basic Books, 1999.

Kempner, Robert M. W., and Jörg Friedrich. *Robert M. W. Kempner, Ankläger einer Epoche. Lebenserinnerungen.* Frankfurt: Ullstein, 1986.

Kershaw, Ian. *Hitler: 1936–1945 Nemesis.* New York. W. W. Norton, 2000.

———. *The Nazi Dictatorship. Problems and Perspectives of Interpretation.* 4th ed. New York: Oxford University Press, 2000.

Krausnick, Helmut, and Harold C. Deutsch, eds. *Helmuth Groscurth: Tagebücher eines Abwehroffiziers 1938–1940*. Stuttgart: Deutsche Verlags-Anstalt, 1970.

Krausnick, Helmut, and Hans-Heinrich Wilhelm, *Die Truppe des Weltanschauungskrieges. Die Einsatzgruppen der Sicherheitspolizei und des SD 1938–1942*. Stuttgart: Deutsche Verlags-Anstalt, 1981.

Levi, Primo. *The Drowned and the Saved*. Raymond Rosenthal, transl. New York: Vintage International, 1989.

———. *Survival in Auschwitz*. New York: Simon & Schuster, 1993.

Lifton, Robert Jay. *The Nazi Doctors. Medical Killing and the Psychology of Genocide*. New York: Basic Books, 1986.

Longerich, Peter. *Die braunen Bataillone. Geschichte der SA*. Munich: Verlag C. H. Beck, 1989.

Lozowick, Yaakov. "Rollbahn Mord: The Early Activities of Einsatzgruppe C." *Holocaust and Genocide Studies* 2, 2 (1987): 221–41.

Maier, Charles S. *The Unmasterable Past: History, Holocaust, and German National Identity*. Cambridge, Mass.: Harvard University Press, 1988.

Maksudov, Sergei, "The Jewish Population Losses of the USSR from the Holocaust." Lucjan Dobroszycki and Jeffrey S. Gurock, eds. *The Holocaust in the Soviet Union*. London: M. E. Sharpe, 1993.

Marrus, Michael R. *The Holocaust in History*. New York: Penguin Books, 1987.

Mayer, Arno J. *Why Did the Heavens Not Darken? The "Final Solution" in History*. New York: Pantheon Books, 1988.

Messerschmidt, Manfred. *Die Wehrmacht im NS-Staat. Zeit der Indoktrination*. Hamburg: R. v Decker, 1969.

Milgram, Stanley. "Behavioral Study of Obedience." *Journal of Abnormal and Social Psychology* 67, 4 (1963): 371–78.

———. *Obedience to Authority. An Experimental View*. London: Pinter & Martin, 1974.

Miller, Arthur G. *The Obedience Experiments. A Case Study of Controversy in Social Science*. New York: Praeger Publishers, 1986.

Mommsen, Hans. *Die verspielte Freiheit. Der Weg der Republik von Weimar in den Untergang 1918–1933*. Berlin: Prophyläen Verlag, 1989.

———. "The Realization of the Unthinkable." Gerhard Hirschfeld, ed. *The Policies of Genocide*. Boston: Allan & Unwin, 1986.

———. "The Thin Patina of Civilization." Robert R. Shandley, ed. *Unwilling Germans? The Goldhagen Debate*. Jeremiah Riemer, transl. Minneapolis: University of Minnesota, 1998.

Niewyk, Donald L., ed. *The Holocaust. Problems and Perspectives of Interpretation*. Boston: Houghton Mifflin Company, 1997.

Nolte, Ernst. *The Three Faces of Fascism: Action Franciase, Italian Fascism, and National Socialism*. New York: Holt, Rinehart, and Winston, 1965.

Rhodes, Richard. *Masters of Death: The SS-Einsatzgruppen and the Invention of the Holocaust*. New York: Alfred A. Knopf, 2002.

Richmond, Theo. *Konin. A Quest*. New York: Vintage Books, 1995.

Ruge, Wolfgang. *Weimar—Republik auf Zeit*. Berlin: VEB Deutscher Verlag der Wissenschaften, 1982.

Rüter, C. F., and D. W. de Mildt, eds. *Die Westdeutschen Strafverfahren wegen nationalsozialistischer Tötungsverbrechen 1945-1997.* Amsterdam and Maarssen: Holland University Press, 1998.

Schleunes, Karl A. *The Twisted Road to Auschwitz. Nazi Policy Toward German Jews 1933-1939.* Urbana: University of Illinois Press, 1970.

Shandley, Robert R., ed. *Unwilling Germans? The Goldhagen Debate.* Jeremiah Riemer, transl. Minneapolis: University of Minnesota, 1998.

Streim, Alfred. "The Tasks of the SS Einsatzgruppen." *Simon Wiesenthal Center Annual* 4 (1987): 309-28.

———. "Correspondence." *Simon Wiesenthal Center Annual* 4 (1989): 311-47.

Streit, Christian. *Keine Kameraden.* Bonn: Verlag J. H. W. Dietz Nachf. GmbH, 1991.

United States Holocaust Memorial Museum. *The Historical Atlas of the Holocaust.* New York: Macmillan Publishing, 1995.

Van Dam, H. G., and Ralph Giordano, eds. *KZ-Verbrechen vor deutschen Gerichten.* 2 vols. Frankfurt: Europäische Verlagsanstalt, 1966.

Volkogonov, Dmitri. *Stalin.* New York: Grove Weidenfeld, 1991.

Von Hassell, Ulrich. *Vom andern Deutschland. Aus den nachgelassenen Tagebüchern 1938-1944.* Zürich: Atlantis Verlag, 1946. Gibson, Hugh, ed. *The Von Hassell Diaries 1938-1944. The Story of the Forces against Hitler inside Germany as Recorded by Ambassador Ulrich von Hassel, a Leader of the Movement.* London: H. Hamilton, 1948.

Wilhelm, Hans-Heinrich. *Die Einsatzgruppe A der Sicherheitspolizei und des SD 1941/42.* Frankfurt: Peter Lang, 1996.

Wise, Edward M., ed. *The Penal Code of the Federal Republic of Germany.* Joseph J. Darby, transl. Littleton, Colo.: Fred B. Rothman & Co., 1987.

Internet

De Mildt, D. W. *Justiz und NS-Verbrechen die westdeutschen Strafurteile wegen nationalsozialistischer Tötungsverbrechen auf CD-ROM (Nazi Crimes on Trial: The German Judgments on Nazi Capital Crimes 1945-1999 on CD-ROM).* English Manual to the CD-ROM edition of Bauer et al. Vol. 20. Amsterdam: Amsterdam University Press, 1998. Available at http://www1.jur.uva.nl/junsv/brd/brdengfiles/brdeng588.htm.

Militärstrafgesetz (Military Penal Code). Available at http://zoom.mediaweb.at/material/milstgb.html.

INDEX

ghettos, *continued*
  Schaulen (Siaulai), 146; Vilnius, 67–68, 69, 73
  (passing); Warsaw, 94
Giordano, Ralph, 181
Goebbels, Josef, 11, 46, 80, 123, 184
Göring, Hermann, 11, 46, 130, 137. *See also* Jewish
  Question
Goldhagen, Daniel Jonah: arguments, 4–6, 40,
  70–75, 98, 101–102, 176; Einsatz-gruppen, 8, 45,
  70; eliminationist anti-Semitism, 7, 74, 99;
  Hitler's Willing Executioners, 4–6, 70–75, 182;
  Reserve Police Battalion 103, 4–7, 182–83
Government General (Generalgouvernement), 25,
  27, 48, 82; camps, 14, 110; *map 2. See also*
  Frank, Hans
Graalfs, Hans, 28, 154, 176
Grasdübel, Kuno (pseud.), 130, 137–38
Greiffenberger, Wilhelm: career, 77–79, 91–92, 95,
  161; character, 83, 91; motivation, 101; sentence,
  98; testimony, 59, 96. *See also* First World War;
  Reich Security Main Office
Greiser, Arthur, 14. *See also* Kershaw, Ian
gypsies, 33, 58–59, 89. *See also* elimination order

H., 129–30, 132–34, 147–48
Hamburg District Court, 4
Harder, Karl, 159, 161–62, 176–77. *See also* Reich
  Security Main Office
Harms, Harm Willms, 122, 158–59, 164, 169. *See
  also* Angleichungsdienstgrad; First World War
He., 131–32, 139, 142–46, 150, 165
Helfsgott, Walter, 178
Hering, August, 67, 77–78, 83–84, 97, 101
Herrscht, Günther (pseud.), 153
Hersmann, Werner, 85, 88, 113–14, 125, 176. *See
  also* anti-Semitism
Heuser, Georg: executions, 119–20, 160, 162, 177;
  in court, 153, 159
Heydrich, Reinhardt: care for Einsatzgruppen,
  39–40, 147; Chief of Security Police and Security
  Service, 17; commission to prepare Final Solu-
  tion, 46; control over SS formations, 42; co-
  ordination of police, 17, 154; elimination of
  the Jews, 3, 11; Fahnemann, Walter (pseud.), 109,
  123; front duty, 148, 184; Higher Police and SS
  Leaders, 41–42; Heydrich-Wagner agreements,
  26, 29, 31, 46; Kluge, Hermann (pseud.), 155;
  Kroeger, Erhard, 78; Nazi Party Security Service,
  17, 21; occupation of Czechoslovakia, 23–25;
  occupation of Poland, 25–27; occupation of
  Soviet Union, 27–29; and Operational Situation
  Reports, 33; orders to Einsatzgruppen, 11–12, 26,

33, 39, 45, 47–48; Police Battalion 124, 139; Reich
  Security Main Office, 193; responsibility for
  crimes, 3, 11–12, 46, 189; Rosenberg, Alfred, 46;
  selection of personnel, 27–28, 175; and Stark,
  Franz, 63; *figure 1; figure 2. See also* Einsatzgruppen, orders to; Göring, Hermann; Himmler,
  Heinrich; Hitler, Adolf; Reich Security Main
  Office; Wagner, Eduard; Wehrmacht
Higher SS and Police Leaders: appointment, 40;
  function, 18, 41; and Heydrich decree, 33, 41, 45;
  relation to Einsatzgruppen, 41–42, 47; Russia
  Center, 64, 129, 139. *See also* Bach Zelewski,
  Erich von dem; Russia North, 41; Russia South,
  92, 164; Wehrmacht, 200n. *See also* Bach Zelew-
  ski, Erich von dem; Jeckeln, Friedrich; Prütz-
  mann, Hans Adolf
Hilberg, Raul, 28, 43, 59, 90–91, 182
Himmler, Heinrich: care for his men, 40; control
  of police forces, 17, 42, 144; elimination of the
  Jews, 3, 11–12, 27; Filbert, Alfred, 56; front duty,
  184; Higher SS and Police Leaders, 18; Kroeger,
  Erhard, 78; orders to Einsatzgruppen, 26, 33, 45,
  148; Rapp, Albert, 61; reaction to insubordination, 144–45, 148; Race and Resettlement Main
  Office (Rasse- und Siedlungs-hauptamt), 19;
  Reich Security Main Office, 18; Reich Leader SS
  and Chief of German Police, 6, 17; Reich Commissioner for the Strengthening of Germandom,
  78; responsibility for crimes, 3, 11–12, 189;
  sadists, 181; speeches, 123, 125, 135–37, 148;
  St., 156; Streckenbach, Bruno, 147; strenghtening
  of Einsatzgruppen, 13; Zenner, Carl, 158, 166;
  figure 1. See also Heydrich, Reinhardt; Hitler,
  Adolf
Hitler, Adolf: amnesty of SS officers, 27; attempts
  on, 56, 108–109, 168; anti-Semitism, 11, 13, 56;
  appointment of Himmler, Heinrich, 17; decree
  on military jurisdiction, 30; devotion to, oath,
  loyalty to, 19–20, 59, 170; disregard, for existing
  law, 166; division of eastern Europe, 78; elimination of Jews, 3, 11, 13, 27, 43, 191; historical task,
  135; ideology, goals, and policies, 13, 30, 46, 185;
  legitimate authority, 174; life, 129; Operational
  Situation Reports, 33; orders to Einsatzgruppen,
  12, 33, 45, 93, 135; power, rise to, and seizure
  of, 79, 105, 131, 154, 176; propaganda, 123–24;
  prophesy, 11, 14, 123; responsibility for crimes, 3,
  11–12, 189; rule, 185; savior, 79; successes, 126;
  weak dictator, 12; will, 52. *See also* functionalist;
  Heydrich, Reinhardt; Himmler, Heinrich;
  Mommsen, Hans
Hitlerjugend (Hitler Youth) , 21, 79, 131, 134

ISBN 1-58544-285-2

90000